The Year of Living Biblically

One Man's Humble Quest
to Follow the Bible
as Literally as
Possible

A. J. Jacobs

SIMON & SCHUSTER

New York London Toronto Sydney

Simon & Schuster
Rockefeller Center
1230 Avenue of the Americas
New York, NY 10020

Copyright © 2007 by A.J. Jacobs

First Simon & Schuster hardcover edition October 2007

SIMON & SCHUSTER and colophon are registered
trademarks of Simon & Schuster, Inc.

For information about special discounts for bulk purchases,
please contact Simon & Schuster Special Sales at
1-800-456-6798 or business@simonandschuster.com.

Designed by Karolina Harris

Manufactured in the United States of America

10 9 8 7 6 5 4 3 2 1

Library of Congress Cataloging-in-Publication Data

ISBN-13: 978-0-7432-9147-7
ISBN-10:   0-7432-9147-6

The Year *of* Living Biblically

Introduction

As I write this, I have a beard that makes me resemble Moses. Or Abe Lincoln. Or Ted Kaczynski. I've been called all three.

It's not a well-manicured, socially-acceptable beard. It's an untamed mass that creeps up to my eyeballs and drapes below my neckline.

I've never allowed my facial hair to grow before, and it's been an odd and enlightening experience. I've been inducted into a secret fraternity of bearded guys—we nod at each other as we pass on the street, giving a knowing quarter-smile. Strangers have come up to me and petted my beard, like it's a Labrador Retriever puppy or a pregnant woman's stomach.

I've suffered for my beard. It's been caught in jacket zippers and been tugged on by my surprisingly strong two-year-old son. I've spent a lot of time answering questions at airport security.

I've been asked if I'm named Smith and sell cough drops with my brother. ZZ Top is mentioned at least three times a week. Passersby have shouted "Yo, Gandalf." Someone called me Steven Seagal, which I found curious, since he doesn't have a beard.

I've battled itch and heat. I've spent a week's salary on balms, powders, ointments and conditioners. My beard has been a temporary home to cappuccino foam and lentil soup. And it's upset people. Thus far, two little girls have burst into tears and one boy has hidden behind his mother.

But I mean no harm. The facial hair is simply the most noticeable physical manifestation of a spiritual journey I began a year ago.

My quest has been this: To live the ultimate Biblical life. Or more precisely, to follow the Bible literally as possible. To obey the Ten Commandments. To be fruitful and multiply. To love my neighbor. To tithe my income. But also to abide by the oft-neglected rules: To stone adulterers. To avoid wearing clothes made of mixed fibers. And, naturally, to leave the edges of my beard unshaven (Leviticus 19:27). I am trying to obey the entire Bible, without picking and choosing.

To back up: I grew up in an extremely secular home in New York City. I am officially Jewish, but I'm Jewish in the same way the Olive Garden is an Italian restaurant. Which is to say: Not very. I attended no Hebrew school, ate no matzoh. The closest my family came to observing Judaism was that classic of assimilation: a Star of David on top of our Christmas tree.

It's not that my parents badmouthed religion. It's just that religion wasn't for us. We lived in the 20th century, for crying out loud. In our house, spirituality was almost a taboo subject, much like my father's salary or my sister's clove cigarette habit.

My only brushes with the Bible were brief and superficial. We had a next-door neighbor, Reverend Schulze, a kindly Lutheran minister who looked remarkably like Thomas Jefferson. (By the way, Reverend Schulze's son became an actor and, oddly enough, went on to play the part of the creepy priest on The Sopranos.) Reverend Schulze told great stories about college sit-ins during the sixties, but whenever he started talking about God, it just sounded like a foreign language to me.

I attended a handful of bar mitzvahs where I zoned out during services and spent the time trying to guess who had bald spots under their yarmulkes. I went to my paternal grandfather's funeral, which was, to my surprise, presided over by a rabbi. How could the rabbi eulogize a man he'd never met? It was disconcerting.

And as far as childhood religion, that was about it.

I was agnostic before I even knew what the word meant. Partly, it was the problem of the existence of evil. If there is a God, why would He allow war, disease, and my fourth-grade teacher Ms. Barker, who forced us to have a sugar-free bake sale? But mostly, the idea of God seemed superfluous. Why do we need an invisible, inaudible deity? Maybe He exists, but we'll never know in this life.

College didn't help my spiritual development. I went to Brown, a secular university where you were more likely to study the semiotics of Wicca rituals than the Judeo-Christian tradition. And when we did read the Bible, it was as literature, as a fusty ancient book with the same truth quotient as The Faerie Queene.

We did, of course, study the history of religion. How the Bible has been the force behind many of humankind's greatest achievements: the civil rights movement, charitable giving, the abolition of slavery. And how, of course, it's been used to justify our worst: war, genocide and the subjugation of others.

For a long time, I thought that religion, for all the good it does, seemed too risky for our modern world. The potential for abuse too high. I figured it would slowly fade away like other archaic things. Science was on the march. Someday soon we'd all be living in a neo-Enlightenment paradise where every decision was made with steely, Spock-like logic.

As you might have noticed, I was spectacularly mistaken. The influence of the Bible—and religion as a whole—remains a mighty force, perhaps even stronger than it was when I was a kid. So in the last few years, religion has become my fixation. Is half of the world suffering from a massive delusion? Or is my blindness to spirituality a huge defect in my personality? What if I'm missing out on part of being human, like a guy who goes through life without ever hearing Beethoven or falling in love? And most important, I now have a young son—if my lack of religion is a flaw, I don't want to pass it onto him.

So I knew I wanted to explore religion. I just needed to figure out how.

The germ of the idea came from my own family: My uncle Gil. Or ex-uncle, to be exact. Gil married my aunt and divorced her a few years later, but he remains the most controversial member of our family. If the rest my relatives are ultra-secular, Gil makes up for it by being, quite possibly, the most religious man in the world. He's a spiritual omnivore. He started his life as a Jew, became a Hindu, appointed himself a guru, sat for eight months on a Manhattan park bench without speaking, founded a hippie cult in upstate New York, turned into a born-again Christian, and, in his latest incarnation, is an ultra-Orthodox Jew in Jerusalem. I may have missed a phase—I think he was into Shinto for a bit. But you get the idea.

At some point along his spiritual path, Gil decided to take the Bible literally. Completely literally. The Bible says to bind money to your hand

(Deuteronomy 14:25), so Gil withdrew $300 from the bank and tied the bills to his palm with a thread. The Bible says to wear fringes on the corners of your garment (Numbers 16:38), so Gil bought yarn from a knitting shop, made a bunch of tassels and attached them to his shirt collar and the ends of his sleeves. The Bible says to give money to widows and orphans, so he walked the streets asking people if they were widows or orphans so he could hand them cash.

About a year and a half ago, I was telling my friend Paul about Gil's bizarre life over lunch at a sandwich shop, and I had my epiphany. That's it. I needed to follow the Bible literally myself. I needed to do it for several reasons.

First, since the Bible requires me to tell the truth (Proverbs 26:28), I must confess that part of the reason is to write this book. A couple of years ago, I came out with a book about reading the Encyclopaedia Britannica, all of it, from A to Z—or more specifically, from a-ak (East Asian music) to Zywiec (a town in southern Poland known for its beer). What could I do next? The only intellectual adventure that seemed a worthy follow-up was to explore the most influential book in the world, the all-time bestseller, the Bible.

Second, this project would be my visa to a spiritual world. I wouldn't just be studying religion. I'd be living it. If I have what they call a God-shaped hole in my heart, this quest will allow me fill it. If I have a hidden mystical side, this year will bring it out of the closet. If I want to understand my forefathers, this year will let me live like they did, but with less leprosy.

And third, this project would be a way to explore the huge and fascinating topic of Biblical literalism. Millions of Americans say they take the Bible literally. According to a 2005 Gallup poll, the number hovers near 33 percent; another poll puts it at 55 percent. A literal interpretation of the Bible—both Jewish and Christian—shapes American policies on the Middle East, homosexuality, stem cell research, education, abortion—right on down to rules about buying beer on Sunday.

But my suspicion was that almost everyone's literalism consisted of picking and choosing. People plucked out the parts that fit their agenda, whether that agenda was to the right or left. Not me. I thought, with some naiveté, I would peel away the layers of interpretation and find the true Bible underneath. I would do this by being the ultimate fundamentalist. I'd be fearless. I would do exactly what the Bible said, and in so doing, I'd discover what's great and timeless in the Bible and what is outdated.

I told my wife, Julie, my idea, and warned her it might affect our life in a not-so-minor way. She didn't gnash her teeth or tear out her hair. She just emitted a little sigh.

"I was kind of hoping your next book would be a biography of Eleanor Roosevelt or something."

Everyone—family, friends, co-workers—had the same concern: That I'd go native. That I'd end up as a beekeeper at a monastery or I'd move into my ex-uncle Gil's spare room in his Jerusalem apartment.

In a sense, they were right to worry. You can't immerse yourself in religion for 12 months and emerge unaffected. The Bible is too powerful. Put it this way: If my former self and my current self met for coffee, they'd get along okay, but they'd both probably walk out of the Starbucks shaking their heads and saying to themselves, "That guy is kinda delusional."

As with most Biblical journeys, my year has taken me on detours I could never have predicted. I didn't expect to herd sheep in Israel. Or fondle a pigeon egg. Or find solace in prayer. Or hear Amish jokes from the Amish. I didn't expect to confront just how absurdly flawed I am. I didn't expect to discover such strangeness in the Bible. And I didn't expect to, as the Psalmist says, Take refuge in the Bible and rejoice in it.

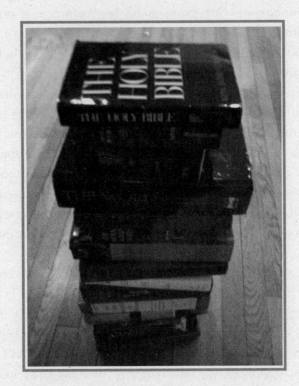

The Preparation

And he shall read in it all the days of his life
DEUTERONOMY 17:19

On the admittedly random day of July 7, 2005, I begin my preparations. I pull out a Bible that is tucked away in the corner of my bookshelf. I don't even remember where I got it, but it looks like the Platonic ideal of a Bible. Like a Bible they'd use in a fifties Western to stop a bullet from piercing the hero's chest. On the front, it says "Holy Bible" in faded gold embossing. The tissue-thin pages remind me of my beloved encyclopedia. The black leather cover smells exactly like my parents' 1976 Plymouth Valiant. It feels good, comforting.

I crack the Bible open. The title page says "This Bible is presented to . . ." and then, in handwritten bubble letters, the name of my ex-girlfriend. Huh. Somehow, I had inadvertently pilfered my ex-girlfriend's childhood Bible. I hope inadvertently. It's been a decade since we broke up and I can't remember. Regardless, that's not a good sign. At the very least, I need to return it when I'm done.

I've read bits and pieces of the Bible before, but never the whole thing, never straight through from Genesis to Revelation. So that's what I do for four weeks, five hours a day. Luckily, I'm used to marathon reading from my Britannica project, so it felt pleasantly nostalgic.

As I read, I type into my PowerBook every rule, every guideline, every suggestion, every nugget of advice I found in the Bible. When I finish, I have a very long list. It runs 72 pages. More than 800 rules. The scope is astounding. All aspects of my life will be affected—the way I talk, walk, eat, dress and hug my wife.

Many of the rules will be good for me and will, I hope, make me a better person by the end of the year. I'm thinking of: No lying. No envying. No coveting. No stealing. Love your neighbor. Honor your parents. Dozens of them. I'll be the Gandhi of the Upper West Side.

But plenty of other rules don't seem like they'll make me more righteous at all. Just more strange, more neurotic, more likely to alienate friends and family:

Bathe after sex. Don't eat fruit from a tree planted less than five years ago. Pay the wages of a worker every day.

And a good number of the rules aren't just baffling, but federally outlawed:

As in: Destroy idols. Kill magicians. Sacrifice oxen.

This is going to be a monster project. I need a plan of attack. I need to make some decisions.

1. Which version of the Bible should I use?

The Bible I pulled from my bookshelf is called "The New Revised Standard Version," which it turns out is a well-respected translation, an offspring of the famed King James Version from 1611, but stripped of most of the 'thees' and 'thous.'

It's a good start. But it's just one of many, many versions—an estimated 7,000 of them. One of my goals is to find out what the Bible really says, so I decide I can't rely on any single translation. I want to compare and contrast at least some of those 7,000.

I go to a Bible bookstore in midtown Manhattan. It's a huge, Wal-Mart-sized store with fluorescent lighting and a long counter of cash registers at the front. My salesman is named Chris, a soft-spoken guy with the body of an Olympic power lifter. He shows me tables covered with dozens of Bibles of all shapes, sizes and linguistic slants—from the plain-spoken English of The Good News Bible to the majestic cadence of The Jerusalem Bible.

He points out one Bible I might want—it's designed to look exactly like a Seventeen magazine: an attractive (if long-sleeved) model graces the front, next to cover lines like "What's Your Spiritual IQ?" and sidebars such as "Rebecca the control freak."

"This one's good if you're on the subway and are too embarrassed to be seen reading the Bible," says Chris. "Because no one will ever know it's a Bible."

It's an odd and poignant selling point. You know you're in a secular city when it's considered more acceptable for a grown man to read a teen girl's magazine than the Bible.

I leave the store with two shopping bags packed with Bibles. But my buying spree isn't over. When I get home, I click on Amazon.com and get several Jewish translations of the Bible, and a half-dozen Bible commentaries. To be safe, I order The Bible for Dummies and The Complete Idiot's Guide to the Bible—anything aimed at those with a sub-80 IQ.

That's not to mention the Bibles sent to me by friends. One gave me the waterproof Outdoor Bible so that I could study the Scripture even during floods and other Old Testament weather patterns. Another sent me a hip-hop version, where the 23rd Psalm reads "The Lord is all that." (The more traditional translation is "The Lord is my shepherd.").

In short, I've got the proverbial stack of Bibles, almost waist-high.

2. What does it mean to follow the Bible literally?

To follow the Bible literally—at face value, at its word, according to its plain meaning—isn't just a daunting proposition. It's a dangerous one.

Consider: In the third century, the scholar Origen is said to have interpreted literally Matthew 19:12—"There are eunuchs who have made themselves eunuchs for the sake of the kingdom of heaven"—and castrated himself. Origen later became a preeminent theologian of his age—and an advocate of figurative interpretation.

Another example: In the early 1900s, when painkillers were first introduced for women in labor, there was an uproar. Many felt it violated God's pronouncement in Genesis 3:16: "I will greatly multiply your pain in childbearing; in pain you shall bring forth children." If Julie and I ever have another child, would I dare get between her and the epidural needle? Not a chance.

It's a good bet that, at some time or other in history, every single passage in the Bible has been taken as literal. I've decided I can't do that. That'd be misleading, unnecessarily flip and would result in permanent bodily harm and prison time. No, instead my plan is this: I will try to find the original intent of the Biblical rule or teaching, and follow that to the letter. If the passage is unquestionably figurative—and I'm going to say the eunuch one is—then I won't obey it literally. But if there's any doubt whatsoever—and most often there is—I will err on the side of being literal. When it says don't tell lies, I'll try not to tell lies. When it says to stone blasphemers, I'll pick up rocks.

3. Should I obey the Old Testament, the New Testament or both?

Many, perhaps most, of the teachings in the two testaments are similar, but some are significantly different. So I've decided to split up my quest.

I will devote most of my year—eight months or so—to the Old Testament, since that's where you'll find the bulk of the Bible's rules. The Old Testament consists of 39 books that mix narrative, genealogy poetry, and lots and lots of laws. The first five books alone—the books of Moses—have hundreds of decrees, including the crucial Ten Commandments, as well as some of the more seemingly atavistic ones about executing homosexuals. That's not to mention divinely-inspired advice in later Old Testament books. The Proverbs—a collection of King Solomon's wisdom—offer guidance on child-rearing and marriage. The Psalms tell you how to worship. I'll be abiding by everything. Or trying to.

Being officially Jewish, I feel much more comfortable living and writing about the Old Testament. (Or, as many Jews prefer to call it, the Hebrew Bible, since "old" implies outdated, and "new" implies "improved"). But in the final four months of my year, I want to explore—in at least some way—the teachings of the Christian Bible, the New Testament.

To ignore the New Testament would be to ignore half of the story. The evangelical movement and its literal interpretation of the Bible holds enormous sway, both for the good (they were powerful advocates for aiding Darfur) and, to my secular mind, the not-so-good (far-right fundamentalists are driving the creationism movement).

Naturally, there's the most famous of all Christian literalists—the conservatives in the Falwell mould. I plan to meet them later this year. But I also want to look at evangelical groups such as "The Red Letter Christians" that focus on what they see as literal adherence to Jesus' teachings about compassion, non-violence and the redistribution of wealth.

It's debatable whether the New Testament even has a legal code—it depends on your definition of 'law'—but it has many teachings that have been followed with varying degrees of literalness, from Jesus' 'turn the other cheek' and 'love your enemy' to the Apostle Paul's decree that men should have short hair. Frankly, I haven't hammered out all the details of my New Testament plan, but hope to hone it once I get my spiritual footing.

4. Should I have guides?

The Bible says "It is not good for man to be alone." Plus, I'm flying blind here.

So over the course of a couple of weeks, I assemble a board of spiritual advisers—rabbis, ministers and priests, some of them conservative, some of them one four-letter word away from excommunication. Some are friends of friends, some are names I stumbled across in Bible commentary books. I'll be talking to them as much as possible.

Plus, I make a pledge to get out of the house. I'll visit a bunch of groups that also take the Bible literally—the ultra-Orthodox Jews, the ancient sect of Samaritans, and the Amish, among others.

My guides will give me advice and context. But they won't be the final word. The Bible will. I don't want to follow any single tradition exclusively. As naïve or misguided as it may be, I want to discover the Bible for myself, even if it entails trekking down some circuitous paths. DIY religion, as my friend calls it. Perhaps I'll find the beauty of a particular tradition fits me best. Or perhaps I'll found my own sect of Judeo-Christianity. I don't know.

As I expected, not everyone thinks my project is a great idea. My aunt Kate—who has remained an Orthodox Jew even after her divorce from the controversial Gil—told me I was, as our people say, meshugga.

I first broke my plan to Kate in early August. We were at my grandfather's house sitting around his big dining room table. Kate had just finished changing after a dip in the pool (she won't wear a bathing suit for modesty reasons, so she plunged in with her long billowy dress, which impressed me. The thing looked heavy enough to sink a lifeguard). When I explained the premise of my book, her eyebrows shot up to her hairline. "Really?" she said.

Then she laughed. I think part of her was happy that someone in our godless family was showing some interest in religion.

After which she got concerned: "It's misguided. You need the oral law. You can't just obey the written law. It doesn't make sense without the oral law."

The traditional Jewish position is this: The Bible—known as the written law—was composed in shorthand. It's so condensed, it's almost in code. Which is where the oral law comes in. The rabbis have unraveled the Bible for us in books such as the Talmud, which are based on the oral teachings of the elders. When the Bible says to "rest" on the Sabbath, you need the rabbis to tell you what "rest" means. Can you exercise? Can you cook? Can you log onto drugstore.com?

Without the rabbis, I'm like the protagonist of the early 80s TV show The Greatest American Hero—he found a bright red suit that gave him all these superpowers, but lost the instruction manual, so he was always flying into walls.

Some conservative Christians were also baffled by my undertaking. They said I couldn't truly understand the Bible without accepting the divinity of Christ. They said that many of these laws—like the ones about animal sacrifice—were nullified with Jesus' death.

And I did start to have doubts. These were good points. I felt torn, anxious about my approach, my monumental ignorance, my lack of preparation, about all the inevitable blunders I'd make. And the more I read, the more I absorbed the fact that the Bible isn't just another book. It's the book of books, as one of my Bible commentaries calls it. I love my encyclopedia, but the encyclopedia hasn't spawned thousands of communities based on its words. It hasn't shaped the actions, values, deaths, love lives, warfare and fashion sense of millions of people over three millennia. No one has been executed for translating the encyclopedia into another language, as was William Tyndale when he published the first widely distributed English-language edition. No president has been sworn in with the encyclopedia. It's intimidating to say the least.

Fortunately, I got a couple of pep talks from two of my favorite advisers. The first was Elton Richards, the father of my friend David, who just retired as minister of his Lutheran congregation in Des Moines. He calls himself a "Pastor out to pasture." I told him about the doubters.

"You just have to tell them that you have a hunger and a thirst. And you may not sit at the same banquet table as them, but you have a hunger and thirst. So they shouldn't judge you."

I love the way he talks. By the end, perhaps I'll be able to speak in majestic food metaphors like Pastor Richards.

I also had breakfast with Rabbi Andy Bachman, a brilliant man who heads up one of Brooklyn's largest synagogues, Congregation Beth Elohim. He told me a Midrash—a story or legend that is not in the Bible proper, but which deals with Biblical events. This Midrash is about the parting of the Red Sea.

"We all think of the scene in The Ten Commandments movie with Charlton Heston, where Moses lifted up his rod and the waters rolled back. But this Midrash says that's not how it happened. Moses lifted up his rod and the sea did not part. The Egyptians were closing in and the sea wasn't moving. So a Hebrew named Nachshon just walked into the water. He waded up to his ankles, then his knees, then his waist, then his shoulders. And right when water was about to get up to his nostrils, the sea parted. The point is, sometimes miracles occur only when you jump in."

So I did. And here is what happened.

Month One: September

Fear God and keep his commandments,
for this is the whole duty of man.

ECCLESIASTES 12:13

It's the first day, and I already feel like the water is three feet over my head.

I chose September 1 to start my project, and from the moment I wake up, the Bible consumes my life.

I can't do anything without fearing I'm breaking a Biblical law. Before I so much as inhale or exhale, I have to run through a long mental checklist of the rules.

It begins when I open my closet to get dressed. The Bible forbids men to wear women's clothing (Deuteronomy 22:5), so that comfortable Dickinson College sweatshirt is off-limits. It was originally my wife's.

The Bible says to avoid wearing clothes made of mixed fibers (Leviticus 19:19), so I have to mothball my polycotton Esquire T-shirt.

And loafers? Am I allowed to wear leather? I go to the living room, click on my Macintosh and open my Biblical Rules file. I scroll down to the ones about animals. Pigskin and snakeskin are questionable, but it looks like regular old cow leather is permissible.

But wait—am I even allowed to use the computer? The Bible, as you might have guessed, doesn't address the issue specifically, so I give it a tentative 'yes.' Maybe sometime down the road I could try stone tablets.

And then I stumble. Within half an hour of waking, I check the Amazon.com sales ranking of my last book. How many sins does that comprise? Pride? Envy? Greed? I can't even count.

I don't do much better on my errand to Mail Boxes Etc. I want to Xerox a half-dozen copies of the Ten Commandments so I can Scotch tape them up all over the apartment, figuring it'd be a good memory aid.

The Bible says "Be slow to anger" (Proverbs 19:11). So when I get there at the same time as this wiry fortyish woman, and she practically sprints to the counter to beat me in line, I try not to be annoyed.

And when she tells the Mail Boxes Etc. employee to copy something on the one and only Xerox machine, I try to shrug it off. And when she pulls out a stack of pages that looks like the collected works of J.K. Rowling and plunks it on the counter, I say to myself:

Slow to anger, slow to anger.

After which she gives some complicated instructions involving paper stock . . .

I remind myself: Remember what happened when the Israelites were waiting for Moses when he was up on the mountaintop for 40 days? They got impatient, lost faith, and were swallowed up by the ground.

Oh, and she pays by check. And asks for a receipt. And asks to get the receipt initialed.

The Proverbs—a collection of wisdom in the Old Testament—say that smiling makes you happy. Which is actually backed up by psychological studies. So I stand there with a flight-attendant-like grin frozen on my face. But inside, I am full of wrath.

I don't have time for this. I have a 72-page list of other Biblical tasks to do.

I finally make it to the counter and give the cashier a dollar. She scoops my 38 cents of change from the register and holds it out for me to take.

"Could you, uh, put the change on the counter?" I say.

She glares at me. I'm not supposed to touch women—more on that later—so I am simply trying to avoid unnecessary finger-to-finger contact.

"I have a cold," I say. "I don't want to give it to you."

A complete lie. In trying to avoid one sin, I committed another.

I walk home. I pass by a billboard advertising a local gym with two well-toned naked people clutching hungrily at each other's bodies. The Bible's teachings on sexuality are complicated, and I haven't figured them out yet. But to be safe, I figure I should avoid lust for now. I keep my eyes on the ground for the rest of the walk home.

When I get back to my apartment, I decide to cross Numbers 15:38 off my list: Attach tassels to the corners of my garment. Inspired by my ex-uncle Gil, I had purchased some tassels from a website called "Tassels without Hassles." They look like the kind of tassels on the corners of my grandmother's needlepoint pillows. I spend ten minutes safety-pinning them to my shirt.

By the evening, I'm bushed. I barely have the energy to listen to Julie talk about the US Open—and even that conversation is fraught. I have to be sure to avoid mentioning the words "Venus Williams," since she's named goddess of love, and it would violate Exodus 23:13 (make no mention of other gods).

As I go to bed, I wonder whether or not I took a step toward enlightenment today. Probably not. I was so busy obsessing over the rules—a lot of which still seem thoroughly insane—that I didn't time to think. Maybe I'm like a student driver who spends every moment checking the blinkers and speedometer, too nervous to contemplate the scenery. But it's just the first day.

Be fruitful and multiply

GENESIS 1:28

Day two. My beard grows fast. I'm already starting to look a little seedy, somewhere between a Brooklyn hipster and a guy who loiters at the OTB all day. Which is fine by me. I'm enjoying the hiatus from shaving. I may be spending all sorts of time on Biblical duties, but at least I'm not wasting three minutes each morning in front of the mirror.

For breakfast, I grab an orange from the refrigerator. Food is going to be tricky this year. The Bible bans many things—pork, shrimp, rabbit, eagle, and osprey, among others. But citrus is fine. Plus, oranges been around since Biblical times—one of my books even says that the forbidden fruit in the Garden of Eden was an orange. It certainly wasn't an apple, since there were no apples in the Middle East of Adam's day.

I sit down at the kitchen table. Julie is flipping through the Arts & Leisure section trying to decide on a movie for Saturday night.

"Should we see The Aristocrats?" Julie asks.

Huh. The Aristocrats is the documentary about the dirtiest joke ever. It contains at least half a dozen sex acts specifically banned by the Book of Leviticus. Julie could not come up with a worse suggestion of an evening activity. Is she testing me? She's got to be.

"I don't think I can. It doesn't sound very Biblical."

"You serious?"

I nod.

"Fine. We'll see something else."

"I don't know if I should be seeing movies at all. I have to think about that."

Julie lowers her gaze and looks at me over the top of her glasses.

"No movies? For a year?"

I'm going to have to choose my battles these next twelve months. I decide I'll bend on this one for now—I'll phase out movies slowly, giving Julie a little grace period.

Things, after all, are a little tense in our house right now. Julie had a hard time getting pregnant with our first child, as I mentioned in my last book. We did eventually succeed (we have a son named Jasper), but apparently, practice did not make perfect, because the second time around is just as much of an ordeal.

In the last year, I've been—as the Bible says—uncovering Julie's nakedness. A lot. Too much. Not that I dislike it, but enough is enough, you know? It gets tiring. Plus, Julie's getting increasingly frustrated with me because she thinks I'm micromanaging—always quizzing her about ovulation times and basal temperatures and her five-day forecast.

"You're stressing me out, and it's really counterproductive," she told me the other day.

"I'm just trying to stay involved."

"You know what? The more stressed out I am, the less chance there is that I'll get pregnant."

I tell her I want our son Jasper to have a little sibling.

"Then please stop talking about it."

So we're in this weird elephant-in-the-room phase where we're both thinking about having a second child, but not saying a word.

This is especially hard for someone who spends as much time as I do reading and pondering the Bible. Fertility is one of the most dominant themes in the Bible—probably the dominant theme of Genesis. If you believe some of the more modern Biblical scholars, Genesis comes from a nature/fertility stage of monotheism, an influence of the pagan sects. In fact, the very first command that God gives to Adam is "Be fruitful and multiply." It's the alpha rule of the Bible.

Now, if I were taking the Bible absolutely literally, I could be "fruitful" by loading up on peaches at Whole Foods and "multiply" by helping my niece with her algebra homework. I could scratch this commandment off my list in twenty minutes flat.

This hammers home a simple but profound lesson for me: When it comes to the Bible, there is always—but always—some level of interpretation, even on the most seemingly basic rules. In this case, I'm pretty sure the Bible was talking about fertility, not algebra, so that's what I'll continue to pursue.

Conception was a huge preoccupation of the ancients. If you think about it, many of the Bible's most famous stories center on the quest to get pregnant. Abraham and Sarah probably had the hardest time conceiving of anyone in the Bible, if not history. At one point, the seemingly barren Sarah became so distraught, she lent her Egyptian handmaiden to Abraham as a concubine. That union produced Ishmael, the forefather of Islam. A few verses later, God sent three angels to Abraham and Sarah's tent to announce that Sarah would soon be pregnant. Sarah's reaction? She laughed, presumably with skepticism. In her defense, she was 90 years old. But God fulfilled his promise, and the nonagenarian matriarch gave birth to Isaac—Hebrew for 'he laughs.'

And then there's Rachel. Rachel and her older sister Leah were both married to the clever shepherd (and my namesake), Jacob. Leah was a procreation machine—giving birth to no fewer than six sons and a daughter. But Rachel remained childless and heartbroken. At one point, she said to Jacob "Give me children or I shall die!" Another time, Rachel bought some mandrakes from her sister—mandrakes are a middle-eastern fruit once thought to be a fertility cure. But it was to no avail. Finally, God "opened Rachel's womb" and she gave birth to Joseph, he of the multi-colored coat.

There is an upside to the Bible's infertility motif: The harder it was for a woman to get pregnant, the greater was the resulting child. Joseph.

Isaac. Samuel (whose mother had to pledge her son to God's service in order to conceive). These are some of the giants of the Hebrew Scriptures.

Yesterday, I broke Julie's gag rule to inform her that if we do have another kid, he or she could be one for the ages. Which made her smile.

"I think that's true," she said. "Good things come to those who wait." Which sounds like a Biblical proverb, but is actually from Henry Wadsworth Longfellow.

You shall have no other Gods before me

EXODUS 20:3

Back to day two. Julie has a meeting, so I'm left alone with my breakfast orange, my list of rules and my stack of Bibles. I've got a half hour before our son Jasper wakes up. Now seems a good time to embark on the more spiritual part of my quest: Prayer.

As I said, I've always been agnostic. In college, I studied all the traditional arguments for the existence of God: The design argument (just as a watch must have a watchmaker, so the universe must have a God), the first cause argument (everything has a cause; God is the cause of the universe). Many were dazzling and brilliant, but in the end, none of them swayed me.

Nor did a new line of reasoning I heard from my cousin Levi a couple of weeks ago. Levi—the son-in-law of my Orthodox aunt Kate— told me he believes in God for this reason: The Bible is so strange, so utterly bizarre, no human brain could have come up with it.

I like Levi's argument. It's original and unsanctimonious. And I agree that the Bible can be strange—the command to break a cow's neck at the site of an unsolved murder comes to mind (Deuteronomy 21:4). Still, I wasn't convinced. Humans have come up with some astoundingly bizarre stuff ourselves—biathlons, turducken, and my son's Chicken Dance Elmo, to name a few.

In short, I don't think I can be debated into believing in God. Which presents a problem. Because the Bible commands you not only to believe in God, but to love Him. It commands this over and over again. So how do I follow that? Can I turn on a belief as if it flows out of a spiritual spigot?

Here's my plan: In college, I also learned about the theory of cognitive dissonance. This says, in part, if you behave in a certain way, your beliefs will eventually change to conform to your behavior. So that's what I'm trying to do. If I act like I'm faithful and God-loving for several months, then maybe I'll become faithful and God-loving. If I pray every day, then maybe I'll start to believe in the Being to whom I'm praying.

So now, I'm going to pray. Even though I'm not exactly sure how to pray. I've never prayed before in my life, not counting the few perfunctory uplifted gazes when my mom was sick.

For starters, what do I do with my body? The Bible describes a multitude of positions: People kneel, sit, bow their heads, lift their heads skyward, put their head between their knees, lift up the hands, beat their breast. There's no single method.

Sitting is tempting, but it seems too easy. I'm of the no-pain-no-gain mindset. So I settle on holding my arms outstretched like a holy antenna, hoping to catch God's signal.

As for what to say, I'm not sure. I don't feel confident enough to improvise yet, so I've memorized a few of my favorite prayers from the Bible. I walk into our living room, stand in front of our brown sectional couch, hold out my arms, bow my head, and, in a low but clear voice, recite this passage from the Book of Job: "Naked I came from my mother's womb and naked I will depart. The Lord gave and the Lord has taken away; may the name of the Lord be praised."

It's a beautiful passage, but I feel odd uttering it. I've rarely said the word "Lord", unless it's followed by "of the Rings." I don't often say "God" without preceding it with "Oh my."

The whole experience is making me uncomfortable. My palms are sweaty. I'm trying to speak with earnest intent, but it feels like I'm transgressing on two separate levels. First, I feel like I'm breaking some sort of taboo issued by the agnostic high priests. Worse, what if I'm breaking the Second Commandment? If I don't believe the holy words I'm saying, isn't that taking the Lord's name in vain?

I glance at the clock. I've only been praying for a minute. I've promised myself I'd try to pray for at least ten minutes three times a day.

So I get back to work. I squint my eyes and try to visualize Him. It's a fiasco. My mind goes to a series of clichés: The Universe, a.k.a the view from inside the Hayden Planetarium; a fog-shrouded middle-east-ern Mountain; something akin to the multi-color special effects from Stanley Kubrick's 2001: A Space Odyssey when the rocket went into hy-perspace. Pretty much everything but the guy in the flowing white robe and the basso profundo voice.

All I can say is, I hope I get better.

And it is possible I will. When I was in high school, I had a handful of what might qualify as quasi-mystical experiences. Surprisingly, none involved a bong. They would happen unexpectedly, and they would only last for a moment, about as long as a sneeze, but they were memorable.

The only way to describe them makes me sound like I'm leading an est seminar, but so be it: I felt at one with the universe. I felt the bound-ary between my brain and the rest of the world suddenly dissolve. It wasn't that I intellectually comprehended that everything and everyone is connected, I felt it, the way one might feel cold or carsick. The epipha-nies would descend on me without warning: One came while I was lying on a blanket in Central Park's Great Lawn, another while I was riding the Bullet Train on a family trip in Japan. They were at once utterly humbling (my life so piddling and insignificant) and totally energizing (but it's also part of something so huge). The glow from these mental or-gasms would last several days, making me, at least temporarily, more serene and Buddha-like.

For no reason I can think of, my epiphanies suddenly stopped around senior year of high school. Perhaps this year will give me the map to find them again. Or else make me conclude my brain was playing two-bit mind tricks on me.

Nor shall there come upon you a garment of cloth made of two kinds of stuff

LEVITICUS 19:19

Day five. I've made a list of the Top Five Most Perplexing Rules in the Bible. I plan to tackle all five this year, but I figured I'd start with one that requires neither violence nor pilgrimages. Namely: The ban on wearing clothes made of mixed fibers. It's such an odd proscription, I figured there was zero chance anyone else in America was trying to follow it.

Of course, I was flat wrong.

My friend Eddy Portnoy—who teaches history at the Jewish Theological Seminary—told me he recently spotted a flyer in Washington Heights advertising a shatnez tester. Shatnez, he informed me, is the Hebrew word for mixed fibers. A tester will come to your home and inspect your shirts, pants, sweaters and suits to make sure you have no hidden mixed fibers.

So today, I dial the number, and a man named Mr. Berkowitz agrees to make a house call. Mr. Berkowitz arrives right on time. He has a gray beard that descends below his collar, large glasses, and a black tie tucked into the top of his pants, which rest a good six inches above his navel. His yarmulke is slightly askew.

Mr. Berkowitz clicks open his black American Tourister rolling suitcase. Inside, his tools: a microscope, an old canister with the faded label "vegetable flakes", and various instruments that look like my mother's sewing kit after a genetic mutation. He spreads them out on my living room table. Mr. Berkowitz reminds me of an Orthodox CSI. God's wardrobe detective.

He gives me a shatnez primer. Shatnez is not just any mixed fiber. Poly-cotton blends and lycra-spandex blends—those are fine. The problem is mixing wool and linen. That's the forbidden combination, according to Deuteronomy 22:11 (the Bible's only other verse that talks about mixed fibers).

"How do you tell when something is shatnez?" I ask.

Well, you can't trust the clothing labels, says Mr. Berkowitz. They're often inaccurate. "You have to look at the fibers yourself. All the fibers look different under the microscope," he says.

He draws me a diagram: linen looks like a piece of bamboo. Wool is like a bunch of stacked cups. Cotton resembles twisted streamers. And polyester is smooth, like straw.

I bring out a pile of sweaters, and he goes to work. He snips some fibers off a black V-neck sweater and puts them under the microscope.

"See if you can tell," he says.

I squint into the microscope.

"It's polyester," I say.

"No. Look. The stacked cups? It's wool."

He seems disappointed. Clearly I'm not a shatnez inspector protégé. Mr. Berkowitz is kind, gentle, but persistently frazzled. And I wasn't helping matters.

Mr. Berkowitz makes some notes on a sheet that looks like a hospital chart. The sweater is kosher, he tells me. So is the next one I bring out.

"Look," he says, motioning to the microscope.

"Wool?" I say.

"No. Cotton."

Damn!

I bring out my wedding suit. This could be trouble, he says: wool suits often have linen hiding somewhere in them, especially Italian suits, which this was.

Mr. Berkowitz gets out a tool that resembles a fondue fork and begins digging into various parts of my suit—the collar, the pockets, the sleeves—with something approaching ferocity. This suit is the only suit I own, and it cost me about a third of my salary. I'm a little alarmed. I'm glad Julie's not here to see this.

"Is it shatnez?" I ask.

He doesn't answer for a minute. He's too busy with the microscope. His beard is squashed around the eyepiece.

"I have a strong suspicion this is linen," he says. The alleged culprit is some canvas that was hiding under the suit's collar

Mr. Berkowitz spins the fabric with his fingers.

"I'm sending it to the laboratory to make sure, but I am almost convinced it is linen." He tells me I'll have to put my only suit into storage, or get it de-linened by a tailor.

Mr. Berkowitz seems suddenly unfrazzled. He is relieved.

"It's joyous," he says. "If I save someone from breaking a commandment, it gives me a little high." He does a fist-pump. "I never took drugs, but I imagine this is what it feels like."

His joy is infectious. I feel momentarily happy too. But then return to my baseline bewilderment.

"It's really that important not to wear linen and wool?" I ask.

"Absolutely."

"Are some commandments in the Bible more important than others?"

"All equal," he says. Then pauses. "Well, I can't say that. Not murdering is at a very high level. So is adultery and not worshiping idols."

He seems torn. On the one hand, all the rules are from the same place. The Orthodox Jews follow a list of 613 rules originally compiled by the great medieval rabbi Maimonides from the first five books of the Bible. On the other hand, Mr. Berkowitz also has to admit that homicide is worse than wearing an unkosher blazer.

Before Mr. Berkowitz leaves, I ask him the obvious, staring-us-in-the-face question: Why? Why would God care if we wore mixed fibers?

The answer is: We don't know.

There are theories. Some say it was to train the ancient Hebrews to keep things separate so they'd be less inclined to intermarry. Some say it's an allusion to Cain and Abel's sacrifice—Cain offered flax to God and Abel offered sheep. Some say that the heathens used to wear the combination, and the Hebrews were trying to distinguish themselves from the pagans in any way they could.

Bottom line, though: We don't know.

"This is a law that God gave us. We have to trust him. He's all-powerful. We're like children. Sometimes parents have laws children don't understand. Like when you tell a child not to touch fire, he doesn't understand why, but it is good for him."

In Judaism, the Biblical laws that come without explanation—and there are many—are called "Chukim." This is such a law. The point is, you can never know what is important in the long term. God might have a different measuring scale than us. In fact, some say it's more crucial to follow the inexplicable ones, because it shows you're committed, that you have great faith.

The notion of obeying laws that have no rational explanation is a jarring one. For most of my life, I've been working under the paradigm that my behavior should, ideally, have a logical basis. But if you live Biblically, this is not true. I have to adjust my brain to this.

You shall not covet

EXODUS 20:17

Day six. After a day devoted to the obscure, I'm craving some good old-fashioned Ten Commandments to bring me back into the mainstream.

Since I break this commandment every day, I decide "Thou shalt not covet" is most in need of immediate attention. This commandment is the final one of the ten, and the only one to regulate a state of mind, not behavior. It's also arguably the hardest, especially in modern-day New York. This is a city that runs on coveting.

It's 2 p.m. and here's the list of things I've coveted since I woke up:

—Jonathan Safran Foer's speaking fee (someone told me he gets $15,000 per lecture)

—The Treo 700 PDA

—The mental calm of the guy at the Bible bookstore who said he had no fear because he walked with God.

—Our friend Elizabeth's sprawling suburban front yard.

—The Clooney-level fame that allows you to say whatever you feel like, moronic or not.

—The brilliant screenplay for Office Space. (I sometimes have a weird fantasy that I could go back to 1997 with a videotape, transcribe the dialogue, and beat writer Mike Judge to the punch).

Plus, ever since I became a father, I've been introduced to a whole new level of coveting. I'm not just coveting for myself, I'm coveting for my son. I'm trying to keep up with the Jones' kid.

Like with Jasper's vocabulary. I love the kid, but he's distressingly behind the curve in the speaking department. He communicates mostly by using eight different types of grunts, each one with its own meaning. I feel like the ethnographer who had to decipher the nuances of the 23 Eskimo words for snow. A medium-pitched grunt means "yes." A lower-pitched grunt means "no." A brief, chimp-like grunt means "come here now!" Jasper's a great walker and ball-thrower, but words—those things I'm supposed to arrange for a living—they're not so interesting to him.

Meanwhile, his friend Shayna—three months his junior—knows words like "helicopter" and "cabinet." She's practically got her own blog. I covet Shayna's vocabulary for Jasper.

To sum up, I expend a lot of mental energy breaking this commandment. And I'm not even including 'coveting' in the sexual sense—though

I certainly did that with the woman in purple flip-flops on the street. Or the woman with the low-riding Calvins. Or . . . I'll return to that topic later, since it deserves its own chapter.

The full anti-coveting commandment reads like this: "You shall not covet your neighbor's house; you shall not covet your neighbor's wife, or his manservant, or his maidservant, or his ox, or his ass, or anything that is your neighbor's."

The ox and the ass aren't a problem in post-agrarian Manhattan. But the phrase "anything else that is your neighbor's"—that pretty much covers it all. No wiggle room.

But how do you stop yourself from coveting?

The word 'covet' is a translation of the Hebrew root "hamad", roughly equivalent to desire or want. There are two schools of thought on what the commandment is preventing.

Some interpreters say that coveting in itself isn't forbidden. It's not always bad to yearn. It's coveting your neighbor's stuff that's forbidden. As one rabbi puts it, it's okay to covet a Jaguar—but you shouldn't covet your neighbor's Jaguar. In other words, if your desire might lead you to harm your neighbor, then it's wrong.

But others say that coveting any Jaguar is wrong, whether it's your neighbor's or the one at the dealership. A moderate interest in cars is okay. However, coveting means you are overly desirous of the Jaguar, you are distracted by material goods, you have veered from the path of being thankful for what God provides. You have, no doubt, fallen victim to advertising, the tenth commandment's arch-nemesis.

To play it safe, I'm trying to avoid both types of coveting.

Julie rejects one of my strategies—I asked her to censor the newspapers and magazines by ripping out all the ads for iPods and Jamaican vacations and such. Instead, I've been forced to cut down my magazine consumption to a trickle.

But coveting material goods in ads isn't the big hurdle for me. My real weakness is jealousy of others. The relentless comparison to my peers. Am I more successful than Julie's ex-boyfriend who invented a lighting gadget that fits over the page of a book so you can read it at night? It's been featured on the cover of the Levenger catalog, as my mother-in-law reminds me often.

If it's not the ex-boyfriend, it's someone else. And this type of coveting will never be assuaged. If by some crazy quirk or twist of fate or accounting error, I were to get J.S. Foer's speaking fee, then I'd move right onto coveting Madeleine Albright's speaking fee. The Bible is right. Jealousy is a useless, time-wasting emotion that's eating me alive. I should focus on my family and, nowadays, God.

Of course, stopping an emotion is not easy. The prevailing paradigm is that we can't control our passions. As Woody Allen said when his affair with Soon-Yi was discovered, "The heart wants what it wants." But I can't just give up—I need a new point of view. So I consult my spiritual advisory board.

One recommended method is to tell yourself the coveted car/job/house/speaking-fee/donkey is just not a possibility. A medieval rabbi—Abraham ibn Ezra—uses this example (he's talking about the sexual sense of covet, but you can apply more broadly): When you see a pretty woman married to another man, you have to put her in the same class as your mother. She's off-limits. The very notion of her as a sex partner is repulsive, unthinkable, except to perverts and/or those who have read too much Freud. Or else, think of the woman as a peasant would a princess. She's pretty, but she's so far out of your realm, your admiration is abstract, not lascivious. I try to do this with J.S. Foer's speaking fee. It's outside of my realm, I say. The strategy runs counter to you-can-do-anything-you-set-your-mind-to ambition, but maybe it's better for my mental health.

And then there's this tactic: If you're intently focused on following the rules of the Bible, you don't have time to covet. Not as much, anyway. You're just too busy. A couple of weeks ago, my daily coveting list would have taken up a third of this book. Now, I've trimmed it down to half a page. Progress, I think.

You shall rejoice before the LORD your God seven days.

LEVITICUS 23:40

Day seven. It's been a week. My spiritual state: Still agnostic. My beard state: itchy and uneven—I've got these bald patches that resemble tiny crop circles. My wardrobe state: I've traded my usual T-shirts and jeans for khakis and Oxfords because it feels somehow more respectful. My emotional state: strung out.

The learning curve remains crushingly steep. I continue to second-guess everything I do and say. I've noticed my speech has slowed down, as if I'm speaking English as a second language. This is because I mentally check every word before allowing myself to utter it: Is it a lie? Is it a boast? Is it a curse? Is it gossip? What about exaggeration? Does the Bible allow me to say "My friend Mark's been working at Esquire since 1904?" (He's been there a mere 17 years). I censor about 20 percent of my sentences before they leave my mouth. The Bible's language laws are rigorous.

I'm poring over religious study books, desperately trying to get a handle on this topic and every other. My reading list grows exponentially. Every time I read a book, it'll mention three other books I feel I have to read. It's like a particularly relentless series of pop-up ads.

I still read the Bible itself, taking it with me wherever I go. That Bible salesman was right—I should have gotten that version of the Scriptures that's camouflaged as a magazine. When I read my Bible on the subway, I can feel the hostility emanating from the secular commuters. They look at me with their lips taut and faces tense, like they expect me to tackle them at any moment and forcibly baptize them.

In addition to the Bible, I also carry around a stapled print-out of my rules, which I scan frequently. My original plan had been to pay equal attention to all the rules every day. This turned out to be impossible. That's like trying to juggle 800-plus balls. The brain can't handle it. I was too scattered.

So my revised plan is this: I will still attempt to follow all the rules simultaneously. But on a given day, I'll hone in on a particular rule, and devote much of my energy to that rule, while keeping the others in my peripheral vision.

How to choose the right time to focus on a particular rule? It's not a science. I've opted instead to go where the spirit takes me. I imagine a lot of factors will come into play—life's curveballs, my whims, logistics, my day job (I write for Esquire magazine, which I know will force me to confront the lust rules soon enough). And variety. I want to alternate obscure with mainstream, physical with mental, hard with easy. I need variety. I don't have the stamina to spend a month focused solely on the 45 rules of idolatry.

With the humble is wisdom

PROVERBS 11:2

Day 11. I'm going to take a bunch of Biblically-themed road trips this year, and today is my first: Amish country. It seems a good place to start. Not only are the Amish tied with the Hasidic Jews for the title of most easily-spotted Bible followers, but they are also interesting in this sense: They strictly adhere to rules in both the Old and the New Testaments. For instance:

—Their famous beards are the result of the Old Testament's ban on trimming the beard. (The Amish do, however, shave their moustaches, because the moustache was thought to have military associations).

—They refuse to pose for or take photos, since it would violate the Old Testament's Second Commandment: "You shall not . . .make any likeness of anything that is in heaven above, or that is in the earth beneath.." This is why, if you click on an Amish website, you'll often see photos of the backs of their heads. (And yes, the Amish have websites; go ahead and chuckle if you must. To be fair, the Amish don't run the sites themselves. It's a third party promoting their woodworks and quilts).

—Amish women wear bonnets in keeping with the New Testament's 1 Corinthians 11:5, which states that women's heads must be covered while praying.

—The Amish perform a foot-washing ritual, in accordance with the New Testament's John 13:5, which says "If I then, your Lord and Teacher, have washed your feet, you also ought to wash one another's feet. For I have given you an example . . ."

The Amish version of Biblical living is combined with what's called the Ordnung—the traditions that have built up since the Amish origins in

16th century Switzerland. The Ordnung is what dictates the Amish dress code and its ban on electricity.

Julie and I rent a car and drive down to Lancaster County. Julie may not be a huge fan of my project, but she figures she can at least take advantage of a road trip or two. Our destination is called Smucker's Farm Guest House. It's one of the few bed and breakfasts actually owned and operated by an Amish family. Most inns just offer some sort of vague proximity to Amish people. This is the real thing.

The trip takes four hours. Incidentally, I'm proud to say that I have absolutely no urge to make a double entendre when we passed Intercourse, Pennsylvania, which I see as a moral victory.

We pull into the driveway, and the first thing I see is a woman in full Amish regalia—ankle-length blue dress and a white bonnet—wielding a gas-powered leaf blower. This isn't an image I expected to see. She doesn't have a video iPod, but still. It punctures my Amish stereotypes right up front.

The woman—Anna—brings us to meet her father Amos, the head of the household. Amos Smucker is tall, wiry and slope-shouldered. He's dressed exactly as you'd expect: Black suspenders, straw hat, pants pulled high above his waist. His snow-white hair is shaped in the traditional Amish style—a modified bowl cut that curves over the ears and then angles down, becoming just a bit longer in the back.

I introduce myself. He nods, gives me a quiet "Hello" and walks us to our room.

Amos talks slowly and carefully, like he only has a few dozen sentences allotted for the weekend, and he doesn't want to waste them up front. I read later in the Amish book Rules of a Godly Life that you should "let your words be thoughtful, few and true." By adopting minimalism, Amos has mastered those speech laws I'm struggling with.

I tell Amos that I'd love to talk to him about the Amish. He obliges. I wonder how sick he is of answering the same annoying questions from curious outsiders. At least I pledged to myself not to bring up Witness or that Randy Quaid movie about a one-armed Amish bowler.

We sit in Amos' kitchen—sparse, of course, with a wooden table and a three-ring binder that says "A Journal of By-Gone Years: The Smuckers."

"When did your family come over?" I ask.

"My ancestor Christian Smucker came over from Switzerland in the 18th century."

And yes, Amos is a distant cousin of the strawberry jam Smuckers, though that branch is no longer Amish.

"How many brothers and sisters do you have?"

"There were 17 of us," says Amos.

"Seventeen?"

He nods.

"And where were you in the order?"

"I was the baby," Amos says. "Once my mother got me, she said, 'I'm done. I got what I wanted.'"

Did he just make a joke? I think so. Amos allows himself just the slightest, faintest wisp of a smile.

I explain the premise of my book to Amos. He stares over my left shoulder in silence. No reaction. From my brief visit with the Amish, I got the feeling that they are not enamored of talking about theology, at least not with the English, at least not with me. Best stick to more practical topics.

"Are you working now?"

"I used to be a dairy farmer, but I don't do so much anymore. I'm not retired. I'm just tired."

I think Amos just made another joke. You haven't seen deadpan delivery till you've seen the Amish.

"What's your schedule?" I ask.

"I go to sleep at 8:30 or so, and wake up at 4:30. I can't sleep after five. I was a dairy farmer, and that's the way my computer is programmed."

An interesting metaphor for a man who doesn't use electricity, I think to myself.

Amos drums his fingers on the table. He has amazing hands. Knotty, but somehow elegant, with thumbs that curve around like a candy canes and practically brush up against his wrist.

We sit silently.

Finally, Julie asks if maybe he could show us the property. He nods. Our first stop is the garage. Amos owns three black buggies, all of them lined up against the wall, their red fluorescent triangle facing outwards. His daughter Anna is polishing the middle one.

The garage opens into the stables, where Amos keeps his horses. He has two of them—they're beautiful and chocolate-brown and they trot over to greet Amos.

"They used to be racehorses," says Amos, patting the neck of one horse. "Ninety percent of the horses the Amish have were once racehorses."

This is the only time during the weekend that Amos approached being prideful. Humility is absolutely central to the Amish way of life, and it's one of the most beautiful things about the community. But if you're going to be proud of anything, I figure these horses are a pretty good choice.

Amos grew up in this house, he tells us.

"What was your childhood like?"

"It was cold. There was no insulation, so it got to be two below in our room."

"Wow," I say.

"Two below the covers."

This time he can't suppress the corners of his mouth from turning slightly upward. That was definitely a gag.

Back in the kitchen, I ask about his kids. He has seven, all of them still Amish, many of them nearby or across the street. Before coming, I had read that the Amish population in America—now at almost 200,000—had doubled in the last twenty years. They are in no danger of fading away.

"Are there a lot of conversions to the Amish faith?"

"Very few." Amos pauses, then says: "Do you want to hear an Amish joke?"

"Sure."

This is great. The Amish have been an easy, go-to punchline for far too long. In fact, I almost didn't come to Amish country because I didn't want to fall into the trap. So it'll be a delight to hear an Amish joke from an actual Amish person.

"What happened when the Mennonite man married the Amish woman?"

Julie and I don't know.

"She drove him buggy."

We laugh. It's not Chris Rock, but you have to remember: Amos is working with some pretty stringent preconditions.

"Ba-dum-bum," says Julie.

I wonder if the rimshot reference made any sense to him, or if he just thought Julie made odd sounds.

I try to bring up spirituality once more. I tell him that the Book of Amos is one of my favorite parts in the Bible. Again, silence. For a long thirty seconds.

"Do you know 'Amazing Grace?'" he finally says.

We nod.

"Help us out then."

Amos fishes a harmonica out of his pocket, takes a deep breath, and starts playing the most astounding version of the hymn I've ever heard. He was working that harmonica, his hand flapping, playing notes on both the inhale and the exhale.

Julie and I fumble the words bit in the middle, but we end strong: "I once was lost, but now am found. Was blind, but now I see."

"Do you play at church?" I ask, when he stops.

"No, we don't play instruments," he says. "It might encourage pride. You might get some thoughts. Try to show off for other people."

Amos holds up his harmonica. "This is just for home use."

A pause. "Well, I best get moving," says Amos. "Supper is at 5:30."

And with that, Amos disappears into his dining room.

Julie and I drive to a local tourist-trap restaurant that serves butter-soaked vegetables and shoofly pie. On the way, we see another startling sight, right up there with the leaf blower: It is an Amish teen, his hands behind his back, Rollerblading leisurely down a country road.

I found out later that some of the Amish allow Rollerblades. Rubber tires are forbidden, so bikes are out, but Rollerblade wheels are made of plastic. Likewise, though electricity is banned, tools using batteries, solar power, or gas are sometimes okay. Hence the leaf blower.

The lesson from my weekend with the Amish is this: you cannot stop religion from evolving. Even here, where customs and dress were suppos-edly frozen in the 16th century, they will still find a way. It makes my quest to rewind my life to Biblical times that much more daunting. Can I really scrape off all those millennia of accumulated tradition?

Before we arrive at the restaurant, Julie and I spot a cluster of about 30 buggies. We pull over to see what's happening. We have stumbled onto an Amish baseball game. Amos tells us that many Amish—him included—discourage competitive sports.

But here are 18 Amish teenage boys, their sleeves rolled up, their shirts and suspenders dark with sweat. Julie and I watch for a long time. These kids are good, but something is off about the game. I realize after a few minutes what it is: This is the quietest baseball game I've ever seen. No trash talk. No cheering from the parents in the stands. Near silence, except for the occasional crack of the bat. It is eerie and peaceful and beautiful.

Do not now be stiff-necked as your fathers were,
but yield yourselves to the LORD

2 CHRONICLES 30:8

Day 13. Back in New York, the Bible is keeping me overscheduled. The mornings are particularly crammed. I have to attach my fringes. Say my prayers. Tie a Xeroxed copy of the Ten Commandments to my forehead and hand in accordance with Exodus 13:9 (more on that later). The rest of the day Is consumed with Bible study, mid-day prayer, perhaps a good deed, Biblical shopping (today I plan to buy a walking stick), a few hours devoted to secular Esquire matters, a Scripturally-approved dinner, then prayers at night.

Oh, and my spiritual advisory board. I try to meet or talk with at least one sage per day. Today is a doubleheader. It starts with breakfast with my friend Roger Bennett.

Roger is a Liverpudlian who ends all conversations with "Rock on." He has about eight jobs—writer, documentarian, foundation head— most of which have to do religion in some way.

Roger doesn't mind that my morning rituals made me ten minutes late, but he does want to tell me something: "You're going into this thinking that it's like studying the Sumo wrestlers in Japan," Roger says.

"You're saying to yourself, 'I won't really become one. I'll maintain my distance.'"

I start to protest. Roger continues.

"You're dealing with explosive stuff. People a lot smarter than you have devoted their lives to this. So you have to admit there is a possibility that you will be profoundly changed by the end."

He's right. And it scares me. I hate losing control. I like to be in command of everything. My emotions, for instance. If I'm watching a love story and I start to get too weepy, I'll say to myself: "Okay, there's a boom mic right over Audrey Hepburn's head, see if you can spot its shadow," and that'll snap me out of the movie and I'll regain my composure. I also spend a lot of time trying to control my health, mostly by obsessing about germs. I have a mild case of OCD (a disease that has, I'm afraid, become a bit trendy, thanks to Larry David et al). My medicine cabinet is packed with a dozen bottles of Purell at all times. I haven't touched a subway pole with my bare hands in a decade—I usually just plant my feet wide apart in the subway car and pretend I'm a surfer.

The problem is, a lot of religion is about surrendering control and being open to radical change. I wish I could stow my secular worldview in a locker at the Port Authority bus terminal and retrieve it at the end of the year.

After breakfast with Roger, I take a subway downtown to have lunch with the Brooklyn rabbi Andy Bachman at a diner. It's back-to-back mentoring today. Andy's easy to relate to. He also grew up in a secular home, though that home was in Wisconsin (Jews there are known as the "frozen chosen," by the way). He was drawn to religion when he first saw the beautiful typography of the Talmud. He's youngish, 42, and insists I call him Andy, which seems disrespectful, but I try.

"How's it going?" asks Andy.

I tell Andy about Mr. Berkowitz and the mixed fiber inspection.

"I was riveted," I say. Maybe too riveted, actually. I know myself. I'm drawn to the weird. In my last book on the encyclopedia, I made seven references to philosopher Rene Descartes' fetish for cross-eyed women, which I think and hope is a record.

"I'm worried I could spend the whole year on the strange parts of the Bible and neglect the parts about goodness and justice," I say.

Andy thinks about it for a half-minute. He takes a sip of coffee.

"My advice is: Don't forget the prophets."

The prophets, he explains, are twenty extraordinary men and women found in the Hebrew Scriptures. They come onto the scene several hundred years after the age of Moses. By then, the Israelites were living in the Promised Land, but they'd botched it all up. They'd gotten corrupt and lazy. They were oppressing the poor just like their former masters in Egypt. The prophets were the Martin Luther King Jr.'s of their day, railing against the crooked system. Not so coincidentally, MLK liked to quote them—including Amos' amazing words: "Let justice roll down like waters and righteousness like an ever-flowing stream!"

"Try to make everything you do measure up to the moral standards of the prophets," Andy told me. "Remember what Micah said. He said that the animal sacrifices weren't important. The important thing is to 'Do right. And to love mercy. And to walk humbly with your God.'"

. . . .and he gave him a tenth of all

GENESIS 14:20 (JPS)

Day 14. Andy's correct, of course. I have to be more moral. I have to do something that would please the prophets. The next morning, I flip through my list of rules and find an excellent candidate on page 28. Give away 10 percent of your income.

"I'm going to tithe," I announce to Julie over breakfast.

She seems concerned. In general, she's much more magnanimous than I am. She's a sucker for those charities that send you free sheets of return-address labels with little cartoons of a rollerblading Ziggy, along with a heartbreaking brochure about lymphoma. I tell her it's emotional blackmail. She ignores me and mails them checks.

But even for Julie 10 percent is high, especially with Jasper and, God willing, another kid to come. She asks me whether I can count my literary agent's fee as a tithe. She's only half-joking.

Unfortunately, I doubt even the most brilliant rabbi could figure out a way to classify International Creative Management as 'the poor' (especially after they raised their commission to 15 percent a couple of years ago).

"Can you at least do 10 percent after taxes?" she says.

That night, I call my spiritual advisory board to ask. I reach Elton Richards, the pastor out to pasture.

"You shouldn't get too legalistic with it," says Elton. "Give what you can afford. And then give some more. It should feel like a sacrifice."

I study my Bible for insight. It seems that in the time of ancient Israel—before the Romans took over—no one paid taxes per se. The tithes were the taxes. And the tithing system was as complicated as any 1040 form. You gave portions to the priests, the temple-keepers, the temple itself, the poor, the widows and the orphans. So, I suppose, at least for now, after-tax tithing is probably okay.

I calculated 10 percent of my projected salary. It's not a huge number—but that's precisely the problem. If I were making $10 million a year and had to give away $1 million, that'd be easier.

That night, I spend three hours browsing a website called Charity-navigator.org. It's sort of a Zagat's guide to aid organizations. (Even this leads to coveting—they list the salaries of these charity CEOs, and some break half a million).

I settle on several organizations—Feed the Children and Save Darfur among them—and donate about two percent of my income. That's as much as I can do in one shot.

When the confirmation emails ping in, I feel good. There's a haunting line from Chariots of Fire. It's spoken by Eric Liddell, the most religious runner, the one who carries a Bible with him during his sprint. He says: "When I run, I feel His pleasure." And as I gave away money, I think I might have felt God's pleasure. I know. I'm agnostic. But still—I feel His pleasure. It's a warm ember that starts at the back of my neck and spreads through my skull. I feel like I was doing something I should have done all my life.

On the other hand, like a hard sprint, the pleasure is mixed with pain. I have just carved off two percent of my salary; and I've got 8 percent left to go. So here's the mental strategy I've adopted: If it weren't for the Bible, I wouldn't be living a Biblical year. I wouldn't have a book deal. No Bible, no income. So it's only fair to give 10 percent to God's people. It's the most righteous finder's fee around.

*He who spares the rod hates his son, but he who loves him is
diligent to discipline him.*

PROVERBS 13:24

Day 23. As I mentioned, one of my motivations for this experiment is my recent entrance into fatherhood. I'm constantly worried about my son's ethical education. I don't want him to swim in this muddy soup of moral relativism. I don't trust it. I have such a worldview, and though I have yet to commit a major felony, it seems dangerous. Especially nowadays. Within a couple of years, Jasper will be able to download Tijuana donkey shows on YouTube while ordering OxyContin from an offshore pharmacy.

So I want to instill some rock-solid, absolute morals in my son. Would it be so bad if he lived by the Ten Commandments? Not at all. But how do I get him there?

This morning, it's clearer than ever that I need help. I'm exhausted, a direct result of the fact that I'm the worst disciplinarian in America.

At about 2 a.m. Jasper woke up, so I let him climb into bed with me and Julie—already a sucker move. Instead of lulling him to sleep, this gave him lots of new activities. For instance, grabbing my sleep mask, pulling it away from my eyes till the elastic band is fully extended—a length of about two feet—then releasing it. The mask would shoot back onto my face with alarming force, producing an eye-watering snap. (Note: Contrary to what you might think, my sleep mask does not violate the Bible's prohibition against wearing women's clothes. It came in a box featuring a photo of a very masculine and well-rested man sleeping next to his attractive wife).

I told Jasper to stop, but my tone was about as menacing as Fred Rogers. So he did it again and again.

This is probably un-Biblical. At the very least, my leniency is a violation of The Proverbs. The Proverbs are the Bible's collection of wisdom attributed to King Solomon, and they come down clearly on the side of disciplining kids. As in corporal punishment.

Proverbs 22:15: "Folly is bound up in the heart of a child; but the rod of discipline drives it far from him."

Proverbs 23:14: "Thou shalt beat him with the rod, and shalt deliver his soul from hell." (KJV)

Proverbs 23:13: "Do not withhold discipline from a child; if you beat him with a rod, he will not die."

Some Americans hew to these proverbs literally. Until 2005, you could buy "The Rod," a 22-inch nylon whipping stick that sold for $5. It was the creation of an Oklahoma-based Southern Baptist named Clyde Bullock, who advertised it with the motto: "Spoons are for cooking, belts are for holding up pants, hands are for loving, and rods are for chastening," He shut down the business partly because of an outcry from more liberal Christians, and partly because he couldn't buy the cushioned grips anymore.

Other not-quite-as-literal literalists say paddles are an acceptable alternative. James Dobson—founder of Focus on the Family, the ultra-conservative Christian group—recommends paddling, especially if you want to keep your hand as 'an object of love.'

I don't own a rod or a paddle. In fact, corporal punishment of any sort is deeply counter to my parenting philosophy. I've always considered walloping your kid the H-Bomb of parenting—it's in the arsenal, but shouldn't be deployed.

Even for Project Bible, I can't deploy it. At least not yet. I've reached my first limit. So what to do? I decided this is one of those times when I should fulfill the letter of the law, if not the spirit. It's better than fulfilling nothing at all.

A few days ago, I Googled "flexible rod" and "soft rod," I ended up ordering a very unmenacing Nerf bat. I try it today on Jasper. After dinner, he grabs a handful of nickels off the dresser and chucks them across the room.

So I take the Nerf bat and smack Jasper's butt with it. I've never spanked him before, despite several temptations to do otherwise. When I swing my paddle—even though a it's spongy and harmless paddle—I break some sort of barrier. I have now punished my son physically. It's an unsettling feeling. It drives home just how lopsided the relationship is: Parents have God-like physical dominance over their kids, at least when those kids have yet to hit puberty.

Jasper seems undisturbed by all this. He responds by laughing hysterically, grabbing his whiffle bat and attempting to smack me back. So I'm basically sanctioning violence here.

The rod is a fiasco. But here's the thing: I agree with the Proverbs' gist. I need to discipline my son more. I need to give Jasper some tough love, dispense more Time Outs, or risk having him turn into a three-foot-tall monster. Julie has become the family disciplinarian, which is causing tension in our marriage, as she's not fond of being the bad cop. I've got to get stricter.

Look at the example set by God. The God of the Bible treats his children—the human race—with both justice and mercy. Right now, I'm out of whack; I'm 10 percent justice and 90 percent mercy. If I had been in charge of the Garden of Eden, Adam and Eve would have gotten three strikes, then a fourth, then a stern warning, then had their bedtime moved up 20 minutes. God, as you know, kicked them out. As a sign of His compassion, he clothed them in animal skins before the eviction, but he still kicked them out.

Make me understand the way of thy precepts, and I will
meditate on thy wondrous works.

PSALM 119:27

Day 30. It's the end of Month One. Physically, I feel okay. The beard's itchiness has receded, and, at least for the moment, it's looks more comparative-literature-professor than guy-who-stopped-taking-his-meds.

As for my spiritual life, the word that comes to mind is disconnected. I've been playing the role of the Bible man for a month—but that's what it still feels like. A role. A character. Like the time at summer camp when I was 12, and, for reasons I no longer remember, I adopted a deep Southern accent—a real Foghorn Leghorn twang—and spoke it exclusively for a month.

This Biblical alter-ego of mine is such a separate being, I've taken to calling him a different name: Jacob. It seemed the most natural choice, close but not identical. I've been observing this Jacob guy, studying him.

And here's what I've found: He too has a split personality. On the one hand, Jacob is much more moral than I am. He attempts to fulfill Leviticus 19:18—Love thy neighbor as thyself. Which means he's doing things like holding the elevator door for slow-moving passengers. Or giving a buck to the homeless guy outside the Museum of Natural History who says he's seeking donations for the 'United Negro Pizza Fund.'

He pays attention to the hundreds of small, almost unnoticeable moral decisions we make every day. He turns the lights off when leaving the room. He refrains from gawking at odd-looking passersby—the 400-pound man, the guy with the banana-colored pants, the woman who's eight inches taller than her boyfriend—something that I, as a lifelong people-watcher, would love to do. Jacob stares straight ahead like a Buckingham Palace guard.

He's not getting shortlisted for the Nobel yet, but he's a better man than my secular self.

On the other hand, my alter-ego is engaging in some deeply strange behavior. He says "Maybe we could have lunch on the fourth day of the workweek," since "Thursday" is forbidden. It comes from the Norse god Thor.

He rubs a dab of olive oil in his hair each morning, as instructed by Ecclesiastes ("let not oil be lacking on your head"), which leaves these unfortunate green stains on all my baseball hats.

And he's developed this byzantine method of paying our babysitter Des. The Bible says the "wages of a hired servant shall not remain with you all night until the morning," so she gets cash every night. But my secular self needs to pay her by weekly check so that she can properly file for taxes. Which means I have to ask that she bring all the cash back at the end of the week and exchange it for a check. Des has already started trying to slip out at night without saying goodbye to me/Jacob.

My alter-ego's behavior points to one of the biggest mysteries of the Bible. How can these ethically advanced rules and these bizarre decrees be found in the same book? And not just the same book. Sometimes the same page. The prohibition against mixing wool and linen comes right after the command to love your neighbor. It's not like the Bible has a section called "And now for some Crazy Laws." They're all jumbled-up like a chopped salad.

I hope all will become clear by the end of the year.

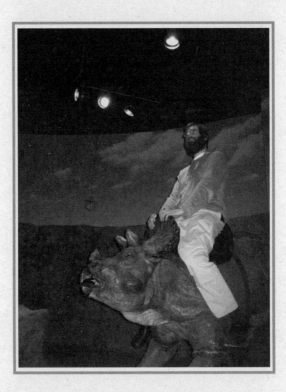

Month Two: October

Three times each year, every male among you must appear
before God the Lord . . .
EXODUS 23:14 (NAB)

Day 31, morning. I spent a half an hour checking airfares to Israel. I need to go this year. I can't devote a year living Biblically without making a pilgrimage to the birthplace of the holy book itself.

I've been once before. When I was 14, my parents wanted to take us to Israel and Egypt, so we signed up for a tour group whose members consisted of my family, a couple of dozen retired orthodontists, and an unmarried 27-year-old woman who had been led to believe this would be a singles tour, which it was, if you count the high percentage of widows and widowers.

I don't remember much about the tour. I remember the long bus rides, with the Israeli tour guide asking us "Does anyone want to stop at the smile room?" That was Israeli tour guide slang for the bathroom, since "everyone smiles when they walk out of the smile room." I remember preferring the Egyptian portion of the trip; I'd always been fascinated by the pyramids and had some knowledge of the Nile culture, or had at least memorized the lyrics to Steve Martin's "King Tut" song.

But Israel itself made little impression on my secular mind at all. At the time, I was going through an ill-thought-out Marxist phase. Religion was the opiate of the people. And not just that: I was sure the opiate-pushers—the rabbis, the bishops, the ministers—were in on the con, and were only trying to pay for their Benzes. Israel was the center of the corrupt system.

By default, this trip has to be more meaningful. Plus, it will give me a chance to meet my ex-uncle Gil. Yes, as in meet him for the first time. Here's the weird thing: He was married to my aunt for years, but I've never seen him face-to-face. The family considered him such an unstable character, such a fraud, that no one wanted him around at reunions or birthday parties. They didn't see him as a harmless eccentric. They thought he was dangerous. There were rumors of his Svengali-like, abusive techniques when he was a cult leader.

The main strategy was to pretend he didn't exist. In her semimonthly family newsletter, my grandmother couldn't even bring herself to type Gil's name. She referred to him only as "He." As in "He and Kate will be visiting in March," which I always found it an ironic echo of the Orthodox refusal to write the name God (usually written "G-d.") The only time I remember my grandmother talking about Gil was when she told me about a disturbing conversation she'd had with Kate. "She told me she'd be happy to stare into his eyes all day," said my grandmother. "That's not how a marriage should be. You should be side by side, facing the world, not looking into each others eyes all day."

So Gil has always been this mysterious, forbidden, slightly scary figure to me. Gil met Kate in 1982, and she became Orthodox soon after. I don't remember much about her from her pre-Gil life. I remember her waist-length hair (now tucked under a headdress), her creepy UFO expert boyfriend, and her gift of a whoopee cushion from France, which I guess was way more sophisticated than any whoopee cushion than we yokel Americans could make.

I remember her giggling a lot. And she still does—Orthodox Judaism hasn't erased her sense of humor. She has a great, loud, whooping laugh. But her passion nowadays is for two things: Her four children and the Torah.

It's a tricky and guilt-inducing proposition, meeting Gil. The truth is, I'm rebelling against my family. No one wants me to meet him. Early on, my mom asked point blank: "You're not going to talk to Gil, are you?" I didn't answer.

She thinks if I meet Gil, it'll give him some sort of legitimacy he doesn't deserve. I don't know about that. I don't think I'm in the position to bestow legitimicy on anyone. Regardless, I can't resist the chance to visit him. The man helped with the genesis of this quest. For better or worse, he could be a pivotal figure in my struggle to understand religion. At the end, I'll beg my family's forgiveness.

Blow a trumpet at the new moon

PSALM 81:3

Day 31. October 1, afternoon. The Bible commands me—or Jacob, or whoever I am—to blow a trumpet at the start of every month. (To be safe, I'm also blowing a trumpet at the start of every Hebrew month).

I find a ram's horn at the Jewish Community Center gift shop. It's a small shofar—$30 will only get you so much—about three times the size of a kazoo, and shaped like an elbow macaroni.

There's no doubt it's from a ram, though. It smells like a barn that hasn't been cleaned for days. I stand in my living room and blow. No sound. Just loudly exhaled air. These ram's horns are surprisingly hard to play. I'm still working under the assumption that the Bible didn't ban computers, so I spend a half hour on the Internet picking up tips:

—Separate the lips as if you were making a raspberry
—Keep your jaw in the position you would if you were spitting a watermelon seed
—wet your lips
—but not too much
—if you do wet them too much, spittle is best removed by a coffee brush or an aquarium brush
—put the shofar on the corner of your mouth, not in the center.

I sip a glass of water, part my lips, jut out my jaw, and blow the shofar again. It sounds like a dying fax machine. But, I remind myself, I still have 11 more months.

I did a little research, and as I suspected, I'm not alone. There are a handful of 21st century people who also blow a trumpet to kick off each month. But they are admittedly on the religious fringe. Mainstream Judaism and Christianity have both discontinued the practice, along with the observance of hundreds of other obscure Biblical rules. The reason?

Christians believe that Jesus was the ultimate sacrifice. His crucifixion made animal sacrifice unnecessary. And not just animal sacrifice, but many of the ceremonial laws of the ancient Hebrews. This is why Christians can eat bacon and shave their beards with impunity. And why they don't need to blow a trumpet to the new month.

Most—but not all—Christians draw a distinction between 'moral laws' and 'ritual laws.' They still adhere to the Old Testament's moral laws, such as the 10 commandments (and sometimes, the ban on homosexuality), but they scrap many of the ritual laws. Of course, there's a good amount of debate in Christianity over which should be considered moral laws and which ritual. Is the Sabbath a moral law? Or ritual? What about the ban on tattoos? I read a long tirade by one Christian against so-called Christian tattoo parlors.

Modern Judaism has a different take. It says that you could only sacrifice goats and oxen in the ancient era of the Jerusalem Temples. The Romans destroyed the Second Temple in 70 CE. And with the Temple, went the relevance of more than 200 sacrifice-related rules. (Including blowing a trumpet to the new moon, which was originally done along with a sacrifice). Plus, Americans are off the hook with regard to another 45 laws that believe they only apply in the land of Israel—many of them agricultural.

When I started this project, I vowed to try to follow all the Bible's rules—ritual, moral, agricultural and sacrificial—and see where it takes me. But, to use a food metaphor in honor of my adviser Pastor Richards, I think I've bitten off more than I can chew.

When a woman has a discharge of blood, which is her regular discharge from her body, she shall be in her impurity for seven days, and whoever touches her will be unclean until the evening.

LEVITICUS 15:19

Day 34. In case you were wondering, Julie got her period yesterday—which is bad news in two senses. First, it means our attempt to be fruitful and multiply has failed yet again. Second, it ratchets up the Biblical living to a whole new level of awkwardness.

The Hebrew Bible discourages the faithful from touching a woman for the week after the start of her period.

So far in my year, adhering this rule has been only mildly uncomfortable, nothing worse. In fact, it's got an upside: it dovetails quite nicely with my lifelong obsessive compulsive disorder and germaphobia, so it's turned out to be a brilliantly convenient excuse to avoid touching 51 percent of the human population.

A female friend will come in for a cheek kiss, and I'll dart my head out of the way like Oscar de la Hoya. A colleague will try to shake my hand, and I'll step backwards to safety.

"I'm sorry, I'm not allowed to."

"Oh. Um. Okay."

Usually, that's the end of it. Usually, but not always. Consider this conversation I had with Julie's Australian friend Rachel, whom we met in Central Park last week.

"You're not allowed to? What do you mean?"

"Well, you might be . . .impure."

"What do you mean 'impure.'"

"You know. In your cycle."

I paused. She looked perplexed. I decided this was a good time to avoid eye contact and study the pavement.

"Oh, you mean I might be menstruating? Don't worry, I menstruated last week."

At which point she hugged me. No escaping it.

Oddly, Rachel is not alone. A small but surprisingly vocal minority of Julie's friends have volunteered detailed information about their biological cycles. The photo editor at Esquire took the considerate step of emailing me her schedule. Did I perhaps want an Excel chart as well, she wondered?

I even managed to flatter this one woman I met at my sister-in-law's party. When I explained to her why I couldn't shake her hand, she told me "Well, that's the nicest compliment I've heard in a long time." I looked at her again: Gray hair, crow's feet, sixtysomething—yes, probably long past needing to worry about unplanned pregnancies.

Julie, however, is not flattered at all. She finds the whole ritual offensive. I'm not loving it either. It's one thing to avoid handshakes during flu season. But to give up all physical contact with your wife for seven days a month? It's actually quite exhausting, painful and lonely. You have to be constantly on guard—no sex, of course, but also no hand-holding, no shoulder-tapping, no hair-tussling, no goodnight-kissing. When I give her the apartment keys, I drop them into her hand from a safe six inch height.

"This is absurd," she tells me, as she unlocks the door. "It's like cooties from seventh grade. It's theological cooties."

I tell Julie that I can't pick and choose what I follow in the Bible. That'd negate the whole point of my experiment. If I'm trying to get into the mindset of the ancient Israelites, I can't ignore even the most inconvenient or obscure. I also point out that I didn't send her to a red tent.

She's not amused. "I feel like a leper."

"Actually leprosy in the Bible is a mistranslation. It's more likely a generic name for skin disease. Some even claim it's syphilis."

This is the wrong thing to say. It's a vestigial reflex from my days as an encyclopedia-reading know-it-all: Whenever I run out of things to say, I crowbar random facts into the argument.

Julie walks out of the room. When she's annoyed, she walks with heavy stomping footsteps. I felt Richter-level tremors throughout the apartment.

Since I understand Julie's objection and kind of agree with it, I figure it'd be good to get some historic and cultural context. I consult my spiritual advisory board and read up on the literature. As with all of the baffling Bible rules, there is a wealth of positive spin.

First, if done properly, the no-touching ban isn't bad for your marriage. Quite the opposite. Orthodox Jews still follow a version of the original menstruation laws and many told me they like the enforced sex hiatus. "It's like honeymoon sex every month," said an Orthodox woman I met one day in Central Park. "It's like makeup sex. You only appreciate what you have when you don't have it."

Second, the avoidance of your wife in this time of month is not misogynist. It actually has to do with a reverence for life. When a woman has her period, it's like a little death. A potential life has vanished. This is a way of paying respect, like sitting shiva.

In fact, words like 'impurity' and 'unclean' are mistranslations. Some Orthodox Jews find such terms offensive. The Hebrew word is 'tameh,' a state of spiritual impurity that doesn't have the same negative connotations.

(By the way, the history of impurity laws is fascinating but complex. Let me try to cram an hour-long talk I had with a rabbi into three lines: The purity laws date from the Jerusalem Temples. Back then, you had to be pure to make a sacrifice. When the Second Temple was destroyed, many of the purity laws fell out of use. Many, but not all. Jewish men still steer clear of their wives during menstruation. But they cite a different motivation: Touching might lead to sex, and sex during that time of the month, temple or no temple, is forbidden by another law, Leviticus 20:18. Also, to be extra-safe, the no-touching-ban today has been extended from a week to twelve days).

None of this positive spin appeases Julie, especially since I've decided to abide by another law that makes the no-touching-impure-women seem like a breeze. It's found in Leviticus 15:20: "And everything upon which she lies during her impurity shall be unclean; everything also upon which she sits shall be unclean." You shouldn't lie on a bed where a menstruating woman has lain, and you can't sit on a chair where she has sat.

It's a rule that no one follows to the letter anymore. But again, I want the ultimate ancient Israelite experience. And it can't hurt to be pure, right?

As for the no-lying-on-unclean-beds, I'm off the hook. Julie and I don't share a bed. Apparently, when I sleep, I thrash around like a beached marlin, so Julie has opted for two twin beds pushed together, a disturbing echo of my parents and 50s sitcoms.

The no-sitting-on-impure-seats presents more of a challenge. I came home this afternoon, and was about to plop down on my official seat, the gray pleather armchair in our living room.

"I wouldn't do that," says Julie.

"Why?"

"It's unclean. I sat on it." She doesn't even look up from her TiVo-ed episode of Lost.

Okay. Fine. Point taken. She's still not appreciating these impurity laws. I move to another chair, a black plastic one.

"Sat in that one too," says Julie. "And the ones in the kitchen. And the couch in the office."

In preparation for my homecoming, she had sat in every chair in the apartment, which I found annoying but also impressive. It seemed in the Biblical tradition of enterprising women—like Judith, who seduced the evil general Holofernes only to behead him when he was drunk.

I finally settle on Jasper's six-inch-high wooden bench, which she had overlooked, where I tap out emails with my knees up to my chin.

The next day I do an Internet search and find a $30 solution to the chair problem: The Handy Seat. This is an aluminum cane that unfolds into a three-legged miniature chair. It's marketed to the elderly, as well as "individuals who suffer from asthma, arthritis, hip or leg surgery, fibromyalgia, back injury" and various other ailments.

My Handy Seat arrives a few days later, and man, do I love it. I've started bringing it everywhere. First, it's a cane, which is sort of like a staff, which feels very Biblical to me. Plus, if you think about it, every subway seat, every bus seat, every restaurant seat—almost certainly impure. The Handy Seat is the foolproof solution. It's not overly comfortable (the plastic part for sitting is only about the size of a Frisbee and I've got minor back pain from the hunching posture it causes). And there's the inevitable problem of raised eyebrows from passersby and scolding from lobby security guys. ("What are you doing?" asked the guard at the Time Warner Center. "Just sitting, waiting for my friend." "Well, you can't sit here. Stand up please"). But The Handy Seat is my little island of cleanliness. There's something safe and comforting about it.

O God, thou art my God, I seek thee

PSALM 63:1

Day 36. A spiritual update: I'm still agnostic. I am feeling a little more comfortable saying the word "God"—thanks to sheer repetition, it no longer makes me sweat. But the anxiety has been replaced by frustration. And frankly, boredom.

The God of the Bible is an amazingly interactive deity. He's not aloof—He talks to people all the time. God spends 40 days with Moses on a mountaintop telling him the commandments. God instructs Ezekiel to make bread, and even gives him a recipe of wheat, lentil and spelt. God wrestles—physically wrestles—with Jacob on a patch of desert called Penuel. Jacob comes out of the fight with a broken hip and a new name: Israel, which means "wrestles with God." (Incidentally, some say it wasn't God himself who wrestled, but one of God's angels; the point is, there was contact with the divine).

I don't expect the level of interaction that the patriarchs had. I don't think God is going to put me in a half-nelson. But I'm having trouble even sensing the presence of God.

I'm praying three times a day. In the Bible, to my surprise, there's no agreed-upon per-day prayer quota, but morning, afternoon and night seems a safe, traditional schedule. I'm still praying with the prefabricated prayers provided by the Bible. Today, I use a moving passage from the Psalms.

> *O God, thou art my God, I seek thee,*
> *my soul thirsts for thee;*
> *my flesh faints for thee,*
> *as in a dry and weary land where no water is.*
> *So I have looked upon thee in the sanctuary,*
> *beholding thy power and glory.*
> *Because thy steadfast love is better than life,*
> *my lips will praise thee.*

I love the prayer. It's got two powerful metaphors at work—first, thirsting for God and second, loving God like a man loves his wife. And yet, despite the prayer's power, my mind wanders as I read it. "I have to remember to charge my cell phone . . . We need more quarters for the laundry room."

> *He who is slow to anger has great understanding,*
> *But he who has a hasty temper exalts folly.*
>
> PROVERBS 14:29

Day 39. I've noticed that a lot of Biblical living is about constant reminders. That's the purpose of the tassels I've safety pinned to my clothing—the Bible says they are to remind me of the commandments, like a
Biblical version of the string around the finger.

In the spirit of reminders, I've taped a list on my bathroom mirror.
It's my Most-Violated List. We'll see if it helps me stop breaking them.
The list includes the following classics:

—Lying.

most recent violation: I told my friend that the book he lent me was at
my mother-in-law's, when in fact I'd lost it.

—Vanity

I check my temples every day for signs of hair loss.

—Gossip

Julie and I talked about how her brother Doug still wears these loud,
multicolored sweaters right out of The Cosby Show.

—Coveting

I did a signing at a book fair a few days ago, and at the next table was
Anthony Bourdain, the rakish celebrity chef/author. My table got such
visitors as: My mother, my father, my wife, my son. Meanwhile, the line
in front of Bourdain's table resembled opening night of the Phantom
Menace, though without as many Darth Maul costumes.

—Touching impure things

Handy Seat aside, it's just too hard to avoid.

—Anger

A couple of days ago, I realized I had to devote more time to the Bible's
teachings on anger. I realized it because I gave the finger to an ATM. The
ATM charged me $1.75 fee for withdrawal. $1.75? That's bananas. So I
flipped off the screen. As Julie tells me, when you make rude gestures to
inanimate objects, it's time to start working on anger.

Mine is not the shouting, pulsing- vein-in-the-forehead rage. Like my dad, I rarely raise my voice (again, I like to be emotionally in control at all times). My anger problem is more one of long-lasting resentment. It's a heap of real or perceived slights that eventually build up into a mountain of bitterness.

Did I really need to get so angry at the juggler at the street fair who stopped juggling to take a cell pone call? And then talked for like 15 minutes while Jasper looked on all eager and hopeful? Yes, it's annoying, but worse things have happened.

Or what about the guy in Starbucks who monopolized the bathroom for 45 minutes? (in my defense, he was also wearing a black beret; this was 2006 Manhattan, not 1948 rive gauche). I was fuming.

And what about the incident at the soup kitchen?

I've been volunteering at Holy Apostles soup kitchen in Chelsea. It's an incredible place, the largest soup kitchen in new York, the second-biggest in the country; they serve more than 1,100 meals a day. The man who runs it is a charismatic tough-love leader who I could see leading a rebellion against the Roman centurions.

And usually, I get a little ethical head rush from working at the soup kitchen. This, I tell myself, is biblical living at its best. I'm following the inspiring words in Deuteronomy 15:7: "If there is a poor man with you, one of your brothers, in any of your towns in your land which the LORD your God is giving you, you shall not harden your heart, nor close your hand from your poor brother;"

And yet . . .even at the soup kitchen, I'm able to find slights.

At my most recent visit, first, I get assigned to kitchen duty—then immediately demoted. They tell me it's because of my beard.

I understand. No one wants an unpleasant surprise in their rice pilaf. I am fine with it, until I spot some other volunteer working in the kitchen—despite having his face covered with a big bushy beard of his own.

Why the discrepancy?

"Oh, I'm shaving my beard tomorrow," explains my rival volunteer.

Which makes exactly no sense. Does gravity somehow stop working the day before you shave?

I get reassigned to garbage duty. My job is to take the plastic trays from those who have finished lunch, remove the cutlery, then bang the trays forcefully against the side of the garbage can—clearing out all the mashed potatoes and string beans—and hand them to the stacker.

I think I am doing a pretty decent job, which is confirmed by the garbage team captain, a guy in a Jets t-shirt who tells me 'good job.' I am feeling pumped.

Then, after an hour and a half, I'm the victim of a soup kitchen power play.

This older guy named Max—he has a droopy face and a perma-scowl—comes up to me, hands me an iced tea in a particularly aggressive manner, and says: "Drink this. Then go away."

I don't want iced tea, and I don't want to go away. I just stare at him.

'Drink this. then go away,' he repeats, glowering.

As far as I can tell, he is no higher on the volunteer food chain than I am; for reasons unknown, he just wants my garbage duty spot.

The Bible says respect your elders and do not quarrel. So I leave. But I stew about it for a good two days. Drink this. then go away. What a bastard.

I've been battling my anger since this project started. I want to let go of my resentment. I know it's healthier, a better way to live.

But how to do this when faced with a real-life soup-kitchen Nazi? The best biblical inspiration I've found is in the book of Jonah. A quick recap for those (like me) who know only the whale part:

God calls on Jonah to preach to the evil city of Nineveh (now in Syria). Jonah refuses. He tries to flee God by boarding a ship. This doesn't work: God creates a mighty tempest, and the frightened sailors throw Jonah overboard. God then sends a whale to swallow Jonah (actually, the bible says 'big fish,' not whale) and spit him safely out onto land.

Chastened, Jonah agrees to go to Nineveh. Jonah preaches there and it works. More than 120,000 men, women and children—repent. God forgives them.

You'd think Jonah would be happy with God's forgiveness, but he's actually angry. He wanted the evil ones smote. He wanted fire and brimstone. He gets so furious at God, he no longer wants to live. God says "Do you do well to be angry?"

Jonah doesn't answer, but goes off to the outskirts of Nineveh to sulk. So God decides to teach Jonah a lesson: God grows a plant that shields the prophet from the harsh desert sun. Jonah is exceedingly glad. But the very next day, God causes a worm to kill the plant. Once again, Jonah is exposed to the harsh sun and gets very angry. Again, God asks Jonah: "Do you do well to be angry?"

God then drives home his point: Jonah lost his temper over a plant "for which he did not labor" and which lasted but a day. God says "And should I not be concerned about Nineveh, that great city, in which there are more than a hundred and twenty thousand persons who do not know their right hand from their left, and also many animals."

In other words, get some perspective.

So that's what I try to do. I ask myself the question God asked Jonah. "Do you do well to be angry?" I ask it out loud to myself. No, I don't, I answer. So I got elbowed aside by a strangely competitive soup kitchen volunteer. The world will not end.

I should remember the modern-day Ninevehs where thousands of lives are in danger—the crowd of homeless out the door at Holy Apostles, for instance, or pretty much anywhere in East Africa.

There is such a thing as biblically-acceptable anger—righteous indignation. Moses gets angry at the Israelites for worshiping a false idol. Jesus gets angry at the money changers for profaning the temple. The key is to ratchet up your righteous anger and mute your petty resentment. I'll be happy if I can get that balance to 50/50.

> *In the beginning God created the heavens and the earth.*
>
> GENESIS 1:1

Day 40. I told my friend Ivan—a good Catholic—that I was considering visiting a creationist museum and he let out a loud groan. "Those people give Christianity a bad name."

I understand what he's saying. It's the way many Jews feel when we see a billboard announcing Rabbi Menachem Schneerson as the Messiah. Or the way many gay men feel when they see a Rip Taylor tossing a handful of confetti. It's kind of embarrassing. Like Ivan, I've always taken evolution to be a cold, hard truth. As indisputable as the fact that sun is hot or that Charles Darwin married his first cousin (the latter of which I learned in the encyclopedia and can't get out of my head).

But creationism is Biblical literalism at its purest, so I need to check it out. I researched various creationist hotspots—both Jewish and Christian—and found a handful of possibilities. But nothing came close to Answers in Genesis. This is the $25 million, soon-to-open Kentucky-based museum—the Louvre for those who believe God made Adam less than 6000 years ago from dust—started by an Australian evangelical named Ken Ham. (A note on timing: I'll be spending more time with evangelicals—both conservative and liberal—in Month Nine when my New Testament portion begins; but since creationism is so tied to the Old Testament's Genesis, I'm doing it early).

AiG is still under construction, which is fine by me. There's something appropriate about seeing the creation of a creationist museum. So I flew down to Cincinnati, a few miles from the site.

At the airport, I realize once again how Biblical symbolism has seeped into every nook in my brain. As I exit, I see a strange FAA sign that ominously warns: "Don't Look Back." It doesn't say how you'd be punished if you do—I'm guessing body cavity search, not getting turned to a pillar of salt—but I still find it a bizarre echo of God's warning to Lot as he fled the destruction of Sodom: "Do not look back."

A half hour later, I pull up to the museum—a low building with thick yellow columns perched on a gentle Kentucky hill. In the parking lot, I spot a bumper sticker of a Jesus fish gobbling up a Darwin fish.

I'm greeted by the publicist Mark Looy, a gray-haired man with a gentle, schoolteacher voice who guides me to a door that lets us into the lobby. It is, in a word, awesome.

The place is still deep in construction. Hard hats everywhere, the smell of sawdust, the whine of drills. But even in its unfinished state, you can tell this is going to send the media into a Michael-Jackson-trial-like frenzy.

The first thing I see is an life-sized diorama of an Edenic scene. There's a waterfall, a stream, and weeping-willow trees. An animatronic caramel-skinned cavegirl giggles and cocks her head to look straight at me, which is odd and impressive and disturbing all at once. She's playing awfully close to a fierce-looking, razor-toothed dinosaur. Don't worry,

Mark tells me. In the beginning, humans and dinosaurs lived together in harmony. The scary incisors are for coconuts and fruit, just like pandas' teeth.

When AiG opens, they expect thousands of visitors. And they'll probably get them—polls say that as many as 50 percent of Americans believe in creationism. Not intelligent design. We're talking strict, the-earth-is-less-than-10,000 years old creationism. (The creationists I met scoffed at Intelligent Design, which says the world was designed by superior being, but not necessarily in seven literal days. The creationists think of it as some sort of nebulous theological mumbo jumbo).

Mark introduces me to Ken, the founder of AiG. Ken is a wiry and energetic 56-year-old with a red Van Dykish beard. He quizzes me about my last book, the one about reading the encyclopedia, and I end up telling him about my ill-fated appearance on Who Wants to Be a Millionaire? I was stumped by the question "What is an erythrocyte."

"It's a red blood cell," says Ken.

He's right. I'm thrown off-guard. A creationist who trumps me in science knowledge—that's unexpected and unsettling.

Ken was born to religious parents in Queensland, Australia, and still has a thick Aussie accent despite his 20 years in America. We start walking through the rooms. "The guy who designed the museum also designed the Jaws exhibit at the Universal theme park," Ken says. And it shows. The place is professional. We stroll past more than a dozen robotic dinosaurs. A statue of Eve with her flowing hair placed conveniently over her pert breasts. A partly-built ark. A room with a circular slope like the Guggenheim, a subtle reminder of man's fall from Paradise. A theater with sprinklers to simulate the flood. A huge crocodile (a prop from the movie Crocodile Dundee). The future home of a talking Virgin Mary robot. A medieval castle-themed bookstore. Medieval? Because the dragons of medieval times were actually still-living dinosaurs.

As we step among the animatronic Roman Centurion and the currently-headless giraffe, I ask Ken the questions he's been asked 1000 times.

If Adam and Eve gave birth to two boys Cain and Abel, how did Cain and Abel have kids?

"That's an easy one. Adam and Eve didn't just have Cain and Abel. It says in Genesis 5:4 that Adam had 'other sons and daughters.'"

When it says 'day', does that mean a literal 24-hour day?

"Yes. You've got to go back to the original word in Hebrew, which is 'yom.' It's the same word that's used for a 24-hour day. If you don't take that to mean 'day,' it's a slippery slope."

What about scientific dating that says the world is millions of years old?

"Ninety percent of age-dating methods are faulty."

Which version do you use?

"Usually the King James. But you have to be careful with translations."

Ken explains that, for instance, many versions say 'the rabbit chews its cud' (Leviticus 11:6). "The skeptics say the rabbit doesn't chew its cud. But you look at the original language, it says 'the rabbit re-eats its food.' And look at what a rabbit does. It excretes rabbit pellets and then eats the pellets. The Bible is correct."

We walk into a room with a brick wall covered with menacing-looking graffiti. This room is devoted to modern ills, among them drugs and racism. "There is only one race, the human race," says Ken.

The creationists I meet are surprisingly liberal on race matters. Racial intermarriage is considered just fine. In fact, they think Darwin's theory can lead to racism because minorities are sometimes seen as evolutionary lower forms of homo sapiens. They are also progressive on Darfur. On other topics—including abortion and gay marriage—they are down-the-line conservatives.

We pass a dinosaur with a saddle on it. This display was mocked by my own magazine—Esquire—which called it a dressage dinosaur because of the English saddle. Ken downplays it. "It's just a novelty. Just something for the kids." He ushers me through. "This way, AJ." (That's one thing I notice: They say "AJ" here a lot. It seems common among certain types of very religious people to say your name all the time. It makes me think of God's first words to Moses, which were "Moses! Moses!", but it's probably unrelated).

Speaking of dinosaurs, if they really were on the ark, how did Noah squeeze them all in?

"He put them in when they were younger and smaller. The equivalent of teenagers."

I later bought a paperback at the AIG bookstore called Noah's Ark: A Feasibility Study, which spends 300 pages outlining the brilliant engineering that made the boat possible. There are chapters on the ventilation system, on-board exercise for the animals and the myth of explosive manure gases.

The book is beautifully argued—and I don't believe a syllable of it. Which I know is counter to my quest. I had told Mark I was coming in with an open mind, but while down here, I realize my mind won't open that far. I can understand being open to the existence of God and the beauty of rituals and the benefits of prayer. But the existence of a juvenile brontosaurus on the ark? And an earth that's barely older than Paul Newman? I have to go with 99 percent of scientists on this one.

Of course, the creationists cite plenty of scientific evidence of their own. Or more precisely, they interpret the same evidence as being proof of creation. Mark told me about a T-Rex bone in Montana that broke open and had blood vessels. No way that could be millions of years old.

The article Esquire ran was called "Greetings From Idiot America," and it was very funny. But I have to disagree with the headline. The AiG folks aren't idiots. And despite a British news show that scored its segment with Deliverance-style banjo music, they aren't hillbillies. Everyone I met had a full set of well-orthodontured teeth and blinked at regular intervals. I can't prove it, but I'd wager there's no difference in the average IQ of creationists and evolutionists.

The thing is, their faith in the literal Bible is so strong, they will squeeze and distort all data to fit the Genesis account. In fact, you have to be quite sharp to be a leading creationist. The mental gymnastics can be astonishing.

Consider AiG's resident astrophysicist, Jason Lisle. Mark introduced me to him proudly. "A real, live PhD who believes in creationism. Here he is, in 3-D."

Jason has meticulously parted hair, looks a bit like Paul Rubens, and is sweet in an unforced way. He tells me it wasn't easy being a creationist PhD student. He had to stay closeted about his beliefs and write for the

AiG magazine under a pseudonym.

Now here's the interesting part: Like mainstream scientists, he thinks the universe is billions of light years big. But if it's that big, and only 6000 years old, the light rays from distant stars wouldn't have time to travel to the earth. Shouldn't the night sky be black?

"That's a tough one," he says. "But it's not a killer." There are several possibilities.

1. The speed of light may not have always been 186,000 miles per second. Perhaps it was faster when the universe began.

2. The time zone analogy. "You can leave Kentucky and arrive in Ohio at 4 p.m. In the same way, there may be something to continuous time zones in space.

3. Something called gravitational time dilation. I didn't quite understand it, but it had to do with our galaxy having a special place in the universe.

After Jason the astrophysicist, I'm brought across the hall to meet another creationist named Carl Kerby. Carl is a big guy—turns out his dad was a pro wrestler. He's wearing a Hawaiian shirt and gives off a casual, feet-on-the-desk vibe. His specialty: He is creationist museum's resident expert on pop culture. Carl monitors movies and TV shows for subtle, or not so-subtle, pro-evolution content so that he can alert fellow creationists to the danger.

On his list: Finding Nemo (namely, the line "Give it up old man, you can't fight evolution, I was built for speed."). And Gilligan's Island (they used the word 'prehistoric" twice in one episode; "There's no such thing as prehistoric," Carl says). Other violators include Bugs Bunny, Lilo & Stitch, Bob the Builder and The Incredible Mr. Limpet.

"It used to be my favorite movie," he says of Limpet. "And then I played it for my family, and 13 minutes in, there was a nerdy science guy who pulls down a chart and starts talking about how fish were our ancestors. I had to stop the movie and talk to my family and explain."

Of course, when it comes to secular entertainment, creationism's enemy number one is Inherit the Wind, about the famous Scopes Monkey trial. It debuted as a play in 1955, and was later turned into a Spencer Tracy movie. And Carl—along with all his colleagues—insists that it's wildly unfair to Christians.

When I got home, I rented the movie and compared it to the actual court transcripts. And I have to say . . .the movie is wildly unfair to Christians. Or at least this strain of Christianity.

William Jennings Bryan—a deeply religious three-time Democratic presidential nominee who was the prosecuting attorney for the anti-evolution folks—was turned into a total buffoon named Matthew Harrison Brady, played by Frederic March. Brady is a pot-bellied glutton. In one scene, he's gorging on fried chicken out of a basket . . . in the courtroom.

The film recreates the famous showdown over the Bible between the Bryan and the brilliant Chicago lawyer Clarence Darrow. It's a good scene. But if you read the court transcript, it was actually a more interesting and subtle confrontation.

For instance, here's the dialogue from the movie:

Darrow: Do you believe every word of the Bible is true?
Bryan: Yes. Every word is literally true.
And here's the corresponding real exchange:
Darrow: Do you claim that everything in the Bible should be literally interpreted?
Bryan: I believe everything in the Bible should be accepted as it is given there. Some of the Bible is given illustratively; for instance, "Ye are the salt of the earth." I would not insist that man was actually salt, or that he had flesh of salt, but it is used in the sense of salt as saving God's people.

Like creationists today, he admits there is some figurative language in the Bible, even if most of it should be taken as literally true.

And he had wit: "I believe [the Bible] was inspired by the Almighty, and He may have used language that could be understood at that time, instead of using language that could not be understood until Darrow was born. [Laughter and applause.]

Not bad, you know?

As I said, I still believe in evolution. There's nothing that will change that, even if they found Noah's Year-At-a-Glance calendar on a pristinely preserved ark. And yes, I know there's artistic license and all that. But it does seem odd to me that this movie—which is supposed to be a champion for the truth—distorted the truth so much. Why do that?

Especially when you have reality on your side.

I spend my last half hour at AiG in the book shop. I flip through dinosaur books for kids, a Far Side-like cartoon book about the Fallen World, biology books, and theology books. I spend several minutes skimming an astronomy book called Dismantling the Big Bang, which aims to expose the philosophical weaknesses of said theory.

It makes me think of AiG's resident astronomer Jason. Before I left, he wanted to make clear to me that he's not a geocentrist—he doesn't believe the earth is the center of the universe. "Does anyone anymore?" I asked. He said, yes, there a group called Biblical astronomers—they believe the earth is stationary because the Bible says the earth "shall never be moved" (Psalm 93:1). Jason considers them an embarrassment.

That was something I hadn't expected: Moderate creationists who view other creationists as too extreme. But it will turn out to be one of this year's big lessons: Moderation is a relative term.

In the seventh year there shall be a Sabbath of solemn rest for the land

LEVITICUS 25:4

Day 42. On my flight back to New York, I sink into a mini-depression about the museum. All that creativity and enthusiasm—it seems like such misplaced energy.

I feel the need to compensate, to do justice to the Bible itself. So I vow to spend the next few days finding Biblical literalism at its most noble. And today, I may have found it while reading a book about faith-based ethics called The Quiet Hand of God. Namely, the movement by faithful Christians and Jews to apply the Bible's financial laws to the world's poverty crises. Here, the Bible has saved thousands, maybe millions, of lives.

To back up: The Bible says that years—like days of the week—belong in a cycle of seven. The seventh year is called the Sabbath year, and big things happen.

First, that entire year, you must stop working. No farming is allowed. This is so the land can rest, and the needy can come and eat all they want from the vines and olive trees. Second, you must forgive all debts. All IOUs are erased.

After seven consecutive Sabbath cycles—49 years—something even more radical happens: The Jubilee year. During the Jubilee year, you must return all property to its original owner (Leviticus 25:10).

Scholars aren't sure how strictly the Jubilee law was practiced in ancient Israel. It's possible it was practiced only by a devout sprinkling of farmers. And naturally, as my investment banker friend points out, if we followed these today, it would throw the financial markets into chaos.

Even on a personal level, I've found it a challenge to practice. Consider the not working part. I've worked for 16 years straight, so I'm long overdue for a year-long hiatus. The problem is, I've got a deadline for this book and a kid who is obsessed with offensively pricey Thomas the Tank Engine toys.

As for forgiving debts, I try two things

—Since bonds are debts, I try to forgive a bond I have owned for nine years. It was issued by the New York State Dormitory Authority.

"We've never had a request like this before," says the fourth guy I was sent to. He finally suggests I donate some money to my favorite SUNY school.

—To my recollection, the only other outstanding debt that stretches more than seven years is the one owed by my sophomore year college roommate. He owed me at least $20. The weasel would buy yogurt with the communal house money, then hide it from the rest of us in paper bags labeled "PHOTO EQUIPMENT—DO NOT TOUCH." I've always held a grudge. I let it go.

But there is something practical I can do. And that's through an organization called Jubilee USA Network.

Back in the 1990s, two British evangelists named Martin Dent and Bill Peters had an epiphany: They made the connection between the Bible's Jubilee concept and the third world debt crises. Dent and Peters had both worked in Africa for the British equivalent of the Peace Corps. Dent, in fact, had been appointed an honorary chief of a Nigerian tribe. He had seen poverty firsthand. He argued that the developed nations should forgive third world debt. Often these IOUs were leftover from corrupt regimes. The Bible says everyone deserves a fresh start.

The Jubilee movement they started has resulted in massive cancellations of debt by England, France, the U.S. and others. They got a huge publicity boost when Bono and his sunglasses joined the cause. Here's what he said about Jubilee in his speech at the National Prayer Breakfast.

It is such an important idea, Jubilee, that Jesus begins his ministry with this. Jesus is a young man, he's met with the rabbis, impressed everyone, people are talking. The elders say, he's a clever guy, this Jesus, but he hasn't done much . . . yet. He hasn't spoken in public before . . .

When he does, his first words are from Isaiah: 'The Spirit of the Lord is upon me,' he says, 'because He has anointed me to preach good news to the poor.' And Jesus proclaims the year of the Lord's favor, the year of Jubilee. (Luke 4:18)

What he was really talking about was an era of grace—and we're still in it."

I joined a group called Jubilee USA as a volunteer, and have been sending out postcards to congressmen and senators about debt relief.

I know. Call Oslo and alert the Peace Prize committee. But it's better than watching Entourage and eating fruit rolls. Plus, I scored some points with my socially conscious wife, who joined me for several hours of addressing and stamp-affixing. Whenever Julie joins me on my Biblical quest, I get a Berkowitz-like high.

> *You shall not wrong a stranger or oppress him*
>
> EXODUS 22:1

Day 43. Tonight, I invited a Jehovah's Witness into my home. I realize this fact already puts me in an extreme minority.

And mind you, I didn't just idly answer the door and let a Jehovah's Witness inside. I aggressively pursued the Jehovah's Witnesses. I phoned the headquarters and requested that a Jehovah's Witness be sent to my home. After three calls and not a little confusion on their part—it's not a common inquiry—I finally got my wish.

Yes, I'm aware that it doesn't make much sense. It's like volunteering for jury duty or paying to see a David Spade movie.

Okay, enough! The poor Jehovah's Witnesses. Their zeal for ringing doorbells have made them one of America's favorite religious punchlines. So I promise: No more cheap Jehovah's Witness jokes.

But I do want to know more about the Jehovah's Witnesses and what they really stand for. Because they are perhaps the fastest-growing Biblical literalists in the world. Their current membership stands at more than 6.6 million, with more than 300,000 new converts a year. They're also interesting to me because they are usually classified as Christian, but, like the Amish, they lean heavily on the Hebrew Scriptures.

My Jehovah's Witness is named Michael, and he arrives right on the dot, at 7:30 p.m. He wears a brown suit, brown shoes, brown tie, and carries a brown leather case holding a Bible and a pamphlet. He looks somewhat like the actor Gary Busey, if Gary Busey had his hair parted in the middle.

Michael is warm and likeable. He has a deep voice, but it was more soothing than booming, more shrink than football coach.

And he is grateful. So grateful it's almost heartbreaking. He thanks me for having him over. "There are so many misconceptions about Jehovah's Witness. I'm just so glad you're talking to me to find out the truth."

He sits on the living room couch, leaning forward, his hands in the 'fish-was-this-big' posture. "People say ours is a primitive Christianity—and we take that as a compliment." The Witnesses believe they're getting back to the original meaning of the Bible—the pamphlet Michael gives me is called What the Bible REALLY says.

Michael, who works in computers at the massive Jehovah's Witness headquarters in Brooklyn, gives me a crash course in his faith. Here, some of the highlights of the belief (vastly oversimplified, of course).

—God should be called Jehovah, because that's what the Bible calls him. "You can call a person 'man' or you can call him by his name, 'Bob.' God has a name—'Jehovah.'"

—Humans should take literally Jesus' pacifist words. "You won't find any Jehovah's Witnesses in Iraq," Michael says. "Jesus said, 'he who lives by the sword, dies by the sword.'"

—They don't believe in the Trinity. Jesus is not God, but instead God's first creation. (This belief is why they are sometimes seen as belonging outside of Christianity)

—Armageddon is coming soon—and believers will be resurrected and live in paradise. But most righteous people won't live in heaven. Almost everyone will live in a paradise here on earth. Heaven will be reserved for 144,000 pious souls, who will reign with Jehovah as divine administrators.

—The Witnesses don't celebrate Christmas or Easter, as neither holiday is mentioned the Bible. Birthdays are also out: The only two birthdays celebrated in the Bible were those of evil people—one by a Pharaoh and one by a pro-Roman Jewish king. Michael's fine with the ban, especially now. "As I get older, I don't want to be reminded of my birthday."

—There is no hell. The Witnesses believe that is a mistranslation of the Gehenna, which was an ancient garbage dump. They say that nonbelievers simply die at Armageddon, rather than being thrown into an inferno. "How can you have a kind and loving God who also roasts people?" he asks.

I am surprised by the Jehovah's Witness theology. I had always heard they were a fire-and-brimstone sect, but here's Michael telling me they reject the notion of hell. The belief is probably heretical by mainstream standards, but it has a gentleness to it.

It has been an hour and a half, and Michael is glancing at his watch every few minutes now.

"You just tell me when you want me to go," says Michael. "I'm from the Midwest, so I'm conscious of overstaying my welcome."

"No, I'm fine," I say. It's true. I could keep going for hours. I doubt Michael will convert me, but I love discussing the Bible. Can't get enough of it.

I ask him what's the most controversial part of his faith.

"The blood transfusion issue," he says. "People think we're kooks. But we absolutely use the medical system." (Was this a subtle dig at the Christian Scientists, I wondered?) "We just don't take blood transfusions."

The reason is the literal translation of three verses—Acts 15:29, Genesis 9:4, and Leviticus 7:26, the last of which reads "Ye shall eat no manner of blood" (KJV)

The Witnesses make an unusual argument here. They say that the word 'eat' should really be translated as 'consume,' and that transfusion qualifies as consumption.

As Michael says, this is seriously controversial. Critics say the ban has caused numerous deaths, and the Witnesses have been the subject of several lawsuits. In recent years, the church elders have scaled back a bit. Now, elements of blood—such as hemoglobin and interferon—can be transfused. But still, the ban on transfusing whole blood remains.

To me, it boils down to this question: Should you obey the Bible's rules even if doing so endangers your life? I've looked in the Bible to see what guidance it gives. As I suspected, there's no clear-cut "Yes" or "No."

On the one hand, the Bible is filled with martyrs and near-martyrs to their faith. In the Book of Daniel, the evil King Nebuchadnezzar commands three Hebrews to bow down before a golden idol or else get thrown in a fire. The men refuse to bow. Nebuchadnezzar stokes the fire—making it 'seven times hotter'—and tosses the rebels in. But God protects his faithful and they emerge unscorched.

On the other hand, there are plenty of times when life takes precedence over the obeying of rules. Jesus lashes out at the Pharisees who criticize his followers for gathering grain on the Sabbath. Likewise, in modern Judaism, life trumps all. Even the most kosher rabbi would allow his followers to get pigs' valves put in their hearts if necessary (despite a misleading Grey's Anatomy plotline to the contrary).

As you might have guessed, I'd make a horrible Jehovah's Witness. Even in my Biblical year, if I needed a blood transfusion, I'd be rolling up my sleeve before the doctor finishes his sentence. I'm just not faithful/brave/foolhardy enough to do otherwise. The Bible, in fact, has made me more reverent of life.

Finally, at 10:30—three hours after he arrived—Michael says politely that he should let me get to sleep. I'm about to say, no, I could keep going, when his Palm Treo rings. It's his wife.

"Yes, we're just finishing up here. I'm about to leave."

Michael stands up to shake my hand.

And then it hits me: I have just done something few human beings have ever achieved. I have outBible-talked a Jehovah's Witness.

. . .If you can read the writing and make known to me its interpretation,
you shall be clothed with purple

DANIEL 5:16

Day 44. In an effort to cut down on temptation, I've been rationing my news intake, especially when the news concerns Hollywood actresses running off with pilates instructors. But I spotted one news story that seemed worthwhile. It was about Supreme Court justice Antonin Scalia.

Scalia apparently made a speech in Puerto Rico to a student group. He said that those who believe the Constitution should evolve with society are "idiots". Wrong, he says. We should stick to the original intent of the Founding Fathers. As Scalia put it, "Scalia does have a philosophy, and it's called originalism." (By the way, referring to yourself in the third person may not be biblically forbidden, but should be. Unless you have a biblical alter-ego, of course).

This is helpful. I've been trying to focus my mission. Here is my answer: I'll do the Scalia technique on the Bible. I can try to find the original intent. I want to live the original religion.

A lot of people tell me such a quest is a fantasy. The Bible was written thousands of years ago by people with profoundly different worldviews. And I agree, it's hard. Much harder than finding the original intent of the constitution, which was at least written in some form of English, even if the S's and F's look alike. The Bible was originally written in Hebrew, Aramaic, and Greek. Its journey into other languages has been famously bumpy; the Bible could be the most mistranslated text in history.

The Red Sea is a mistranslation of the 'Sea of Reeds.' The idea that Moses (and his descendents) had horns comes from a mistranslation of the Hebrew word qaran. It actually means that Moses' face was shining, or emitted beams of light.

I've been doing my best. I've been told reading the Bible in translation is like watching TV in black and white, so I'm trying to compensate any way I can. I flip between different versions. I have this fancy Bible software with an ancient language dictionary. I have my advisory board. I've bought books on teaching yourself Hebrew and ancient Greek—

which is overly optimistic, given my time frame.

But even if I assume a proper translation, then there's the not-so-trivial matter of changes in the text over time. Most modern scholars (at least those of secular bent) don't believe the medieval scribes were flawless Xerox machines. They made tweaks both intentional and accidental. Similarly, the Hebrew Bible has been stable for centuries, but you can see small variations if you compare, for instance, the Dead Sea Scrolls with the Hebrew Bible.

But I don't want to give up just because it's hard. Especially since the Scalia method of 'original intent' continues to be a major force in Biblical interpretation, both in Christianity and—rather differently—in Judaism.

A 30-second history: For centuries, most believed the Bible was a true account of what happened. It was non-fiction, plain and simple. They were, in the words of author Marcus Borg, "natural literalists"—they had no strong evidence to believe otherwise.

But more and more, science began to butt up against the literal Biblical story. How to reconcile Galileo's universe with Joshua stopping the sun in the sky? Or Darwin's theory of evolution with Noah's ark? You saw several reactions. Two of the major ones that have dominated for a century are:

1) Modernism. This says that science and religion are separate. In the words of Stephen Jay Gould, they are 'non-overlapping magisteria.' The Bible is packed with figurative language and poetry. The creation story, powerful as it may be, is a myth. But religion and the Bible still have a place, because science can't answer questions about faith, purpose and the meaning of life.

2) Fundamentalism. This view continues to assert that the Bible is 100 percent inerrant, both in morals and historical accuracy. Joshua really did make the sun stand still. Noah really did pile the animals onto an ark made of gopher wood. They admit there is some non-literal language in the Bible—when Isaiah says the "trees clapped," it's obviously a metaphor. Same with Jesus' parables. But unless a phrase is clearly figurative, the Bible should be taken at face value.

Like 60s White House advisers, fundamentalists have their own domino theory. If one part of the Bible is proven wrong, why should we believe any of it? It's a good point. And as an agnostic, I had this view from the other side. Why should I follow a book that seems to condone slavery and hand-chopping? The question helped inspire my quest.

The Christian literal movement is, of course, famous for its conservative politics. To oppose homosexuality, for instance, they cite Leviticus 18:22: "You shall not lie with a male as with a woman; it is an abomination."

But not all Christian literalists are conservative; there's a growing progressive movement. One branch calls itself Red Letter Christians—after the color of the text of Jesus' sayings in old Bibles. The Red Letter Christians—such as Reverends Tony Campolo and Jim Wallis—focus not on homosexuality or abortion, but instead on literal adherence to Jesus' teachings about poverty and peace. When I start exploring the New Testament, I'll be consulting both sides.

Jewish Biblical interpretation has taken a slightly different path. I got a crash course in this from a frighteningly smart rabbi named Robbie Harris. Robbie—who talks so quickly that my fingers ache from typing notes—is a professor of the Bible at the Jewish Theological Seminary in upper Manhattan.

When I first met him, Robbie was on his cell with a publicist from The Knitting Factory, the hipster downtown music club.

"Okay," he said. "Great. I'll call you later."

He was playing there next week, he told me. His band is called Shake, Rabbis and Roll (SR2, for short).

"What kind of music is it?" I asked.

"Rock and roll. Do you like rock and roll?"

"Who doesn't?"

Robbie played me a couple of songs from his first album which "went aluminum." I liked them, especially the one about the snobby New York girl. ("She looks at Central Park as the Great Divide/And now she thinks she's slumming on the Upper West Side").

He's an observant Jew, but one whom I can relate to, since—unlike the totally religious Mr. Berkowitz—he straddles the secular and Jewish worlds.

Here's what Robbie taught me: In Judaism there's the literal meaning of the Biblical passage, and then there's the interpretation of the rabbis

There is one sect of Judaism that rejects oral law altogether. They're called Karaites, and they are theological minimalists, adhering only to the Bible. This can result in some ultra-strict behavior. On the Sabbath, they turn off the heat so as not to engage in commerce with the electric company. "I just wear a lot of layers," one Karaite I interviewed told me. "It's not so bad." The Karaites had their golden age in medieval times—an estimated 10 percent of Jews were once Karaite. They have since dwindled in number to about 50,000, mostly in Israel and, oddly enough, Daly City, California.

On this journey, I plan to be mindful or the oral law. But I'm not going to follow it exclusively. I feel I have to try to puzzle out for myself what the Bible means, even if it means I take some wrong turns.

All this makes me realize: In a sense, my project is steeped in Judaism, since I'm spending a lot of time on the Hebrew Scriptures. But in some ways, it's actually more influenced by the Protestant idea that you can interpret the Bible yourself, without mediation. Sola scriptura, as it's called.

Martin Luther advocated sola scriptura in reaction to the Catholic Church. At the risk of muddying matters, Catholicism is somewhere between Judaism and Protestantism in terms of Biblical interpretation. Like Judaism, there's a middle step between you and the Bible—namely the Church Doctrine. But the Church mandates are generally slightly less elaborate and complex than those of the rabbis.

In some ways, going literal is turning out to be easier than Rabbinic Judaism. Do I need to wear a yarmulke? No, the Bible doesn't mandate it. That came from the rabbis. But in some ways, it's infinitely harder. I'm trying to follow the word. When the Bible says, 'an eye for an eye,' I don't want to soften it to the rabbinically-approved 'some money for an eye.' When it says smash idols, I want to smash idols. Plus, already feeling guilty—which is how I know I am actually Jewish. I feel like I'm disappointing my forefathers. I imagine my ancestor the Vilna Gaon—a famous rabbi in Eastern Europe—shaking his head somewhere, sighing, emitting an Oy-yi-yi-yi-yi.

Give strong drink to him who is perishing, and wine to those in bitter distress

PROVERBS 31:6

in books like the Talmud.

Sometimes, these two line up. When the Bible says don't
and linen, that's what it means: Don't mix wool and linen. Here
bis just elaborate on what kind of wool (sheep's) and how fa
must be from the linen.

But other times, the literal meaning is light years from the r
terpretation. For instance, the famous line in Leviticus "an e
eye" doesn't really mean pluck out the other guy's eye. It's m
civilized than that. The tradition says it means this: "cash for
The attacker has to pay the victim the monetary value of the ey

Or consider this passage:

"You are not to boil a young goat in the milk of its mother."

EXODUS 23:19 (NASP

If you take this literally, as I'm trying to do, this is relative
think—with a little willpower and a safe distance from farn
make it for a year without boiling a baby goat in its mother's
friend John suggested that, worse comes to worst, I could boil
goat in its aunt's milk. Thanks, John.

But the rabbis have a far more elaborate interpretation
23:19 actually means to separate milk and meat. Which is wher
the kosher rules banning cheeseburgers. Along with the myr
about how long you must wait between a meat course and a dai
(as many as 24 hours) and whether some hard cheese qualifies
because it's made with an enzyme from cow stomachs (debatab

Strict Orthodox Jews believe God gave these amplificati
'oral laws'—to Moses on the mountain-top. That's why he was
for 40 days. Moses passed on the oral laws to the Israelites,
them to their sons, and so on until they were eventually writt
Traditionally, the laws from the all-important five books of Mo
Torah—come to a total of 613. (My list of rules is slightly lo
cause I included advice from other parts of the Old Testament
Proverbs and Psalms). Other Jews believe that the oral laws ha
oped over thousands of years, but are sacred nonetheless.

Day 44. My Esquire colleague David broke up with his girlfriend. He has sciatica—which I had always thought was restricted to people who drive Crown Victorias and get half-off movie tickets. Also, he wrote a very funny movie script about elaborate Christmas displays—and then had someone sell the exact same idea two days before he sent it out.

Next time I'm at Esquire, I stop by his office with a bottle of Kendall Jackson red wine.

"Here," I say, handing it to him over his desk.

"What's this?"

"It's because you're depressed. The Bible says to bring wine to the heavy of heart."

"The Bible says that?"

"Yes. It also says that you shouldn't sing to people with a heavy heart. That'd be like rubbing salt in the wound."

"So you're not going to sing to me?"

"No."

David seems grateful for the wine, and no doubt the lack of singing as well. I love it when the Bible gives Emily Post-like tips that are both wise and easy to follow.

Remember the Sabbath day, to keep it holy

EXODUS 20:8

Day 45. It's the seventh Sabbath of my Biblical year. Well, actually, it's the day after the seventh Sabbath. I couldn't type this entry on the Sabbath itself because the Bible tells me not to work. (A friend of mine said that even observing the Sabbath might be breaking the Sabbath, since my job is to follow the Bible. That gave me a two-hour headache).

Before my Biblical year, I was among the biggest Sabbath violators in America. I'm a workaholic. It's a trait I got from my father, who scribbles away on his law books without ceasing—on the beach, on the train, while 'watching' old Katharine Hepburn movies on DVD (which means an occasional glance at the screen to make sure the picture is still moving). If the Apocalypse comes, there's no doubt he'd work right on through, looking up to take note of the rising rivers of blood before returning to his case study. I'd probably do the same.

We'd have a lot of company. In the post-BlackBerry age, is there really a boundary between the weekday and the weekend, between work hours and overtime? We work on Saturday, the Jewish Shabbat. We work on Sunday, the Christian Sabbath. We put in more hours than the God of Genesis himself.

It wasn't always so in America. As New York Times writer Judith Shulevitz points out, the Puritans left England in large part for the freedom to follow the fourth commandment. The Puritans took the Sabbath seriously: No sports, no dancing, no smoking, no visiting. You must attend church, but the Puritans "punished anyone who got there with unseemly haste or on too showy a horse." The Sabbath in America survived even after the Puritans faded away. As recently as eighty years ago, writes Shulevitz, "football was considered too vulgar to be played on Sunday."

You can see traces of the Puritan influence today—just try buying liquor on Sunday morning in Manhattan. And the hardcore Sabbath is making a comeback in some evangelical circles. Florida-based minister Dr. D. James Kennedy—whose TV show The Coral Ridge Hour reaches millions—tells his parishioners not to eat at a restaurant on Sunday, because that's encouraging waiters to work, thus breaking God's law.

The strictest Sabbath-keepers today are probably the Orthodox Jews. In post-Biblical times, the rabbis wrote down a complex list of forbidden behavior. It's got 39 types of work, including cooking, combing and washing. You can't plant, so gardening is off-limits. You can't tear anything, so toilet paper must be pre-ripped earlier in the week. You can't make words, so note-taking and Scrabble are off-limits (though one rabbi allows Deluxe scrabble, since the tiles have ridges, which provides enough separation between letters so that they don't actually form words).

I got a firsthand taste of the Orthodox Shabbat when my aunt Kate was visiting my parents house. Kate's very cute, very observant 13-year-old daughter Rivka was over. She'd eaten part of an ice cream sundae, and wanted to store it in the freezer for later. But it was Friday, and sundown was coming fast. (The Jewish Sabbath lasts from sundown Friday to sundown Saturday).

She couldn't open the freezer after sundown, because that would turn on a freezer light, which was illegal.

"Can you unscrew the freezer light bulb?" she asked my mom.

My mom tried to unscrew it, but couldn't reach the bulb without removing every last Eggo and Ben & Jerry's from the freezer drawer.

"I'll tell you what," said my mom. "I'll open the freezer for you."

"You can't. You're Jewish," said Rivka.

"Then I'll ask Joelle to do it." (Joelle is my Catholic great aunt)

"You can't ask her. She just has to volunteer to do it."

At which point, my mom gave up. I'm guessing that the poor kosher sundae is still in there today.

On the face of it, the Sabbath and all of its rules seemed outlandish. And yet, I've opted to reserve judgment till I experience the Sabbath myself.

Or at least the explicitly Biblical version of the Sabbath. Unlike the rabbis, the Bible itself gives few detailed instructions on how exactly to refrain from work. And the ones it does give only apply to farmers and reality show contestants: No kindling of fire, no gathering sticks, no plowing or harvesting.

So I have to figure this one out myself. Since my work is writing, I decide I need to abstain from writing, of course. But also researching, phoning colleagues, and scouting the newspaper for ideas. The thing is, going cold turkey terrifies me. I want to wade into this ocean cautiously, like a Sarasota retiree

The first week, I told myself: No checking of email. I lasted all of an hour, after which I told myself, well, I won't open the emails themselves. I'll just scan the subject headers. That's not really working. So I clicked on the mail. Hmm. An email from my mom. The Bible does say, respect your parents. And maybe it's urgent. Plus, I have another 51 Sabbaths to get it right . . . I clicked on it. It's a joke about a blind man and five blonds at a bar.

Week number two, I tried it again. No email from sundown on Friday to sundown on Saturday. I made it past Friday night, but then broke down on Saturday morning and stole a peek again. Well, I told myself, I've still got 50 Sabbaths left. Unfortunately, I didn't improve with Sabbaths three to six.

This week, I vowed to make it all the way. I felt optimistic. At 6:30

p.m. on Friday night, the sun officially dipped below the New York horizon, I snapped shut my computer, shoved all my books in the corner, silenced the electronic cowbell on my cell phone that I've been meaning to change anyway—and did a little Berkowitz-like fist pump. Something clicked in my brain. It was a school's-out-for-summer feeling. A wave of relief and freedom. No matter how much I want to, I cannot work. I have no choice.

It was a beautiful moment. And short-lived. An hour later, my brain clicked back, and I started to suffer pangs of withdrawal every time I walked past my idle PowerBook. What emails are piling up in my inbox? What if the editor of The New Yorker sent me a surprise job offer? On Saturday at noon, I broke down. I checked. Who's going to know?

I was too embarrassed to tell Julie. Julie loves that I'm trying to break the seven-day-work cycle—the Sabbath is her favorite part of my experiment. So I keep my failure a secret.

Worse, I then used the Sabbath to weasel out of household tasks.

"Can you put the papers in the recycling bin?"

"I really shouldn't. I'm not allowed to carry a burden outside of my house."

As she took out the papers herself, I could hear her footsteps thump down the hallway corridor.

You shall keep the feast of booths seven days

DEUTERONOMY 16:13

Day 47. The Bible does tell us how to build Noah's ark—300 by 50 by 30 cubits, with a roof and three decks. And there's an impressive 12 pages on how to construct the Tabernacle, the tent where the Ten Commandments were stored.

Luckily, I'm exempt from both these projects. They were one-time-only.

But the Bible does command me to build something else. A hut. Once a year, we're supposed to build a hut and dwell in it for a week so that we may be reminded of the huts used by the ancient Hebrews when they wandered the desert for forty years. It's a major Biblical holiday called the Feast of the Ingathering—or Sukkot—and is still practiced by religious Jews. It starts today. (October, incidentally, is a huge month for Biblical holidays. I've also observed Yom Kippur and Rosh Hashanah—but let me return to those later).

Frankly, the idea of building a large three-dimensional structure gives me a stomachache. I'm no handyman. Put it this way: When I watch Bob the Builder with Jasper, I always learn something new (oh, so that's what a strut is).

I try to console myself that the hut will be a nice change from all the negative commands, the "thou shalt nots." Here, a clear "thou shalt." So I dive in and tackle the first issue: Where to put up my hut? The roof seems logical. I call our building's manager and explain my plan.

"I can't let that happen," he says. "Liability issues."

"What about the courtyard?"

"The courtyard isn't accessible to anyone except one apartment."

"Which apartment?"

"It's not going to work. You can't build a hut in the courtyard."

So I go to my backup plan—building the hut in our living room. This is not ideal for two reasons. The first reason is that it's a hut in our living room.

The second is that my hut—called a sukkah, in Hebrew—wouldn't pass muster with even the most laid-back rabbi in America. The rabbis say huts must be built outside, and conform to dozens of other rules as well. This time of year, sukkahs sprout up all over west side roofs.

"Wouldn't it be easier just to use the sukkah on the roof of the Jewish Community Center?" Julie asks.

"Maybe," I say. "But I'd feel like I was cheating."

I explain to Julie that I'm on a solo mission to find the core of the bible. I am a lone adventurer. I must find my own path.

"Okay, but it sounds like you're making work for yourself."

I trek down to a store called Metropolitan Lumber and pick up a dozen two-by-fours, a half-dozen cinder blocks and some canvas. I start to feel better about the project. There's something satisfying about buying lumber. It makes me feel like a guy who builds porches and rec rooms and uses words like "drywall."

Next, I sling my duffel bag over my shoulder and trek off to Riverside Park. I need some more materials. The Bible instructs us to get "the fruit of goodly trees, branches of palm trees, and boughs of leafy trees, and willows of the brook." (In Biblical times, these might have been used to build the huts, though the longstanding Jewish tradition is to wave them in the air).

So off I go and stuff my bag full of branches and willows I collect by the Hudson River. I buy a palm plant the size of a volleyball and a middle-eastern lemon-like fruit called an etrog (traditionally thought to be the fruit in question). It feels good. I'm accomplishing stuff. I'm sweating.

At 11 a.m. I begin hammering crossbeams and holding nails in my mouth and sweating a lot more. Three hours later, thanks to the simpleton's blueprint I downloaded off the Internet, I actually have the skeleton of a bona-fide hut. Which promptly collapses like it's in a Buster Keaton movie and smashes into the wall. I start again, and this time add extra struts and this time it stays up.

"Oh my God," Julie says when she arrives home.

I ask her if she's annoyed.

"A little. But more stunned that you actually built something. It's enormous."

Julie inspects my hut. It's got four wooden poles topped by a big sheet of canvas that just grazes our apartment's ceiling. The interior is spare, but decorated with boughs of leafy trees and willows of the brook. She squeezes between the hut and the radiator to get another view. She eyes the cinderblocks, making sure they didn't scratch the floor.

The Bible says to dwell in the hut, so I plan to dwell as much as possible—eat my meals in my hut, read my books there, sleep there. I invite Julie along, but she says she'll let me "fly solo on this one."

So that night, at 11:30, I spread three blankets out on the wood floor. I lie down, put my hands behind my head, stare at the draped canvas, breathe in the citrus and willows, which smell like something they'd rub into you during a massage at Bliss Spa, and try to figure out what I'm feeling.

First, I realize, I'm still on a high from building the hut. I put the thing up myself. Bertrand Russell—the famously agnostic philosopher—said there are two kinds of work in this world: Altering the position of matter on earth, and telling other people to alter the position of matter on earth. I like doing the former. I like breaking the stereotype of the physically inept Jew, at least for a day.

My elation is tainted with guilt, though. This sukkah is way too comfortable. This is supposed to remind me of the ancient huts in the desert, but here I am in a climate-controlled apartment—no sand, no wind and no lack of food. I don't have to worry about the freezing nights or blistering days or the plague, which killed 40,000 of the 600,000 Israelites.

But that guilt, in turn, is relieved by this epiphany: This holiday is all about living Biblically. God, if He exists, is ordering everyone—not just those with a book contract—to travel back in time and try to experience the world of the ancient Middle East. God created "immersion journalism," as my agent calls it. Maybe God approves of my project after all.

And David danced before the Lord with all his might

2 SAMUEL 6:14

Day 55. It's the night of October 25, and I'm at the loudest, rowdiest, most drunken party of my life. Me and several hundred Hasidic men.

I came for the dancing. There's a part in the Bible where King David celebrates the return of the Ark of the Covenant to Jerusalem. This was an older David, years after he slew Goliath with a rock and sling. He has defeated his increasingly paranoid mentor Saul to become King of Israel. And he brings home the ark, a sacred box containing the Ten Commandments. He celebrates by dancing. And man, does he dance. He dances with such abandon, with such joy, that he doesn't notice that his robe is flying up, exposing his nakedness to the young handmaids in the kingdom.

His uptight wife Michal is appalled. She makes the mistake of scolding King David, and, as a result, is cursed with childlessness.

The unhappy ending seems unduly harsh. But I do love the image of the king doing a wild holy jig. The joy of religion—that's what David was feeling, and that's something I underestimated—or pretty much ignored—in my secular life. I want to feel what David felt, so I took a subway to Crown Heights on a Tuesday evening.

The occasion is a Jewish holiday called Simchat Torah, the last night before the sukkah is taken down. It's not in the Bible proper, but it does celebrate something Biblical—the end to the annual reading of the five books of Moses. And it sounded too interesting to miss.

My guide is a friend of a friend named Gershon—a kind, bespectacled, newlywed Hasid whose outgoing voicemail message said: "Your next action could change the world, so make it a good one."

As we walk, I get to see a side of ultra-Orthodox Jews that I'd never seen before. They always look so somber on the subway, so purposeful. But here they are, well, wasted. They're weaving down the sidewalks, some holding bottles of Crown Royal, some singing loudly Hebrew.

On this holiday, it's not just okay to drink, it's pretty much mandatory. Gershon and I go to his mother's house and pound a few shots of vodka in their front-yard sukkah. It's raining, and the raindrops fall through the gaps in the sukkah roof and splash into our glasses of vodka.

When Gershon says the prayers in Hebrew before drinking, I sneak a peek at him. His eyes are half-closed, his eyelids fluttering, his eyeballs rolled toward the back of his head. Will I ever come close to that spiritual state? Will I get my longed-for epiphany? I'm worried I won't.

After our vodka shots, we head over to the party's headquarters—the huge building known as 770 Eastern Parkway, the nerve center of this sect of Hasidism. (The sect is called the Lubavitchers, and they're the least insular of the Hasidic Jews, committed to bringing unaffiliated Jews into the fold).

I'm wearing black pants and a black sweater to better fit in with the Hasidim. I forgot to bring the crucial yarmulke, but Gershon lends me one of his.

"We dance for our animal nature," says Gershon, as we step across the puddles. "The Torah is for both sides of the nature. The reading is for the divine side, and the dancing is for the animal side."

As we approach within a few yards of 770—as it's called—Gershon asks me:

"You ever been bungee jumping?"

"No."

"Well I have. The instructors say to just jump, don't think about it. That's what you have to do here."

I see what he means. Just getting inside is going to be an extreme sport. The doors are glutted with dozens of revelers in their black coats—all men, no women (the Hasidim aren't much for gender mixing). We have to elbow our way through.

A fat, red-bearded guy comes up to Gershon and hugs him. Red Beard goes off on a drunken I-love-you-man, you-are-the-greatest-guy-I-know rant that lasts a good two minutes.

Gershon finally extracts himself.

"Who was that?" I ask.

"Never met him before in my life."

We squeeze our way inside. And there, an ocean of undulating black hats. Hundreds, maybe thousands of them in a hall the size of a large gymnasium. It's as loud as any concert I've ever been to. But instead of drums and guitar, it's a village of men singing "Ay yi yi yi."

The floor is exactly like a Seattle mosh pit circa 1994. Everyone's bumping, smacking, thumping into each other. One guy barrels into me so hard he sends me stumbling.

"Hey you with the beard!" he says. Everyone looks up. He unleashes a deep laugh.

We are making a slow, huge circle, sort of a holy roller derby. If you look up, you can see the occasional Hasid bouncing up in the air like a pogo stick. When there is a patch of free space on the floor—which isn't often—a reveler will do a somersault. Two men are swapping their black hats repeatedly as if they were reenacting a Laurel and Hardy scene.

I tell you, I've never seen such pure joy. It is thick, atmospheric, like someone had released a huge canister of nitrous oxide into the room. Here we are, hundreds of dancing King Davids. Even for a control freak like me, you there's no choice but to go along with it. You are over-whelmed. You follow the sweaty, bouncing, shouting, ay-yi-yi-ing hordes, or you are trampled.

I swing from emotion to emotion: terror that I'll be crushed, fascination that humans act this way, paranoia that they'll deal with the inter-loper in a manner I'd never forget. (think Deliverance meets Yentl). But occasionally, I swing to delirious happiness. I don't know if I feel God.

And it isn't as intense as the epiphanies I had as a kid. But a couple of times that night, I feel something transcendent, something that melts away the future and the past and deadlines and the MasterCard bills and puts me squarely in the moment. At least for a few moments, there is no difference between me and Jacob, my Biblical alter-ego.

After three hours of dancing—at 1 a.m.—I tell Gershon that I'm going to go, even though the hardcore dancers stay on till 6 a.m. He walks me out. "Remember," he says to me, as we shake hands goodbye on the street corner. "Sometimes you have to look beyond the weirdness. It's like the Temple in ancient Jerusalem. If you went there, you'd see oxen being slaughtered and all sorts of things. But look beyond the weirdness, to what it means."

As I ride the subway home, with the Ay-yi-yi-ing still echoing in my ears, I try to think of the meaning beyond the weirdness. Here's what I decide: Underneath my repression, maybe I have a closeted mystical side. Maybe I'm a rational Presbyterian on the outside, but an emotional Baptist on the inside. Given the right circumstances, maybe everyone is, even Henry Kissinger.

The next morning, I tell Julie about my wild night of dancing with Hasidic men, and how I got a taste of pure joy.

"And where were the women during this thing?"

"Well, they were watching. They have these observation windows."

"Observation windows?" Julie looks pissed.

It's strange. Naturally, I noticed the gender segregation—but there were so many odd and overwhelming things about the night, that I didn't laser in on that one. It's the obliviousness that comes with being in the majority.

"Yeah," I say. "Well, I was trying not to be judgmental."

"Well, seems like they're being judgmental of women."

I can sense Julie becoming more and more skeptical of religion, or at least hardcore religion.

Before my project, Julie was the mildly pro-religion one in the family. She believed in a God of some sort, or at least a universe that wasn't morally apathetic. "Things happen for a reason," she was always telling me when I'd moan about some career setback. She loves the rituals of Hanukkah and Passover. She's already started coming up with themes for Jasper's bar mitzvah (soccer! The Academy Awards!)

But now, I feel her drawing away—even as I start to warm to some aspects religious life. It's the difference between living the Bible and living with someone who is living the Bible.

Keep your tongue from evil

PSALMS 34:13

Day 60. A lot of my friends expect me to speak like a walking King James Bible. They want me—or at least my alter-ego Jacob—to spout words like thou and woe unto and whosoever shall. I get a lot of emails that start 'Give ear, O Jacobs.' And phone calls that begin 'Verily, I ask thee, would you like to meet us for pizza?'

I try to play along as best I can ('yea, I shall rejoice in a feast pizza). But it's not high on my list of priorities. Such language is more a reflection of 17th century England than ancient Israel.

No, speaking Biblically requires a far more radical change than raising my diction a few notches. It requires a total switch in the content of my conversation: No lying, no complaining, no gossiping.

They're all hard, but let me just focus on the gossip for a bit, because that's turning out to be a killer. The Bible has at least 20 passages condemning gossip. In English editions, translators use words such as 'slander' or 'talebearing' or 'unwholesome talk' or 'evil tongue.'

This means I can't join in when my co-workers as they discuss a certain boozy actress who scribbled obscenities on a bathroom mirror, or the rumor that a news anchor is about to ditch his wife for a younger woman. That's a feat in itself, but I expected living Biblically would require that.

The problem is, if you really want to be Biblically safe, you should go much further. You should avoid almost all negative speech whatsoever. Here's how one of my Bible commentaries defines evil tongue:

This refers to any derogatory or damaging statement against an individual—even when the slanderous or defaming remarks are true—which if publicized to others would cause the subject physical or monetary damage, anguish or fear."

In other words, about 70 percent of all conversations in New York.

In Hebrew, 'evil tongue' is called Lashon Hora, and the rabbis compare it to murder. As the Talmud says, "The gossiper stands in Syria and kills in Rome." Many Christians have a similar concept about negative speech. As Paul says in Ephesians 4:29: "Do not let any unwholesome talk come out of your mouths, but only what is helpful for building others up according to their needs, that it may benefit those who listen."

Parts of the Bible do allow some types of badmouthing—a gentle rebuke is okay, as is warning your friend he's about to open a coffee shop with an embezzler. But for the most part, all sniping, snarkiness, disparaging, mocking, scoffing and scorning is off-limits. Which is beyond difficult. I fail on a daily basis. An hourly basis.

Consider the scenario I faced last night. Julie and I went to a wedding on Long Island; the bride and groom, thoughtfully enough, had hired a van to schlep the guests back to New York. However, there would be no napping on this ride. Instead, we would be forced to eavesdrop on a very loud, very drunk goateed guy.

For an hour, without pausing, he pontificates to this pretty blonde he's trying pick up. She hears the following (as does everyone else).

"My one-man show 'Why Try' is a dissertation on suicide," he announces. "It's very funny. I have a very funny mind. Death is funny. I haven't been to a funeral that I haven't laughed at."

She nods politely.

"My teacher said to me, 'You are a great actor. And I said, 'I don't know what that means.' And I don't. All I know is the process."

Oh man, I wanted so much to lean over to Julie and mock this bloviating putz with his greased-back hair and his pretentious Buddy Holly glasses.

He continues:

"Whhhhhy do I admire George Clooney? I'll tell you. He wants to do something for society at large—and beyond."

I want to point out to Julie that he overpronounces his 't's and 'wh's.'

A couple of minutes later, apropos of nothing, he says:

"I've always wanted to write a comic strip called 'Grizelda of Drunkopolis.'"

When it becomes clear—even to him—that this woman was not going to climb into bed with him, he tried to engage the other passengers. Including me. A mutual acquaintance had mentioned that I have written for a trivia magazine called Mental Floss. This is his way in. He shouts:

"MENTAL FLOSS MAN over there! Mental Floss!! Tell us some trivia!"

His tone makes it clear my job is not on the artistic level of his one-man show about suicide. I demur. After we get off the van, I hold back for three minutes. Julie and I just walk silently to our apartment. But there's something to the hydraulic metaphor in human behavior: the steam kept building up and up in my brain. I had to let it out.

"Can you believe that idiot?" I say finally, as we waited at an intersection. "'Society at large—and beyond?' What is beyond society at large? Society at large is beyond."

Julie just nods her head. She knows.

Maybe taming my tongue will be good for me in the end. But it's pretty hard when you've got a world filled with idiots from Drunkopolis. It's like asking me not to breathe or blink. All I can say is, I'll keep trying.

He had done so, walking naked and barefoot

ISAIAH 20:2

Day 62. I'm typing this right after midnight. The Psalms tell us to rise at midnight and praise God, so I've been doing that for a week. I promised Julie I'd only do it for a week, since I've had to set an alarm for 11:58 p.m.

It's the end of my experiment's second month, and here's what I'm feeling: exhilarated, confused, overwhelmed, underqualified, fascinated and scared. Also, embarrassed.

My Biblical alterego Jacob is starting to look freakish. I've got fringes hanging from my garments. I take this purity-insuring Handy Seat everywhere. My beard has gone beyond shaggy. It now hangs a good two inches below my chin, and it's starting to make curlicues and shoot off in unexpected directions. (Julie wanted to go to Halloween with me as Tom Hanks from Castaway and her as the volleyball, but I can't do Halloween because it's a pagan holiday).

Yes, of course, part of me likes the attention. I write memoirs for a living, for Pete's sake. And yes, I know I brought this on myself—no one's forcing me to follow the Bible at knifepoint. But the constant stares and quizzical looks—it'd be enough to make anyone, even me, self-conscious. A bit paranoid, even.

Luckily, I've found inspiration in the Bible. As the Brooklyn rabbi Andy Bachman suggested, I've been re-reading the Prophets. He's right. They are amazing.

I love their message of social justice—especially Amos, Micah and Hosea. Again and again, they berate the hard-hearted rich who lie on beds of ivory and sip wine contentedly and 'trample the heads of the poor into the dust of the earth.' Their days are numbered.

But I also love the way they delivered that message. You see, the prophets didn't just utter their prophecies. They staged what are known as "prophetic acts"—wild, attention-grabbing, God-inspired pieces of performance art. The prophets the inventors of street theater, as Marcus Borg points out in his book Reading the Bible Again for the First Time. They were ancient David Blaines, but with orders from God, not a network executive.

Consider Hosea, who married a prostitute and named his children "Not pitied" and "Not my people." The names were a warning: If Israel continues on its immoral path, God will have no pity and cut them off.

Even more radical was Isaiah, who walked naked and barefoot for three years among the people of Jerusalem. (This was symbolic of what would happen if Judah allied itself with Egypt and Ethiopia; they would be conquered and everyone would end up naked captives). Another prophet Jeremiah wore clothes, but walked the streets with a wooden yoke around his neck to signify the yoke of Babylonian rule.

But eclipsing them all was Ezekiel. He was the master. I knew from reading the encyclopedia that Ezekiel had eaten a scroll to symbolize his appropriation of its message. And yet, that was tame compared to his other performances. One time, for instance, God told Ezekiel to carve a model of Jerusalem into a brick, then lay down beside the model on his left side. He continued lying there. For 390 days. Then, Ezekiel turned to his right side to lie another forty days. These days were to symbolize the years that Israel and Judah would be in exile after the Babylonian conquering.

During his 430-day feat, Ezekiel was to eat a meager diet of bread—cooked over human dung. Ezekiel pleaded with God, and God agreed to let him use cow dung as fuel instead.

As I enter my third month, Ezekiel and his fellow prophets have become my heroes. They were fearless. They literalized metaphors, they turned their lives into protest pieces. They proved that, in the name of truth, sometimes you can't be afraid to take a left turn from society and look absurd.

Maybe my alter-ego Jacob is in the prophetic tradition of Ezekiel. I hope so. On the other hand, he could be way off. I imagine that for every Ezekiel, there were 100 false prophets walking around Jerusalem with, say, loincloths on their heads.

I blow my shofar. It still sounds like a fax machine, but a healthy one.

Month Three: November

They shall be stoned with stones, their blood shall be upon them
LEVITICUS 20:27

Day 64. It's been more than a month since my mixed fiber adventure. Time for me to tackle the second item on my list of Most Perplexing Laws. Capital Punishment.

The Hebrew scriptures prescribe a tremendous amount of capital punishment. Think Saudi Arabia, multiply by Texas, then triple that. It wasn't just for murder. You could also be executed for adultery, blasphemy, breaking the Sabbath, perjury, incest, bestiality and witchcraft, among others. A rebellious son could be sentenced to death. As could a gluttonous or a drunkardly son.

The most commonly mentioned punishment method in the Hebrew Bible is stoning. So I figure, at the very least, I should try to stone. But how?

I can't tell you how many people have suggested I get adulterers and blasphemers stoned in the cannabis sense. Which is an interesting idea. But I haven't smoked pot since I was at Brown University and I wrote a paper for my anthropology class on the hidden symbolism of bong hits. (Brown was the type of college where this paper actually earned a B+).

Instead, I figured my loophole would be this: the bible doesn't specify the size of the stones. So . . .pebbles.

A few days ago, I gathered a handful of small white pebbles from Central Park, which I stuffed in my back pants pocket. Now all I needed were some victims. I decide to start with Sabbath breakers. That's easy enough to find in this workaholic city. I noticed a pot-bellied guy at the Avis down our block had worked on both Saturday and Sunday. So no matter what, he's a Sabbath-breaker.

Here's the thing, though: Even with pebbles, it is surprisingly hard to stone people.

My plan had been to walk nonchalantly past him and chuck the pebbles at the small of his back. But after a couple of failed passes, I realized it was a bad idea. A chucked pebble, no matter how small, does not go unnoticed.

My revised plan: I would pretend to be clumsy and drop the pebble on his shoe. So I did.

And in this way I stoned. But it was probably the most polite stoning in history—I said 'I'm sorry,' and then leaned down to pick up the pebble. And he leaned down at the same time, and we almost butted heads, and then he apologized, then I apologized again.

Highly unsatisfying.

Today, I get another chance. I am resting in a small public park on the Upper West Side, the kind where you see retirees eating tuna sandwiches on benches.

"Hey, you're dressed queer."

I look over. The speaker is an elderly man, mid-70s I'd guess. He is tall and thin and is wearing of those caps that cabbies wore in movies from the Forties.

"You're dressed queer," he snarls. "Why you dressed so queer."

I have on my usual fringes, and, for good measure, have worn some sandals and am carrying a knotty maple walking stick I'd bought on the Internet for $25.

"I'm trying to live by the rules of the Bible. The 10 commandments, stoning adulterers . . ."

"You're stoning adulterers?"

"Yeah, I'm stoning adulterers."

"I'm an adulterer."

"You're currently an adulterer?"

"Yeah. Tonight, tomorrow, yesterday, two weeks from now. You gonna stone me?"

"If I could, yes, that'd be great."

"I'll punch you in the face. I'll send you to the cemetery."

He is serious. This isn't a cutesy grumpy old man. This is an angry old man. This is a man with seven decades of hostility behind him.

I fish out my pebbles from my back pocket.

"I wouldn't stone you with big stones," I say. "Just these little guys."

I open my palm to show him the pebbles. He lunges at me, grabbing one out of my hand, then chucking it at my face. It whizzes by my cheek.

I am stunned for a second. I hadn't expected this elderly man to make the first move. But now there is nothing stopping me from retaliating. An eye for an eye.

I take one of the remaining pebbles and whip it at his chest. It bounces off.

"I'll punch you right in the kisser," he say.

"Well, you really shouldn't commit adultery," I say.

We stare at each other. My heart is racing.

Yes, he is a septuagenarian. Yes, he had just threatened me using corny Honeymooners dialogue. But you could tell: This man has a strong dark side.

Our glaring contest lasts ten seconds, then he walks away, brushing by me as he leaves.

When I was a kid, I saw an episode of All in the Family in which Meathead—Rob Reiner's wussy peacenik character—socked some guy in the jaw. Meathead was very upset about this. But he wasn't upset that he committed violence; he was upset because it felt so good to commit violence.

I can relate. Even though mine was a Stoning Lite, barely fulfilling the letter of the law, I can't deny: It felt good to chuck a rock at this nasty old man. It felt primal. It felt like I was getting vengeance on him. This guy wasn't just an adulterer, he was a bully. I wanted him to feel the pain he'd inflicted on others, even if that pain was a tap on the chest.

Like Meathead, I also knew that this was a morally stunted way to feel. Stoning is about as indefensible as you can get. It comes back to the old question: How can the Bible be so wise in some places and so barbaric in others? And why should we put any faith in a book that includes such brutality? Later that week, I ask my spiritual adviser Uri about stoning. Uri was born in the Midwest, and calls himself a "Jewtheran"— Jewish guilt and Lutheran repression mesh nicely, he told me. He's an ordained Orthodox rabbi, but never practiced, instead opting for the shmatta trade—he sold scarves to, among others, the Amish. He's tall and broad-shouldered with a neatly-trimmed beard. In his spare time, writes wry essays about Jewish life, including a lament about how his favorite snack, Twinkies, recently became non-kosher. I met him through Aish HaTorah, an Orthodox outreach group.

He isn't fazed by my question at all.

We don't stone people today because you need a Biblical theocracy to enforce the stoning. No such society exists today. But even in ancient times, stoning wasn't barbaric.

"First of all, you didn't just heave stones," says Uri. "The idea was to minimize the suffering. What we call 'stoning' was actually pushing the person off the cliff so they would die immediately upon impact. The Talmud actually has specifications on how high the cliff must be. Also, the person getting executed was given strong drink to dull the pain."

Plus, the stonings were a rare thing. Some rabbis say executions only occurred once every seven years, others say even less often. There had to be two witnesses to the crime. And the adulterer had to be tried by a council of 70 elders. And weirdly, the verdict of those 70 elders could not be unanimous—that might be a sign of corruption or brainwashing. And so on.

I half-expected Uri to say they gave the adulterer a massage and a gift bag. He made a compelling case. And yet, I'm not totally sold. Were ancient times really so merciful? I suspect there might be some whitewashing going on. As my year progresses, I'll need to delve deeper.

And you shall eat and be full, and you shall bless the LORD your God
for the good land he has given you.

DEUTERONOMY 8:10

Day 66. A spiritual update: I'm still agnostic, but I do have some progress to report on the prayer front. I no longer dread prayer. And sometimes I'm even liking it. I've even taken the training wheels off and am testing out some of my own prayers instead of just repeating passages from the Bible.

Elton Richards—the pastor out to pasture—broke down prayer for me into four types. It's a handy mnemonic: ACTS. A for adoration (praising God). C for confession (telling God your sins). T for Thanksgiving (being grateful to God for what you have). S for supplication (asking God to help you).

Right now, the one that's working for me best is T, thanksgiving. Adoration feels awkward to me. Confession feels forced. As for Supplication, I'm doing it, but I feel greedy asking God to help my career. Should I really be cluttering His in-box by asking for better placement of The Know-It-All at airport bookstores?

But thanksgiving, that I'm getting into. In Deuteronomy, the Bible says that we should thank the Lord when we've eaten our fill—Grace after meals, it's called. Christians moved grace to the beginning of the meal, pre-appetizer. To be safe, I'm praying both before and after.

Today, before tasting my lunch of hummus and pita bread, I stand up from my seat at the kitchen table, close my eyes, and say in a hushed tone:

"I'd like to thank God for the land that he provided so that this food might be grown."

Technically, that's enough. That fulfills the Bible's commandment. But while in thanksgiving mode, I decide to spread the gratitude around:

"I'd like to thank the farmer who grew the chick peas for this hummus. And the workers who picked the chick peas. And the truckers who drove them to the store. And the old Italian lady who sold the hummus to me at Zingone's deli and told me 'Lots of love.' Thank you."

Now that I type it, it sounds like an overly earnest Oscar speech for best supporting middle eastern spread. But saying it feels good.

Here's the thing: I'm still having trouble conceptualizing an infinite being, so I'm working on the questionable theory that a large quantity is at least closer to infinity. Hence the overabundance of thank you's. Sometimes I'll get on a roll, thanking people for a couple of minutes straight—the people who designed the packaging, and the guys who loaded the cartons into the truck. Julie has usually started in on her food by this point.

The prayers are helpful. They remind me that the food didn't spontaneously generate in my fridge. They make me feel more connected, more grateful, more grounded, more aware of my place in this complicated hummus cycle. They remind me to taste the hummus instead of shoveling it in like it's a nutrition pill. And they remind me that I'm lucky to have food at all. Basically, they help me get outside of my self-obsessed cranium.

I'm not sure this is what the Bible intended, but it feels like a step forward.

> *The fool hath said in his heart, "There is no God."*
>
> PSALM 14:1

Day 67. The ancient Israelites were surrounded by unbelievers. This is clear from the amount of space the Bible devotes to condemning idolatry, paganism and false gods. An impressive 46 of the 613 Jewish laws deal with the topic (give or take a couple, depending on how you classify them). It is, I think, one of the main similarities between ancient Israel and 21st century New York—we live among unbelievers.

I feel tempted all the time—not so much by a cult to Baal, but by the lure of secular humanism. To face my demons, I decide to go deep into the heart of unbelief: The weekly New York City Atheists meeting at a midtown Greek restaurant.

I know a fair amount of atheists, seeing as I live in a relatively godless city. But there's no way you could drag any of my atheist acquaintances to a meeting of New York City Atheists. Some of my friends are atheists precisely because they want to avoid joining a group that meets on a weekend and talks about plans for a cable access TV show.

An atheist club felt oxymoronic, like an Apathy Parade. But against all odds, it exists. The gathering of the godless takes place in a back room with a long table. A big blue Atheism banner hangs from the ceiling—right next to the Christmas decorations of cardboard silver angels, an irony several of the atheists point out.

I meet my neighbors. One is a compact woman with graying hair and a Darwin Cap. How was she converted to atheism? "I grew up with a Methodist Aunt who was basically a Victorian," she tells me. "I couldn't say the word 'leg.' I had to say 'limb.' I once said the word 'constipation' and got smacked. The hypocrisy was too much for me."

Then there was the big guy who looks like he was either a stevedore or hockey coach. "I'm a second-generation atheist," he says. "My dad spat when he walked by churches or synagogues."

There is a short-haired woman who was quite eager to steer the conversation to her self-published book, which is about an atheist arena cleaner in ancient Rome. "The main character's job was to clean up the carnage after the gladiators."

They ask me, eyeing my unkempt beard, why I'm visiting the Atheist's club, and I tell them about my project. They seem relieved, at least, that I'm not an Orthodox Jew or militant Muslim. But further discussion will have to wait.

"Shhhh-shhh."

The shusher is Ken, the leader of New York City Atheists. Ken looks a bit like Jackie Mason, but a strapping, broad-shouldered Jackie Mason. He's at the front of the room, wearing a blue-and-white Atheist baseball cap. My neighbor, the one with the Darwin cap, tells me that Ken worked at IBM for 37 years, and instead of golf, atheism is his retirement hobby.

Ken starts with the week's announcements. They are looking for guests for the weekly Atheist Cable Access TV show.

Also, the weekly movie night will be at 5:30 on Thursday, and they will be watching the Nazi war crime film Judgment at Nuremberg.

"Judgment at Nuremberg?" says a bald guy in the back. He doesn't seem happy.

"Yes," says Ken.

"What does that have to do with atheism?"

"You'll see," says Ken.

"It doesn't seem like it has a lot to do with atheism."

"It has a lot to do with atheism. And a lot to do with skepticism."

The bald guy was, as you might have guessed, skeptical.

Then Ken goes into his sermon proper—the importance of confronting 'believers.'

"We have to stop being polite. We may not make as many friends. But we have to say, 'The Bible is literature not history.'"

"Moussaka! Who has the moussaka!"

Ken pauses while the waiter delivers the moussaka. There's only one server, causing some 'feed the multitudes' jokes.

"You know the saying there are no atheists in a foxhole," says Ken. "You know what? I think they should stop praying and dig a deeper foxhole."

"Greek Salad? Who ordered the Greek salad?"

Ken is a good speaker, even charismatic, as close as you can get to a godless preacher. He has a booming voice, he slaps the palm of his hand to punctuate a point, he all but says "amen." Problem is, no one believes Ken's authority derives from God—which means it's a lot harder to command attention. There's lots of murmuring and crosstalk during his sermon.

I leave early—childcare duties—but return a week later to chat with Ken. He says his road to atheism began when, as a kid, he figured out there could be no Santa Claus.

"It just was not feasible to deliver all those presents," he says. "This was before FedEx."

So Ken was tipped off to the Santa Claus falsehood because of faulty logistics. Very IBM of him, I think.

"I started to ask myself, what else are they telling me that's not true?" says Ken.

I ask him if it's hard to lead a group of atheists. Like herding cats, he says. Atheists aren't, by nature, joiners. "They're individualists," he says. Which perhaps explains why we had 30 separate checks for lunch.

Ken has, in fact, boosted the group's membership and started some programs. But go to an atheist meeting, and you'll see why the religious lobby doesn't have to worry about the atheist lobby quite yet. You'll see why there are no soaring atheist cathedrals and why hotel room drawers don't come with a copy of *Why I Am Not a Christian* by Bertrand Russell. It's hard to be passionate about a lack of belief.

Recently, atheists have made a good effort, with authors like Sam Harris and Richard Dawkins acting as the movement's anti-popes. But still, if organized religion is Goliath, then organized atheism barely qualifies as a David.

You shall not make for yourself a graven image,
or any likeness of anything that is in heaven above,

or that is in the earth beneath,
or that is in the water under the earth.

Exodus 20:4

Day 69. I've added another commandment to my Most-Violated List: No making images. It was a surprise entry. Until I focused on it, I didn't realize the pervasiveness of images, nor how often I made them.

The loose interpretation of the second commandment—which starts out "You shall not make for yourself a graven image"—is that it prohibits idolatry. God is telling us not to bow down to golden calves or carved pillars.

But the more severe interpretation, which still echoes through Judeo-Christian tradition today, is that we should allow no images whatsoever. No drawing or sculpture or photography. No painting, unless you're Rothko or Mondrian. This is because of the second part of the commandment forbids us from making the 'likeness of anything in the sky, or earth, or in the water.' Which pretty much covers it.

The strictest adherents in America right now are probably the aforementioned Amish. Modern-day Islam is also famous for its avoidance of images. It's the reason why the Taliban shut down all movie theaters and riots erupted after that Dutch newspaper published cartoons of Mohammed.

Since I'm following the Bible literally, I figure I should take a rigorous approach, somewhere between the Amish and Taliban. Which is enormously difficult.

I can't absentmindedly doodle. I can't use emoticons, which I never used anyway, but it was nice knowing I had the option. I can't turn on the TV (though I decide that it's okay to watch TV if it's already on, because that cannot be construed as 'making an image').

I used to entertain Jasper by doing Google image searches of his favorite animals; no more. This is probably good, because typing in something like "kitty" inevitably turns up a woman in a skimpy cat outfit licking her hand.

I've tried to stop taking photos. Well, as much as possible anyway. When I balked at snapping a picture of my wife and her mom at her mom's birthday, Julie said "Can we have a sidebar conference please?"

The result of that tense negotiation: I'll take this photo, but after that, I'm done.

Granted, my starvation diet from images can be a headache. This morning, Jasper dumped his Play-Doh on the table. And as usual, he instructed me what to make. He's now moved beyond grunts to a vocabulary of 20-odd words.

"Ball!"

"How about a circle?" I respond.

I figure Platonic shapes are okay. I make a circle.

"Car!"

"You want to see a square?" I make a square.

"Nemo," says Jasper. (Nemo is Jasper's word for any type of fish; as a good proto-consumer, he speaks in brand names).

"Here you go," I say, making an oval. I'm starting to run out of shapes.

Jasper seems disappointed by my Play-Doh geometry. I feel ridiculous for refusing to make him a fish, but I also know I have to do this experiment full-bore, or else I'll risk missing out on making key spiritual discoveries. No cutting corners.

At least I have plenty of historical precedents. After the Reformation, a few protestant leaders—including John Calvin—urged the removal and/or smashing of paintings and statues from churches. Riots erupted in Switzerland and Scotland, among other places. Aside from provoking idolatry, images were thought to be a sign of human vanity. People were trying to compete with the God of Creation.

Jews have also obeyed this commandment on and off. Orthodox Jews still won't make a sculpture of a human. Some Jews of 14th century Germany wouldn't draw people, though they did find my favorite loophole: They illustrated their texts with bird-headed humans. You see, the commandment forbids the likeness of anything in heaven or earth—and technically, bird-headed humans don't exist in heaven or earth. Ingenious, no?

My vacation from iconography has been surprising, even enlightening. Despite the inconvenience, I'm liking image-avoidance.

First, it suits my job. Images are taking over, and writers are a dying breed. The Norman Mailers of today are reduced to writing pun-filled captions for paparazzi photos. Blogs—which were threatening enough to professional writers—are being replaced by video blogs. We writers need to embrace the second commandment as our rallying cry for the importance of words. In a literally biblical world, all publications would look like front page of *The Wall Street Journal*. Or the way it used to look, anyway.

Second, I think there's something to the idea that the divine dwells more easily in text than in images. Text allows for more abstract thought, more of a separation between you and the physical world, more room for you and God to meet in the middle. I find it hard enough to conceive of an Infinite Being. Imagine if those original scrolls came in the form of a graphic novel with pictures of the Lord? I'd never come close to communing with God.

The Bible is right: A deluge of images does encourage idolatry. Look at the cults of personality in America today. Look at Hollywood. Look at Washington. I'd like to see the next presidential race be run according to second commandment principles. No commercials. A radio-only debate. We need an ugly president. I know we're missing out on some potential Abe Lincolns because they'd look gawky and gangly on TV.

A righteous man hateth lying

PROVERBS 13:5 (KJV)

Day 72. Man, do I lie a lot. I knew I lied, but when I started to keep track, the quantity was alarming.

Here's a sample of today's lies:

—I lied to Julie about how much internet access at Starbucks costs. I told her $8 instead of $10 so she'd be 20 percent less annoyed.

—I gave a fake email address to a religious magazine called *Sojourners* because I didn't want to be swamped by junk email.

—I told a friend who writes children's books that my son loved her book about cookies even though we've never even cracked open said book about cookies.

—And I lied to kindly Mr. Berkowitz, the man who tested my fibers.

This I do at least once a week. Mr. Berkowitz calls—usually at 8 a.m. when Julie is still asleep—and asks if he can come over to my apartment to pray with me. If I said yes every time, he'd practically be a roommate. So I lie. "Can't today, Mr. Berkowitz. An important business meeting." "Sorry Mr. Berkowitz, I'm sick today. A throatache, a headache, the whole thing."

I don't tell huge lies. My lies aren't of the "I never met Jack Abramoff" variety, or even the "I spent three years in jail with my friend Lenny" variety. They're little lies. White lies. Half-truths. Sugarcoating.

I'm such an experienced liar, I once wrote an article for Esquire on the art of the "non-committal compliment." When your friend makes a movie that is just dreadful, what do you say? I gave a bunch of options, like "You've done it again!" or "I loved the credits!"

I've always thought that this sort of truth-hedging was necessary in human relations. Without little lies, chaos would erupt. Marriages would crumble, workers would be fired, egos would be shattered. I've seen Liar, Liar with Jim Carrey. I know how it works.

But if you take the Bible strictly, it says to avoid lying on all occasions. It says this several times. (A relevant detour: Some scholars argue that the commandment "Thou Shalt not Bear False Witness" should be interpreted more narrowly—it originally only applied to lying under oath. Unfortunately for liars, there are heaps of other passages banning deceit of any kind, including Proverbs 6:17, which calls "The lying tongue" an "abomination.").

In his book Why the 10 Commandments Matter, conservative Florida minister D. James Kennedy says my little white lies are, in fact, sins. Think of it this way: You have a date with a friend but you just want to stay home and watch TV. You don't want to hurt her feelings, so you say you're sick. The friend comes over with a pot of chicken soup and finds you healthy. She can never trust you again. Just tell her the truth in the first place says Dr. Kennedy.

So at the very least, I should cut back on lying. I decide to do this in stages. My first mission is to stop telling lies to my son, then move on from there. I lie to Jasper all the time, especially at meals. One classic is this: "Just one more bite," I'll say. He'll take a bite. Then I'll say "Okay, just one more bite." And so on.

Mind you, he's equally as deceitful. He's only allowed to watch TV when eating, so he'll try to stretch the dinner out for hours. He'll put a string bean halfway into his mouth, and just dangle it there like a Marlboro Light.

I'll say "Eat, Jasper."

And then he'll gum it for a bit before stopping and getting back to the business of watching Dora explore.

My question is: does the parent-child relationship have to be one of dishonesty? Perhaps there's something to transparent parenting.

I start it this morning. Jasper wants a bagel for breakfast. So I ask Julie where she put the bagels.

"We're out," she says. "Just give him an English muffin and tell him that it's a bagel."

She did it yesterday, and he didn't know the difference.

So I give him a whole-wheat Thomas's English muffin.

"Bagel?" he asks, pointing to the English muffin.

"Actually, it's not a bagel. It's an English muffin."

He looks confused.

"It's still very good. But it's not a bagel."

As it registers that he isn't getting a bagel, his expression turns from confusion to anger. He looks like someone has just circumcised him again.

"Bagel! Bagel!"

"We don't have bagels. We'll get bagels tomorrow."

Within about a minute, this has escalated into a full-blown tantrum. I'm still amazed that kids can live out clichés quite as precisely as they do. When throwing tantrums, Jasper will get down on his stomach and pound the floor with his fists and feet like he's a character in a Peanuts cartoon.

"What's going on here?" asks Julie. As you might have guessed, I had to tell the truth.

There are probably long-term advantages of being completely honest with your kid (he'll know he can't have his way all the time, for one thing. He'll trust you for another). But there are severe short-term disadvantages.

Love not sleep, lest you come to poverty

PROVERBS 20:13

Day 74. The other day, my grandfather asked me "Do you sleep with the beard under the covers or over the covers?" Now that I'm aware of it, I can't stop thinking about it. I switch positions every few minutes.

It's just one of the reasons I'm having trouble sleeping. The problem is, I'm downloading so much spiritual data during the days that I spend my nights awake in bed trying to process it. (Incidentally, the author of the Proverbs would be fine with my lack of sleep; he considers sleep a sign of laziness that will lead to poverty).

As I lie in bed tonight, I think about Answers in Genesis, which just sent me a four-color brochure. Maybe I let myself off the creationism hook too easily. As unlikely as the six-day scenario may be, shouldn't I at least give it the benefit of doubt?

So I do an experiment. I try to put myself into the mind of my Biblical alter-ego Jacob. I convince myself that the earth was formed 6000 years ago. I can't 100 percent believe, but for a few minutes, I almost believe it.

And it is fascinating. The first thing I notice is that I feel more connected. If everyone on earth is descended from two identifiable people—Adam and Eve—then the "family of man" isn't just pablum. It's true. The guy who sells me bananas at the deli on 81st street—he's my cousin.

But even more powerful is this feeling: my life is more significant. If the earth is 10 billion years old, I'm barely a drop of water in the ocean that is the universe. But if the earth is 6,000 years old, then I've been alive for a decent portion of the all history. I'm no bit player. I've got a speaking part in the movie of life.

My thought experiment crystallized a key tension I've noticed in the Bible. On the one hand, the Bible teaches extreme humility. Humans are sinful, barely worthy of praying to God.

On the other hand, there's a certain—I don't know if arrogance quite the right word. Maybe pride. Humans are the pinnacle of Biblical creation, the ones God saved until last on the sixth day, beings that are vastly superior to the beasts and nature. We are made in God's image. (As the philosopher Baruch Spinoza said, if triangles could think, their

God would be eminently triangular).

I think that's a key motivation to creationism—the need to feel less inconsequential . I remember Mark Looy—the publicist for the creation museum—saying, "Evolution says we are the product of random processes. That we evolved via pond scum. When we say that, we're not applying much value to humanity. If we say we're a product of accidents and random processes, how much purpose and hope does that give to our youth?"

Since I'll never convert to creationism, I have to find some dignity and self-esteem and sacredness even with our mucky origins.

> *Speak to the people of Israel, and bid them to make tassels*
> *on the corners of their garments*
>
> NUMBERS 15:38

Day 75. I've bought a lot of books this year, but this new Amazon delivery is a big one: The autobiography of my ex-uncle Gil. When I open the box, the first thing that strikes me is this: Gil is not opposed to graven images. The cover features no less than 11 photos of Gil. Gil in front of his hippie bus, Gil with his eyes shut smelling flowers, Gil perched regally on a red armchair.

The book is called Coming Back to Earth and was published in 2004 by a small Jewish press and was banned by some rabbis in Israel because, among other things, it contains four-letter-words. I start to read. His life is crazier than I anticipated, even if you make allowances for the occasional James Frey-like fabrication.

Gil grew up in a secular Jewish family in upstate New York. He became a financial consultant in Phoenix—and a successful one, by his account. But he felt something missing. So he dropped out and became a hippie.

Some of his adventures are typically hippie, the things you might see in an early Dennis Hopper film: He dropped acid and passed out for three days. He ate nothing but watermelon for two weeks straight in an attempt to cleanse himself. He got high at an opium den in Pakistan. He was arrested for skinny-dipping in Virginia. His wardrobe consisted of a tablecloth.

But other escapades are outlandish even by hippie standards. Gil trekked to an ashram in Northern India where he lived in a squalid yard with 5000 other devotees. The ashram's guru—a man with a huge Afro and a crimson-colored robe—would emerge from his house every day, but never deign to speak to Gil. Gil waited for weeks.

Finally, one day, the guru's pet elephant Gita went on a stampede in the ashram yard. Panic everywhere. Gil stood up, 'threw my hand in the air toward the raging elephant and screamed STOP!' The elephant stopped. From then on, Gil had a place in the guru's inner circle. This allowed him to meet John Lennon and Yoko Ono, who were disenchanted with their own guru—the Maharishi Mahesh Yogi—because, writes Gil, "he couldn't keep his hands off Mia Farrow's butt."

Gil came back to New York and opted to go into the guru business himself. He decided God wanted him to start his sect on a bench on the corner of 86th street and Central Park West. He sat there, gazing at the tip of his nose for eight months, amassing—by his account—dozens of followers who sat at his feet, soaking up his vibes: seekers, stockbrokers, poets and movie stars (Sally Kirkland!).

Did I mention he wasn't speaking at the time? Gil had given up vocal communication, remaining silent for three years. He dispensed wisdom (e.g. "smoke the best bag first") to his followers through a sign language of his own invention.

Eventually, Gil moved his "Family" to Ithaca, New York. He lived in a yurt by a pond meditating for—he says—23 hours a day. All of his needs were attended to by his worshipful followers—who, by the way, had been given brilliantly sixties-ish names like Rainbow, Bliss, and Banana Tree. And I do mean worshipful. They literally fell on their faces in front of him.

Gil's Hindu phase came to an abrupt end when he read a pamphlet someone left in his bathhouse. It was about Christianity. Gil became a born-again Christian leader who, among other things, battled demons and healed a homeless man.

That phase, in turn, came to an equally abrupt end when Gil started to read the Hebrew Bible more closely. It was during this time that Gil followed the Bible literally: When he made tassels of yarn and attached them to every corner he could find on his clothes, and when he tied a wad of cash around his hand.

He eventually switched to more traditional Jewish practices. And nowadays, he spends his days in Jerusalem binding tefillin on tourists at the Western Wall and holding Shabbat dinner for young seekers. But I get the feeling that Gil is a very unorthodox Orthodox Jew. One of his theological precepts is that everything is God, sort of a Semitic pantheism.

Here's how Gil puts it: He writes he was once sent to a psychiatrist who diagnosed him as a "megalomaniac." Gil writes: "I had to look it up in a dictionary. It said 'someone who believes they are God.' I had to agree with that. I not only thought I was God, I thought (and still think) all is God."

Gil's life inspired another obscure book that I figured I should read as well. Called Yea God, this 1987 biography painted a much darker picture of Guru Gil. This was the Grimm's to his Disney version.

Here, we meet a Gil who was sexist (men in his cult got cushy yurts, women had to suffice with tepees) and controlling (he went so far as to instruct his followers how to go to the bathroom properly).

Worse, according to this book, Gil sometimes smacked around members of the Family. And here's the crazy part: They allegedly liked it. "Thank you for loving this one enough to beat him," it quotes one follower saying, in the odd third-person language of the Family. (Gil says he was "out of his mind" during this part of his life, so he can't remember everything, but that the allegations about his violence are overblown).

There's a scene where the author interviews the parents of one of Gil's cult members. They talk about how their son changed his name and stopped speaking about anything but his new "family". It's a heartbreaking story. And it makes me understand what my grandparents must have gone through when Kate became Gil's Number One follower.

It's exactly what I was always most afraid about with religion. To embrace religion, you have to surrender some control. But what if it's a slippery slope, and you lose all control, and slide right past the Judeo-Christian mainstream and end up in a yurt kneeling in front of a guy wearing a tablecloth who has renamed you Lotus Petal?

It's why I don't know what to do with Jasper. If I give him some religion, then he might become obsessed and go Guru Gil on me. Then again, if I give him no religion, he could descend into moral anarchy. They're both so risky. I feel like I can't win.

Train up a child in the way he should go: and when
he is old he will not depart from it.

PROVERBS 22:6

Day 78. I've started to wear sunglasses more often. I can't find anything in the Bible prohibiting them, and they make my beard—which is now down to my Adam's Apple—look slightly hipper. More indie record producer, less Crown Heights. Today, I've taken my shades on a trip to the playground with my wife and son. Julie's reading her People magazine on the bench, and I'm scampering around after Jasper.

He wants to go on the swing.

"Okay, just give me a second," I say.

I take a bottle of Purell anti-bacterial lotion from the stroller bag. These playgrounds, they're like a germ free-for-all. I wipe the chain on the left side of the swing, then start in on the right side. Jasper is whining that he wants to get on already.

"Almost ready," I say.

Julie looks up from her magazine to see the battle in progress. "AJ," she says. "Helmet."

Helmet is Julie's codeword to me that I'm being a crazy overprotective father. We've had so many fights about this, she thought it'd be easier to just sum up her position with a single word: Helmet. She chose helmet because, at one point, without irony, I checked out the prices of baby helmets on the Internet.

It's just that these kids are so fragile, you know? They've only got that mushy little skull separating their brains from the sidewalk. They only have two years of an immune system built up.

Last week, Julie and I got into an argument because I said I didn't want him going to something called "The International Preschool." This is a school where a lot of U.N. workers send their kids.

I said I don't want him to become too interested in foreign countries, because then he might live in one when he grows up.

"You're kidding, right?

"No, I want him to live in the same town I do."

"That's why you don't want him to go there?"

"Yes."

"That's demented."

She told me that I have to back off. Otherwise I'll be cutting his hot dog into tiny pieces when he's 19 and chaperoning him to the prom. That's when she came up with "helmet."

Maybe she's right. Maybe I should treat Jasper more like God treats humans in the Bible. He gave us free will. He relinquished some control because He wanted us to be able to make our own mistakes and have our own victories.

Maybe I should. But I can't. I can't expose him to an unsanitized swing with its millions of microorganisms. So I give the right-hand chain another squirt of Purell. Julie shakes her head.

It is better to go to a house of mourning
than to go to a house of feasting,

Ecclesiastes 7:2

Day 80. The extended family has gathered at my grandfather's apartment in midtown for a late lunch. It's to honor my grandmother, who died two years ago. It's our own secular ritual—we get together once a year to reminisce. My grandmother was an remarkable woman—smart, funny, elegant, organized beyond belief (each of her six children was assigned a different color, and got towels only in that color, left notes in that color, etc.)

And man, was she secular. For her, family was the alpha and omega, so she found the story of Abraham's near-sacrifice of his son Isaac on a mountaintop particularly inexplicable.

"How could a father even think about killing his son?" she once told me when I was a kid. "What a horrible story."

After my aunt Kate's switch to Orthodoxy, my grandmother went from being secular to fiercely anti-religious. I remember walking down

57th street with her. We passed a Hasidic man draped in his black hat and black coat. I looked at my grandmother, who was staring at the man, almost scowling—and then she darted her tongue out. Quick as a snake, just poked it out.

"What was that?" I asked.

"I always stick my tongue out at people like that," she said.

"Do you think he saw?"

"He saw," she said. "He knows."

She was torn between her usual polite, elegant self and her real hatred for what she saw as religious fundamentalism. I often wonder what she would have thought of my experiment.

Everyone is at the lunch, including both Kate and my vegan-feminist aunt Marti from Berkeley. Marti gives me some stern pointers on the politically-incorrect, violence-laden religious words to avoid.

"You shouldn't use the word sacred, because it comes from sacrifice."

"Okay."

"And 'bless' comes the Old English word bletsian, which means consecrate with blood. So don't use that."

"What about Bible?"

"I'm not sure about that one."

"It comes from Byblos, the Egyptian word for papyrus. Made from the corpses of once-living plants."

"Yes, maybe avoid that too," she says.

Kate also gives me suggestions on language. Right before lunch, Jasper wants to show me a fascinating trick in which he jumps from the rug to the wooden floor, so he tugs on my pants and says:

"A.J! A.J!"

"Yes, I'm watching."

"He calls you A.J?" says Kate.

"Yeah. We're on a first-name basis."

I've tried to switch Jasper to the more traditional "Dad" or "Daddy," but he insists on A.J. So I've gotten used to it.

"Children aren't supposed to use their parents first names," says Kate. "It's disrespectful."

Kate's probably right; in Biblical times, their was no such thing as informal I'm-friends-with-my-kid father. Without me knowing it, Jasper was violating the 'honor your parents' commandment.

When we all sit down to lunch, my grandfather asks me: "What's the strangest rule you have to follow?"

I mentally scan my list of Five Most Perplexing Rules. I choose one at random. "Probably the one about how if you're in a fistfight, and the wife of your opponent grabs your private parts, you must cut off her hand."

"That," he says, "is very strange indeed."

And it is. But that's exactly what the Bible says:

"When men fight with one another, and the wife of the one draws near to rescue her husband from the hand of him who is beating him, and puts out her hand and seizes him by the private parts, then you shall cut off her hand; your eye shall have no pity.

Deuteronomy 45:11–12

So far (knock on wood) I've avoided getting in a brawl with man whose wife looks like she has a firm grip. So I guess I'm obeying it by default, and can congratulate myself on that.

But, as with the mixed fibers, it baffles me. Why the specificity? Why does the Bible ban this particular below-the-belt maneuver and not, say, a kidney punch or a kick between the thighs. Julie suggests it's because the writer of Leviticus had this precise unpleasant scenario happen to him, and so decided to forbid it for all eternity.

Unfortunately, Kate is within earshot when I tell my grandfather about the private parts rule. Damn. I thought she had been in the kitchen. I didn't want her hearing me talk about the crazy ones without balancing it with some good ones.

And sure enough, she looks stricken. Like she just discovered her son smokes two packs a day. She had studied the Bible for years, but had never learned about the husband-grabbing part. It's just not one that gets a lot of play at synagogue.

The next day, I get three voicemails. All from Kate. "Is part of your Biblical life that you're not allowed to answer the phone?" she says.

I call her back.

"I talked to my rabbi," Kate says. "And yes, it is in the Torah." But . . . it's supposed to represent something broader: Do not embarrass others. The wife here is embarrassing her husband by assuming he needs help. And the wife is embarrassing the husband's opponent by, well, grabbing his privates. Plus, adds Kate, you didn't actually chop off the wife's hand. That's metaphorical. The woman was only required to pay a fine.

Okay. It does seem more rational if interpreted that way. But my question is: Why didn't the Bible just say that? Why not just say "Don't embarrass others?" Why the mysterious code?

I've asked all of the Jewish members of my spiritual board this question. The best answer I've gotten is this, from a rabbi named Noah Weinberg, a founder of Aish HaTorah, the outreach group: Life is a jigsaw puzzle, he told me. The joy and challenge of life—and the Bible—is figuring things out. "If a jigsaw puzzle came numbered, you'd return it to the store." Same with life.

It's a good answer, but only partly satisfying. I have to keep digging.

Cursed shall you be in the city,
and cursed shall you be in the field.

DEUTERONOMY 28:16

Day 82. Tonight I break the eighth commandment—no stealing—and I pay the price.

It happens when I try to research different types of Biblical incense on the Internet, but our wireless connection is on the fritz. So I go in search of a signal. I take my laptop to the gray-walled emergency stairwell, and descend to the fourth floor. I figure maybe I can latch onto a neighbor's network. I try one called Sonicboy. No dice. Password required. I go down another flight. Zildo y Zelda? Nope. Also requires a password. But down another flight, I find a network with the beautifully generic name of "Wireless." An excellent sign. If they can't be bothered to come up with a name, maybe they don't know about this newfangled thing called passwords. Yes, I get a signal.

But it's not coming in strong enough, so I climb down another two stairs. At which point I trip and slam my knee into the railing and bash my laptop against the wall.

So I deserved it. The Bible says thou shalt not steal; I stole my neighbor's wireless signal. And I'm now limping around the house with a bum knee.

Was this God's punishment? I don't know. I don't honestly think so. Would my ancient Israelite ancestors have thought so (assuming I explained wireless Internet etiquette to them)? Maybe. As with everything Biblical, there's no simple answer about the consequences of sin. You can find several major themes.

The first is that God will punish you, and he will punish you in this life. This motif is best seen in Deuteronomy 28, which contains the three most terrifying pages in the history of publishing. Here you read every horrible disease and weather pattern that will befall you if you don't live by the Bible.

The Lord will "smite you with consumption and with fever, inflammation and fiery heat, and with drought, and with blasting and with mildew."

And that's just some throat-clearing.

"And the heavens over your head shall be brass, and the earth under you shall be iron.

And the Lord will make the rain of your land powder and dust."

It's actually oddly beautiful. Take away the fact that the words condemn you to a life of aching, thirsty, itchy torment, and it's poetic, breathtaking.

"You shall grope at noonday, as the blind grope in darkness . . .

You shall betroth a wife, and another man shall lie with her . . ."

It goes on to say you shall be reduced to eating your own children and trying—unsuccessfully—to sell yourself as a slave. There is also a section of the good things that will happen if you follow the law. But it's only a quarter of the length of the curses. It's the curses that stay with you.

In some hyper-religious circles, this type of thinking persists. Jerry Falwell said 9/11 was God's punishment for America's depravity. Pat Robertson, with all sincerity, blamed Hurricane Katrina on the shirt-lifting antics of Mardi Gras revelers.

I find myself slipping into this mindset now and again. But only for a second. The world doesn't seem to work that way. Just look at the evil people in America. They don't have boils on their legs and they're not eating their children. Many are living in penthouses and some have their own reality shows.

Thankfully, the Bible is a big book, an infinitely complex book, and there are many alternatives. One recurring theme—found mostly in the New Testament—says that you will be rewarded in heaven. Another strain—found in books like Ecclesiastes and Job—takes a modern, almost agnostic, view.

Ecclesiastes is probably my favorite book of the Bible. I first read about it in the Encyclopaedia Britannica, and I have loved it ever since. Called Kohelet in Hebrew, the book is a collection of wisdom and reminiscences from a man who identifies himself as King Solomon. If you believe modern Biblical scholars, the author was probably not Solomon, but instead a now-anonymous third-century BCE poet. Whoever he was, the writing is awe-inspiring.

Every time I read it, I feel myself doing a little silent call-and-response with the text. 'yes.' 'that's right.' I feel the thrill of recognizing thoughts that I have had myself, but that I've never been able to capture in such beautiful language. And I feel the oddity of finding myself on the same wavelength as a man who lived 2000 years ago. It's the closest I've come to proselytizing—telling friends they have to read Ecclesiastes.

In any case, the author of Ecclesiastes says: "The race is not to the swift, nor the battle to the strong, nor bread to the wise, nor riches to the intelligent, nor favor to the men of skill; but time and chance happen to them all"

Ecclesiastes says that life is uncertain. "Vapor, all is vapor." (This is a more accurate translation of the phrase usually rendered "vanity, all is vanity.") We can never hope to plumb the mystery of God's mind. Bad things happen to good people. Idiots and geniuses, saints and sinners—we all die. The best we can do is try to appreciate the grea things that God has given us—food, drink, the pleasure of honest work. We should follow the commandments, but we should do so with no guarantee that they will pay off in this life.

This is so wise. Be good for goodness' sake, as someone once said. It's a pragmatic worldview. The thing is, it's not a solid worldview. It's vapor, all vapor. If I knew for sure I'd be punished for sinning, then I'd have a undeniable reason to follow the God's word. But I doubt I'll ever believe that for certain. So what to do? Part of me wants something more tangible than the vapor. Can I find it by the end of the year? Or is that, as Ecclesiastes says, chasing the wind?

> *He who despises his neighbor is a sinner*
>
> PROVERBS 14:21

Date 84. I've been trying to love my neighbor, but in New York, this is particularly difficult. It's an aloof city. I don't even know my neighbor's names, much less love them. I know them only as woman-whose-cooking-smells-nasty and the-guy-who-gets-Barron's-delivered-each-week, etc .

Well, except for Nancy in 5I. We met because our son and her beagle are about the same age, have pretty much the same vocabulary and share similar interests, such as running around the hall.

Nancy is a former hippie who was once friends with Jimi Hendrix and Janis Joplin. In fact, she looks like Janis Joplin would have looked if Janis Joplin had lived another 30 years. In the sixties, Nancy took a lot of drugs, had a couple of disastrous relationships with men, did some waitressing, wrote some poetry, and now lives alone with her dog and listens to Howard Stern every morning. She almost always wears sundresses and knit caps. She calls herself "the kooky lady with the dog."

She's painfully shy, almost skittish. She'll visit our apartment occasionally, but when I knock on hers, she always just cracks the door open and pokes her head out. "I'm painting one wall at a time," she once explained. "I don't want anyone to see it till it's done." She also once told me that I unnerved her because I kept too much eye contact. (Which is, in fact, a problem for me. I often forget to intermittently glance away during conversations, and have to remind myself to do so, otherwise people will think I'm a psycho who keeps torsos in my freezer).

Nancy was married for awhile after college, but she couldn't have kids. So she's become the unofficial Godmother to our son. For the past few months she's been sketching a portrait of him. "I'll be finished soon," she promises. "By the time he takes his SATs."

And today, she brings Jasper an early holiday present: A wooden Noah's ark with a menagerie of little painted animals. She thought it'd be good to get him a Biblical present. I make Jasper say thank you, a phrase he pronounces without those tiresome consonants so it sounds like 'a-ew.'

"You know, it's interesting," I say to Nancy, as we sit at the kitchen table watching Jasper march the giraffes onto his boat. "I was reading in one of my Bible commentaries about how the flood is such a tragic story—the drowning of millions of people and animals—and how strange it is that it's always made into cute kids' toys."

Nancy looks wounded.

"I didn't . . ." Ugh. What a putz. I had tried to show off my Biblical knowledge, and I ended up insulting my only friendly neighbor. The Bible tells us not to be know-it-all—"A prudent man conceals his knowledge" (Proverbs 12:23).

"I love his ark," I say. "It's adorable . . .."

"Don't worry," she says, recovering. "At least I didn't get him the stuffed 10 plagues."

Nancy is a good neighbor, probably the best I've had in my time as a New Yorker. I decide that this will be one of my missions for the year: Do something righteous—a good deed, a mitzvah—for my neighbor in 5I.

Therefore he may lie with you tonight in return for your son's mandrakes.

GENESIS 30:15 NASB

Day 87. As of this week, Julie and I have officially been trying to be fruitful and multiply for a year. Still no luck. So we've decided to take radical measures. We're going to try in vitro fertilization.

This is more morally fraught than I had realized. Thanks to my religion-soaked life, I now know that several higher authorities condemn the procedure. The Catholic church, for instance, denounces IVF for at least two reasons. First, it requires the man to stimulate himself. Second, it breaks what one Catholic magazine calls "the unity and integrity" of "conjugal fruitfulness." Which means that the conception takes place outside the woman's body, not where God intended it.

On the other hand, most rabbis don't have much of a problem with IVF—and some Jewish scholars even argue that "be fruitful and multiply" means that there's a moral imperative to get pregnant by any means necessary. Which is why New York fertility clinics are often crowded with black hats and voluminous beards.

The Bible, of course, never addresses the issue directly. There's nary a mention of IVF in Scripture, even by its long-forgotten name of 'test tube baby.' There is, however, a Biblical story about fertility drugs—or their ancient equivalent, anyway. You remember Jacob, who was married to two sisters: Leah (the baby machine) and Rachel (the one with the barren womb). At one point, Rachel got so desperate, she pleaded with her sister for some mandrake. Mandrake is an egg-shaped middle-eastern fruit that was thought to be a fertility cure. Rachel got her mandrake—but the scheme backfired. Because Rachel—to secure the mandrake—had traded to Leah a night with Jacob—and on that very night, Jacob was apparently at maximum virility. Leah got pregnant. Rachel got nothing, at least for the time being. So . . .you could argue that the Bible subtly disapproves of fertility treatments.

But honestly, that seems like speculation. If I take the Bible literally—at its word—I can't find any guidance pro or con.

So we're going to try IVF. It helps that my new insurance plan covers it. And it helps too that we have a family connection to the procedure. My cousin David—now 23—was the very first test tube baby in New York State, and he got his little technologically-assisted face on the cover of The Daily News. He seems to have turned out all right. He fits in fine with my family—with the exception of my ultra-liberal aunt Marti, who squabbles with him every time they're in the same room. David—former president of his fraternity—likes manly things like baseball and a big juicy piece of meat. Marti does not. Whenever someone takes a family photo, she tells us all to say "SOY CHEESE!", which always prompts David to shout a gleefully malicious "T-BONE!" (To be technical, Marti has since decided soy causes health problems, so she now prefers us to say 'Vegan").

IVF is a startlingly complicated process. The build-up to the actual fertilization involves 40 days of shots, pills, alcohol swabs and a fearsome array of syringes. Granted, I get the better half of the deal. Julie actually has to be poked by a needle every day. But I do have to be her RN, mixing together white powders and sterile water in what seems the most stressful chemistry experiment of my life.

The first night, a Russian-accented nurse came to our apartment to show me how to inject my wife. She asked Julie to drop her pants and lean over. "It's just like throwing a dart," the nurse told me. Though with this dart, you miss and the target starts bleeding.

"Each night, you alternate cheeks—first right, then left, right, left." And, she advised, you have to make sure the needle hits the sweet spot of the upper butt.

I don't like vagueness. So I opened a drawer, took out a green magic marker and requested the nurse to draw me the exact location of these 'sweet spots' on Julie's butt. Which she did. And which helps me enormously. But not Julie. She complains that whenever she wears white pants, everyone can see two green orbs on her butt.

"I hope this works," Julie told me yesterday. "Because I don't think I can go through this again."

For God is with the generation of the righteous

PSALMS 14:5

Day 92, November 30, the end of month three of Project Bible. My alter-ego Jacob is looking more and more religious. Or, to be precise, more and more Jewish thanks mostly to the beard. I know this because I was stopped by some tourists on the street and asked "Where in New York can I get a good knish?" More to the point, I was told by a guy at the homeless shelter where I volunteer: "You look really Jewish." Hard to misinterpret that one.

On the other hand, my ethical state leaves much to be desired. This occurs to me as I am sitting on the cross-town bus today reading Ecclesiastes.

I'm concentrating hard. Too hard. I feel a tap on my shoulder. I'm annoyed. I don't like strangers touching me. I look up. It is a fiftyish man.

"Excuse me, this lady is feeling sick. Could you give her your seat?"

He points to a tall brunette woman who was standing right in front of me. How did I miss this? The woman looks horrible: Her face is sallow, nearly the color of lima beans. She is doubled over. And she is weeping.

I get up in a hurry with mumbled apologies. To paraphrase Ecclesiastes, there's a time for reading, and a time for getting off your butt.

I realize I was what is known in Hebrew as a Chasid Shote. A righteous idiot. A pious fool. There's a traditional Jewish story in the Talmud about man who is so obedient to the rules, he refuses to save a drowning woman on the beach. She might be impure.

The moral is the same as Jesus' parable about the Good Samaritan: Don't be so caught up in the regulations that you forget about the big things like compassion and respect for life. The Righteous Idiot is what the Christian Bible calls Pharisees—the sanctimonious legalistic scholars who criticize Christ's followers for picking grain on the Sabbath.

As I mentioned in the introduction, one of the reasons I embarked on this experiment was to take legalism to its logical extreme and show that it leads to Righteous Idiocy. What better way to show the absurdity of Jewish and Christian fundamentalism? If you actually follow all the rules, you'll spend your days acting like a crazy person.

I still believe that. And I still plan on making a complete fool of myself to get this point across. But as with everything involving religion, my project has become much more complicated. The spiritual journey now takes up far more of my time.

My friend Roger was right. It's not like studying Sumo wrestling in Japan. It's more like wrestling itself. This opponent of mine is sometimes beautiful, sometimes cruel, sometimes ancient, sometimes crazily relevant. I can't get a handle on it. I'm outmatched.

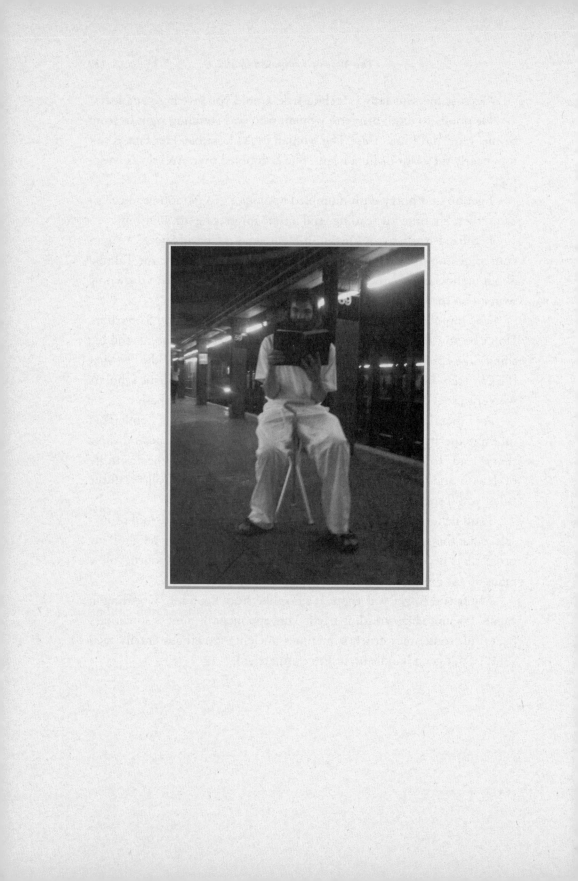

Month Four: December

For everything there is a season
ECCLESIASTES 3:1

Day 93. December has arrived, and everyone is gearing up for the big Judeo-Christian holidays. New York is packed. I tried to walk through Rockefeller Center the other day, and I got flashbacks to the mosh pit at the Hasidic rave.

I feel oddly out of synch. This is because the Bible itself has surprisingly little to say about the December holidays. The New Testament talks about the birth of Jesus, of course. But there's no description of how to celebrate that birth—no tree, no services, no carols, no egg nog, no Frank Capra films. Which means some of the more literalist Christian denominations—including the Jehovah's Witnesses and the Worldwide Church of God—don't celebrate Christmas at all.

Hanukkah doesn't make it into the Bible either. The story of Hanukkah—the revolt of the Jewish rebels the Maccabees against their Greek oppressor Antiochus—appears (though only in a section of the Bible called the apocrypha, which in Judaism is considered non-canonical). But there's nothing in the Scriptures about the lighting eight candles or grease-soaked latkes.

I'll be sitting out this holiday season. Well, as much as I can. I still have to buy some gifts for Julie. I can't get away with skipping that, and the Bible is actually pro-gift-giving ("It is more blessed to give than to receive," Acts 20:35). Fortunately, buying gifts won't take too much time; Julie is so absurdly organized, she always hands me a stack of catalogues with the gifts she wants circled in red magic marker. It's a great thing. As is the conviction with which she says the inevitable "Oh my God! How did you know!"

Let your garments be always white.

ECCLESIASTES 9:8

Day 95. I looked in the mirror today, and decided it's official: I've become someone I'd cross the street to avoid. To complement my beard and fringes, I've begun wearing all-white, as prescribed by King Solomon in Ecclesiastes: "Let your garments always be white." White pants, white T-shirts, a white sweater and a white zip-up jacket from The Gap, obviously without mixed fibers.

Which means that when I say goodbye to Julie in the morning, I get one of two responses. Either

a) A Saturday Night Fever hand twirl and accompanying arm thrust
Or

b) A Fonzie-like "aaaaayyyyyy."
The John Travolta reference I understand, but the Fonzie one stumped me.

"In the first season Fonzie wore white because black leather was considered too menacing," Julie explained. (This is a woman who still has her childhood collection of TV Guides).

Personally, I prefer to think of myself in a more highbrow mold—a Biblical version of Tom Wolfe. Or perhaps a modern Emily Dickinson, who became a recluse in the 1860s and refused to wear anything but white.

Regardless, it's a bizarre sensation walking around the Upper West Side in white garments—or 'tusk' garments, as The Gap calls them. As with many New Yorkers, my regular wardrobe is mostly made up of bleak colors—blacks, browns, a daring splash of navy blue. It seems to suit city's soot and cynicism. Dark clothes for a dark city.

I rarely see New Yorkers wearing all-white unless they're behind a bakery counter. So I'm getting even more wary glances than ever on the subway. I like to play a game: I swivel my head around quickly and see how many starers I can catch. Usually at least two.

But the thing is, I'm enjoying it. My white wardrobe makes me feel lighter, more spiritual. Happier. It's further proof of a major theme of this year: The outer affects the inner. Behavior shapes your psyche as much as the other way around. Clothes make the man. As I walk down

Columbus Avenue on this brisk day, with the wind flattening my white pants and jacket against me, I think to myself: Life can't be too terrible if I'm dressed like I'm about to play a cricket match or attend P. Diddy's birthday party, right?

The 'white garment' line from Ecclesiastes is usually interpreted metaphorically—as a call to remain pure and joyous. But it's not be-yond-a-doubt metaphorical. Maybe it means what it says: dress in white. An ancient Israelite sect called the Essenes dressed in white, as do some Kabbalists. I should have been wearing all-white from Day 1, but it was one of those rules I felt I had to build up to. Now that I'm doing it, I don't want to stop.

Remember the Sabbath day, to keep it holy

EXODUS 20:8

Day 98. It's a Tuesday afternoon in December, but I feel I've just experienced my first real Sabbath.

Let me explain: the doorknobs in our apartment fall off on an alarmingly regular basis. They're mercurial little suckers. We don't even need to be touching them—it's more of a natural-life-cycle type of situation, like icebergs calving or my hairline retreating. I'll be in bed, reading my Bible, and I'll hear a thud, and know that another doorknob succumbed to gravity.

Usually, I screw the knob back on. Problem solved—for a week or two, anyway. No big deal. But this morning, it became a big deal. At 9:30, I stop typing my emails and shuffle over to the bathroom—and close the door behind me. I don't realize what I've done until I reach for the nonexistent inside doorknob. It had molted sometime during the night.

For the first ten minutes, I try to escape. I bang on the door, shout for help. No answer. Julie was away at a meeting and Jasper was out with his babysitter. I've seen Ocean's Eleven, so I know to look for the grill in the ceiling that I could unscrew, climb into, slither through an air chute, drop into my neighbor's bedroom, make a clever comment like "just thought I'd drop in," and then return home. No grill. I'm trapped.

The next half hour I spend going through a checklist of worst-case scenarios. What if I slip, cut my forehead on the bathtub, bleed to death, end up on the front page of The New York Post? What if there's a fire and I'm forced to hang by my fingernails from the window ledge?

Even more stressful to me is that the outside world is speeding along without me. E-mails are being answered. Venti lattes are being sipped. George Bush's childhood friends are being appointed to high-level positions.

At 10:30, the phone rings. I hear a muffled voice leaving a message. This almost qualifies as human interaction. At 10:35, I make a pledge to myself to put more reading material in the bathroom if I ever escape. A Bible would have been nice. I'm stuck with an old Levenger catalog and a candle with a Omar Khayyam poem on the side: "A jug of wine, a loaf of bread and thou." Khayyam seems to be taunting me. I don't have a jug of wine, or a loaf of bread or thou. I have a tube of Neutrogena shaving cream and some towels. That's not paradise enou'.

By 11:00, I've become the world's greatest expert on this bathroom. I know the fake marble tiles with their spider-vein pattern and the power outlet that is rakishly diagonal. I spend half an hour tidying the medicine cabinet. I notice that the ingredients in ChlorTrimeton go all the way from A (acacia) to Z (zein), which, as a former encyclopedia reader, appeals to me.

By noon, I'm sitting on the floor, my back against the shower door. I sit. And sit some more. And something odd happens. I know that, outside the bathroom, the world is speeding along. That blogs are being read. Wild salmon is being grilled. Reggaeton is being explained to middle-aged white marketing executives.

But I'm okay with it. It doesn't cause my shoulders to tighten. Nothing I can do about it. I've reached an unexpected level of acceptance. For once, I'm savoring the present. I'm admiring what I have, even if it's 32 square feet of fake marble and a tilted electrical outlet. I start to pray. And, perhaps for the first time, I pray in true peace and silence—without glancing at the clock, without my brain hopscotching from topic to topic.

This is what Sabbath should feel like. A pause. Not just a minor pause, but a major pause. Not just a lowering of the volume, but a muting. As the famous rabbi Abraham Joshua Heschel put it, the Sabbath is a sanctuary in time.

At about 1:30, I hear Julie come home. I call out and pound on the door.

"Where are you?"

"In here. In the bathroom."

I hear her footsteps approaching. .

"You can't get out?"

"No, I can't get out."

"How long have you been in there?"

"Four hours."

There was a pause. I knew she was weighing her options. A few months ago, when she had trouble opening our bedroom door, I had made her pretend she was in a prison movie and shout "Attica! Attica!"

Julie was the more mature of us. After a few seconds, she just opened the door. I am free. There were emails to return, calls to make. It's kind of a shame.

All my sleep has fled because of the bitterness of my soul.

ISAIAH 38:15

Day 101. Another sleepless night. I lay in bed, adjusting and readjusting my pillow, unable to stop obsessing about this horrible article I read in a magazine. The article said the recidivism rate for meth addicts is 80 percent. This freaks me out. If Jasper someday tries a little meth—'what's the harm?' he'll say to himself, 'my parents were always in favor of experimentation'—he'll get addicted forever and end up hollow-eyed and slack-jawed in a county jail. Maybe it's true. This whole loosey-goosey parenting style is too dangerous.

A couple of months ago, right before my Biblical year began. Julie and I went to Baltimore to attend the wedding of Sara, the daughter of my Orthodox aunt Kate, and I sat next to one of Kate's friends. She had a wide-brimmed white hat that wouldn't be out of place at Prince William's wedding, a peculiar counterpoint to the black-hatted Hasidim who were there.

She told me her background was completely secular. But when she had kids, she and her husband made a deliberate decision to become religious.

"I didn't trust American culture."

"No?" I asked.

"Well, what does American culture teach?"

I wasn't sure what to say. "I think there are lots of different American cultures." This was the wrong answer.

"If you turn on the TV, you see 'buy, buy , buy, sex and violence, buy, buy, buy. We decided to live by a different code."

They explored several religions—including Hinduism—but ended up diving into Orthodox Judaism, since they were born Jewish.

They didn't become ultra-religious because of a charismatic leader or the truth of the Bible—they did it for the structure. And now their kids have grown up into responsible young adults. I met one of them. A nice computer geek.

It's something I should consider. More structure for Jasper. In my pop culture-tainted mind, I keep coming back to this conundrum:

Would I rather have Bart Simpson or one of the Flanders kids? A couple of years ago, I would have chosen the loveably spunky Bart. No question. But nowadays, now that I have my own three-dimensional son, I'm leaning towards the Flanders progeny. Yes, they may be a little creepy, they may sing loud songs about Noah's ark, but at least you know they won't spend their free time burning down the cafeteria or skateboarding off a canyon. I'd sacrifice some individuality for the knowledge that my son will outlive me.

> *Behold, I have taken upon myself to speak to the Lord,*
> *I who am but dust and ashes.*
>
> GENESIS 18:27

Day 103. I'm trying to pray for a half hour a day in three ten-minute intervals, usually in the corner of Julie's office, a couple of feet from the basket full of Real Simple magazines. Half an hour's no record, I know. But at least I'm not glancing at the clock every minute as I did in the beginning.

And once in awhile, I actually find myself looking forward to those 10-minute sessions, especially at night. It's a decompression. When I was a kid, I spent several minutes each night before bed picturing water-skiers slaloming over choppy waves. I don't know how I came up with the ritual. It's not like I was a big fan of waterskiing—I had tried it at camp and ended up swallowing a lot of lake water. But I found visualizing it relaxing. Maybe prayer will serve the same purpose. I get to close the door, close my eyes, and sink into a meditative state, or as close to one as my brain will allow me.

Plus, I've discovered another category of prayer that I like: praying on behalf of others, for the sick, needy, depressed—anyone who's been kicked around by fate. Intercessory prayer, as it's called.

I've read a bunch of articles about intercessory prayer recently—mostly about how it's sprouted up all over the Internet. You can place prayer requests on websites like eprayer.com and cybersaint.org (recent examples include "I am expecting my first child. Please pray for a speedy delivery," and "Please pray for me to complete my thesis work, it is delayed by eight months.")

Intercessory prayer can be found sprinkled throughout the Bible—with everyone from Moses to Paul pleading with God for the sake of others. Abraham is the first to try it—and he's far from successful. It's a curious scene. God announces to Abraham that he's considering laying waste to the wicked cities of Sodom and Gomorrah.

Abraham asks him: Suppose there are fifty righteous within the city; wilt thou then destroy the place and not spare it for the fifty righteous who are in it? . . .

And the LORD said, "If I find at Sodom fifty righteous in the city, I will spare the whole place for their sake."

Abraham answered, "Behold, I have taken upon myself to speak to the Lord, I who am but dust and ashes.

Suppose five of the fifty righteous are lacking? Wilt thou destroy the whole city for lack of five?" And he said, "I will not destroy it if I find forty-five there."

It continues. Abraham is able to haggle the Lord down to ten people—if there are ten good people in Sodom, God agrees not to smite it.

In the end, though, as you know, Sodom didn't meet the quota.

At first, I found the whole passage comical. I mean, here's Abraham sounding like a salesman at a bazaar trying to get rid of his last decorative vase. But on reflection, what's wrong with what he did? It's actually a noble, beautiful—if ultimately doomed—attempt by Abraham to save the lives of his fellow humans.

I'm not done with my year, so I'm withholding judgment, but my rational side says that intercessory prayer today is no more effective than Abraham's effort. I still can't wrap my brain around the notion that God would change his mind because we ask him to.

And yet, I still love these prayers. To me, they're moral weight training. Every night, I pray for others for 10 minutes—a friend about to undergo a cornea operation, my great aunt whose sweet husband just died in their swimming pool, the guy I met in a Bible study class whose head was dented in a subway accident. It's ten minutes where it's impossible to be self-centered. Ten minutes where I can't think about my career or my Amazon.com ranking or that a blog in San Francisco made snarky comments about my latest Esquire article.

The Bible says not to boast, so I'm not going to say I've turned into Albert Schweitzer or Angelina Jolie. But I do feel myself becoming a slightly more compassionate person.

The odd thing, though, is that to be fully compassionate, I might not want to tell these people I'm praying for them. I recently read about a new study of 1,802 coronary artery bypass patients. The patients who knew they were being prayed for actually had more complications than those who didn't. Perhaps they thought, "Well, if I'm sick enough that I need people to pray for me, I must really be in bad shape." In case that's true, I'll pray secretly and hope they don't read this chapter.

The treacherous are taken captive by their lust

PROVERBS 11:6

Day 105. So lust. This week, my job at Esquire has forced the issue.

Before I explain, let me confess that lust has been one of my biggest failings so far this year. Ever since that first day when I spotted that gym ad of two gorgeous sweaty people clutching each other after what appeared to have been a very vigorous workout, I've been trying to smother my libido.

I try not to think about sex. I try not to talk about sex. I try not to glance at women on the street. The problem is, my heart's not in it. Thanks to my 38 years of staunchly secular life, I'm having a hard time adjusting to the worldview that sexuality is sinful. Well, some sexuality is sinful, as anyone with a DSL line can tell you. But I'm having trouble getting worked up over a moderate amount of sexuality in culture.

I'm guessing this has a lot to do with my previous wrestling matches with sex. In high school and college, I experienced some startling dry spells. To justify my unasked-for abstinence, I told myself that I was above such crass human motivations as sex. I had better things to do than think about women. And what is sex, anyway? Just some skin contact necessary for DNA-mixing during procreation. I didn't need it. I tried to turn myself into a neo-Puritan. I was pure intellect, with my body just a shell to transport that brain from place to place.

It didn't work. My attempt to stifle my sex drive didn't make me a more righteous person—I just got more frustrated and unhappy and preoccupied with sex. So for years, I've thought that, as long as I remain faithful to Julie and don't let my libido run rampant, what's the harm in a little sexuality in culture? A racy joke, an unacted-upon fantasy, a movie with partial nudity? It never bothered me much.

But now, everyone expects me—or more precisely, Jacob, my Biblical alter-ego—to embrace extreme modesty and total restraint. No carnal thoughts, no carnal words. It's a reasonable expectation, I suppose. Modesty has been a huge part of the Judeo-Christian tradition for a long time. Orthodox Jews follow rigid modesty rules—women cover their hair and cannot wear a dress revealing their collarbone. Some conservative Christians also conceal flesh and shun R-rated movies.

So I've been trying. The difficulty is, the level of sexual imagery in modern life is astounding. I knew intuitively this was true, but when you tune into it, you just can't believe it. I click on the Yahoo! finance page and there's this blonde model in a low-cut dress looking at a computer screen and nibbling alluringly on the temple of her glasses, apparently very aroused by the latest S&P 500 report. Even the suburban mom character on Dora the Explorer has clothes that are disturbingly form-fitting. Or maybe that's just me.

A few weeks ago, I heard that Billy Graham, before he arrives at a hotel, has his room swept for potentially tempting images. I decided to sweep my own apartment. I stashed away all magazines we had lying around, like the one with Jessica Alba in a blue skintight suit.

Next, I took out a roll of masking tape and got to work censoring the images apartment. Anything that has the potential to stir my libido got covered with a piece of tape.

—The woman in a geisha outfit on the box of Celestial Seasonings tea.

—The photo of a cute chef with the unlikely name of Crescent Dragonwagon on the spine of a cookbook.

—The bosom of Julie's friend Sharon in a photo from our wedding, since said bosom is both ample and prominently displayed.

My censorship raids were actually pleasantly nostalgic. When I was a kid in the 1970s, my dad subscribed to Playboy, which he got, as they say, for the articles. My mom did not approve. Whenever a new Playboy would arrive, my mom would give me a black magic marker, and, while Dad was at work, we'd go to town on the latest issue. We'd scribble thick black bikinis on all of the Playmates of the Month and Girls of the Big 10. I liked this a lot. Too much. Mom eventually caught on that I was spending several minutes inspecting the photo before I censored it. So the raids ended.

And these late-2005 censorship raids are about as effective. In other words, they are completely counterproductive. Every time I spot the masking tape, I'm reminded about what was underneath that masking tape. It makes me think about sex more, not less.

Anyway, back to my job and lust. Esquire is a tastefully lascivious men's magazine, but lascivious nonetheless. So avoiding sexual imagery there is even more difficult than in my home. And it got worse a few days ago. My bosses decided it'd be funny to assign me an article about a hot young actress. You know, tempt the Bible guy.

The actress I'm interviewing is named Rosario Dawson. And to be a properly prepared journalist, I have to rent her movies, which is a quandary in itself. Because from the looks of it, there's a good deal of wantonness and harlotry and coveting.

So I joined a movie rental service called CleanFlicks. A Utah-based company started by a Mormon man, CleanFlicks is the Netflix for the highly religious. They'll send you sanitized Hollywood movies with the violence and sex chopped out. Also, profanity including "the B-words, H-word when not referring to the place, D-word, S-word, F-word, etc." (The S-word and F-word I know. But the B-word? The D-word? So many options. It's like working on a dirty New York Times crossword puzzle.)

A week later, I get a couple of DVD's in bright yellow envelopes of two of Rosario's movies: The 25th Hour and Josie and the Pussycats. I pop them into my player. It is a confusing couple of hours. The Clean-Flix films are full of non sequitur jump cuts and intermittent sound, like what I imagine an VoIP phone call from Tanzania is like. (When I was finish with Rosario's movies, I can't resist ordering Kill Bill on Clean-Flicks, because I figured it'd be about 5 minutes long. It actually broke the hour mark, but made no sense whatsoever).

A couple of Rosario's movies weren't available on CleanFlicks—but they can be found on one its competitors, ClearPlay. This is an even more sophisticated bowdlerizing service. You download the censoring filter from the Internet and then plug that into a specially-equipped DVD. The beauty of ClearPlay is that you can customize which offensive material to block, and which to let through. (Incidentally, CleanFlicks has since shut down; a Colorado court ruled that it was violating copyright laws by slapping fig leafs on the movies. But ClearPlay is still going strong).

I download the filter for one of Rosario's movies—Oliver Stone's Alexander—and it looks like I hit the sin mother lode. Take a look at what it's got:

Non-Sensual/Non-Crude Sex Talk
Thematic Sexual Situation(s)
Homosexual/Lesbian Characters
Implied Marital Sex
Implied Premarital Sex
Implied Extramarital Sex

Revealing Clothing
Some Suggestive Dancing
Some Suggestive Dialogue
Threatening Dialogue
Intense Action/Adventure
Intense Life/Death Situations
Scary Moments
Non-Graphic Injury/Wound
Intense Battle Sequences
Alcohol Consumption
Rape Topic
Intense Thematic Elements
Suicide
Murder Topic
Dysfunctional Relationships

In other words, Thursday night at Tommy Lee's house. (My friend David pointed this out; I can't make such comments myself).

I suppose CleanFlicks and ClearPlay mean well. But they weren't so helpful. I had the same problem as I did with my masking tape endeavor. I was so focused on what they were cutting out, I probably conjured up far more sinful things in my mind than if I had just watched the suggestive dancing and thematic sexual situation(s) all the way through.

> *I have made a covenant with my eyes;*
> *How then could I look upon a virgin?*
>
> JOB 31:1

Day 107. I flew out to Los Angeles yesterday, and drove to the hotel. I notice that my sense of geography has changed. I pay attention to the locations of all the churches and synagogues in the same way I used to pay attention to pop culture landmarks (look, that's where they filmed the mall scene in Fast Times at Ridgemont High!).

Today is my interview with Rosario. I arrive at our meeting place—an aggressively Californian café with organic root beer and whole wheat bagels. Rosario comes half an hour late, as is required by a secret celebrity handbook.

Things start off better than I expected. Yes, she's beautiful with skin out of a Clinique ad, but she's wearing a bulky beige sweater and jeans. Very discreet, not overly revealing. Second, she seems unfazed by my project. This is LA, home to calf implants and Crispin Glover, so the strangeness bar is set pretty high.

And finally, she was one of about three people thus far who claimed my topiary looked good. "I've always loved big beards," she says, adding cryptically, "When I was a kid, I wanted a beard of my own. I thought it'd be nice to stroke it."

So I am feeling good.

And then we start the interview proper. It soon becomes clear that my bosses could not have picked a worse celebrity for me to interview. She is the single most raunchy actress in Hollywood. She has absolutely no ClearPlay-like filter in her brain. Over the course of two hours I hear about her grandmother's sex life, her sex life, her conception with a broken condom, her breasts, her mom's R-rated piercings, her ex-boyfriend's bedroom noises, and on and on.

I feel like there are three people at this interview: Rosario Dawson, my regular old secular journalist self, and my Biblical alter-ego.

Every time she talks about the handcuffs you can buy at the Hustler store, my alter-ego Jacob winces. Meanwhile, the secular journalist does a silent little cheer. Because I know that a racy quote from a beautiful woman is men's magazine gold.

I have two heads, two sets of eyes, two moral compasses. They're battling for supremacy. Maybe one will win—or maybe I can keep both. A friend of mine said that we shouldn't underestimate people's ability to hold totally contradictory opinions and be just fine with it. Like speech and blushing, it's a uniquely human trait.

Sustain me with raisins, refresh me with apples; For I am sick with love.

Song of Solomon 2:5

Day 109. Back in New York, I go out to lunch with Robbie Harris—the rock and roll professor from the Jewish Theological Seminary. I tell him about the racy conversation. And he makes a fascinating point—maybe my secular self and Jacob were fighting each other for no reason.

I had always assumed the entire Bible had an anti-lust, proto-Victorian point of view. And parts of it—especially passages in the New Testament's letters from the Apostle Paul—do say that celibacy is the ideal.

But much of the Hebrew Bible—if you read it carefully—isn't really anti-sex. Robbie directed me to the Song of Solomon, which is probably the bawdiest section of the Bible. It's a collection of love songs that contain, among other things, the B-word: "Your two breasts are like two fawns, twins of a gazelle, that feed among the lilies." And later again: "Oh, may your breasts be like clusters of the vine, and the scent of your breath like apples."

The Song of Solomon has sometimes been interpreted as an allegory about humans' love for God. And it may be one aspect of it. But, says Robbie, don't forget that it's also a paean to erotic love.

"But married love, right?" I say. That's the traditional view, that the Bible sanctions husband-wife marital relations and nothing else.

"They don't sound married to me," says Robbie. "They sound to me like young lovers hightailing it to the woods."

When I get home, I look up Song of Solomon 2:10–12, one the passages Robbie was referring to. It says:

> "My beloved speaks and says to me:
> 'Arise, my love, my fair one,
> and come away;
> for lo, the winter is past,
> the rain is over and gone.
> The flowers appear on the earth,
> the time of singing has come,
> . . .Arise, my love, my fair one,
> and come away."

He's right. It does sound like a couple of not-necessarily-married kids off for a tryst in the wilderness. This is liberating information.

You shall not commit adultery

EXODUS 20:14

Day 108. The Bible isn't a free love manual, though. Not all types of sex are permitted. The Bible forbids orgies and bestiality and incest. It famously calls homosexuality an 'abomination,' a troubling (to put it mildly) notion that I'll talk more about later.

And of course, it bans adultery.

But I should clarify: Adultery in the Hebrew Bible is not what modern Americans think of as adultery. It's a much narrower concept. Adultery applies to married women. Married women aren't allowed to sleep around. They're off-limits. Married men, on the other hand . . .well, they have more leeway—as long as the woman who is the object of their lust doesn't already belong to another Israelite man.

And I use the word belong on purpose. The ancient Israelite culture was passionate about some forms of social justice, but gender equality was not high on the list. Women belonged to men. You can't sleep with a married woman, because it's an affront both to God and to her husband's rights. And if you sleep with a virgin, you should make sure that her father is compensated properly.

The compensation could take the form of paying the father off. Or you could take the woman off his hands and marry her.

Now here's the interesting thing: You could marry the woman even if you already have another wife. Polygamy was, if not the norm, completely accepted. The Hebrew Bible is packed with examples of polygamy. Jacob had two wives (and two concubines). King David had eight. Solomon holds the record with 700 wives. (Solomon's proverbs warn against adultery, which is I find curious, since I can't imagine he had any time or energy for other men's wives).

Ashkenazi Judaism officially banned multiple wives in the 11th century when the great French rabbi Gershom ben Judah laid down the one-spouse-only law. But you can still find a handful of Jews who want a return to the old days. As one pro-polygamy Jewish website says: "Polygamy is a Jewish institution. It is practiced, albeit underground, in Israel today. If the present trend to Orthodoxy among Jews continues, we can expect open polygamy to return soon."

Christianity hasn't had much polygamy in its history, with the famous exception of early Mormonism and a handful of outlying sects of fundamentalist Christianity that got a little bump in publicity when HBO's multiple wives drama Big Love debuted.

One such sect is called the Christian Polygamy Movement. It was founded by an Arizona-based man named Pastor Don Milton. Most of his justification seems to lie in the fact that the great men of the Hebrew Bible had many wives. The New Testament, contrary to popular opinion, does not overturn this, he says.

Yes, the Apostle Paul did say "each man should have his own wife and each woman her own husband." (1 Corinthians 7:2) But here's the catch: Pastor Don says the Greek word for "own" in that sentence doesn't mean "one and only." The marriage is still a sacred covenant between one man and one woman. It's just that the man can have several simultaneous covenants—sort of like psychologist and his clients.

I call up Pastor Don and ask him, "If I'm trying to follow the Bible, and I'm interested in having a second wife, how do I convince my current wife that this is a good idea."

Pastor Don pauses: "You don't want to bring it up unless you have a prospective second wife."

"Why is that?"

"What if you tell your first wife and then never meet anyone that you wanted to be your second wife? You'll end up causing a rift in your current marriage for nothing."

In fact, Pastor Don continues, I might want to consider the preemptive strike—a strategy he's seen successfully employed over the years.

"You find a prospective wife, have a ceremony and consummate the marriage. Then go back and tell the first wife that you have a second. There is conceivably a better chance that your first marriage will survive."

Isn't that a bit . . .sneaky and un-Biblical?

"It can end up being more cruel to put a wife through a year, five years, ten years of worrying that you're going to take a second wife."

Pastor Don's tone is friendly, informal. His website has a lot of fire and brimstone, warning detractors that "You are required by it to confront me in person if you accuse me of sin, then with witnesses to the alleged sin (Deuteronomy 19:15), and finally before a Christian assembly worthy of wielding its authority over us." But on the phone, Pastor Don's tone is that of a married man giving his bachelor buddy some girlfriend advice.

I ask Pastor Don if I should tell the prospective second wife about the first wife. Definitely, he says. You have to. And the good part is, it might even be a turn-on.

"Some women are drawn to men who are bold enough to say they have more than one wife. It's a bad boy thing."

I ask him if he has any other tips about making the first wife see the light.

"First, pray like you've only prayed when you're in trouble. Then, bring her into Bible study."

Show her the Bible doesn't forbid polygamy. And in fact, the Old Testament heroes were often polygamous. "You have to get her to see that the men of the Old Testament were great men. David—he wrote the Psalms! And Solomon—he wrote the proverbs. These are great men. Get that point across. Polygamy is not only acceptable, but it's fabulous, and these women [the wives] are holy."

In fact, says Pastor Don, the father of the human race probably had several ceremonies.

"I think Adam was the first polygamist. Here was the healthiest man in history with the healthiest sex drive ever. And he only had one wife? Come on."

Pastor Don asks me if I had a prospective second wife.

"Well, I do like our nanny," I say. Des is, indisputably, adorable—she's 26 and text-messages me things like "gud am" which take me five minutes to figure out (that's good morning, for all you over-30 people out there). Julie agrees she's ideal, and has given me permission to have an affair with her, a la Curb Your Enthusiasm. Of course, Julie only gave me the offer because she knew there was no chance Des would ever be interested. It's like giving me permission to become a linebacker with the Miami Dolphins. Completely moot.

"What religion is she?"

"She's Catholic."

Pastor Don exhales loudly. Catholics are tough to crack, he said. On the other hand, if I ever do marry Des, I have a good line of reasoning when I tell Julie.

"You can tell her that we can stop paying the nanny. Save on the price."

At one point, Pastor Don's voice rises and I imagine on the other end of the line, his face was red. He was talking about the persecution against polygamists. He was furious that they would put polygamists in jail—next to criminals and homosexuals.

Yes, homosexuality. Apparently, polygamists aren't so tolerant of other types of sexual behavior.

Thou shalt not steal.

EXODUS 20:16

Day 111. When I'm jotting down tips on how to land a second wife, it's clear the pendulum swung too far into the Bible's crazy territory. I need to refocus. Get back to basics. The Ten Commandments. So I'm going to delve into the Eighth again—thou shalt not steal.

Actually, many modern biblical scholars think the word 'steal' is a mistranslation. A closer word would be 'kidnap.' You should not kidnap a person and force them into slavery. This would be easier to follow. I could do that for a year. But it also feels like a cop out.

So I'm going to stick with the traditional on this one—especially since there are plenty of other "do not steal" commands in the Bible (e.g. Leviticus 19:11).

I informed Julie that I can no longer raid the Esquire supply closet for manila folders for personal use. And I've stopped with the wireless piggybacking—we've seen what that can lead to.

Today, I clamp down on some attempted theft at Starbucks. We are out for a walk—Julie, Jasper and Julie's step-dad, who looks and acts exactly like George Burns. We stop for a coffee at Starbucks, and Jasper grabs a handful of straws from the counter. He's got a straw fetish. He loves to unwrap a dozen or so at a shot, perhaps thinking the next one will have a special surprise, maybe a Willy Wonka-like invitation to tour the straw factory.

"No, Jasper. Just one."

Starbucks doesn't have a strict straw policy. But I think there's an implicit contract—you are supposed to take one straw for every beverage.

Does Starbucks need my money? Not so much. But the Bible's command is absolute. It doesn't say "Thou shalt not steal except small things from multinational corporations with faux Italian name for 'medium.'" It says, "Thou shalt not steal." There's no such thing as "petty theft."

"Just one," I repeat.

"Let him take 'em," says Julie's step-dad.

"No, we're only supposed to take one. Otherwise it's stealing."

"Let him take a few. It's not stealing."

"What if I took 5,000 straws in a Starbucks every day," I say. "Would that be stealing?"

"Well, there's got to be a relative . . ."

"Why? Why should it be relative?"

"Well, look," says Julie's step-dad. "One murder is okay. But fifty murders isn't okay."

I'm stopped short.

"Got you there, huh?" he says.

I'm not sure how to answer a man who has stolen my argument.

Jasper screams and grunts and points for about 45 seconds. I stand my ground; I've got to ratchet up that justice-to-mercy ratio. Finally, I give him a napkin to rip up, which calms him down.

I could have rationalized the straws. That's one thing I've noticed this year. I can rationalize almost anything. For instance, I could take the utilitarian approach:

The amount of pleasure it gives Jasper outweighs the couple cents it'll cost Starbucks. Or I could argue to myself that, in the end, it helps out the straw industry.

Same with when I stole the Internet connection in my apartment building—I could have rationalized it by saying that I'm using the Internet to learn about God and make myself a better person.

I have a tendency towards ends-justify-the-means thinking.

But this year isn't about that. It's about following the rules. Strictly. To the letter. And seeing what happens.

I know of only one other person I know who follows the "no steal-ing" commandment to the letter. My dad. Whenever we're on a road trip, he refuses to pull over at any old Holiday Inn or McDonald's to use the bathroom. Not unless we buy something. Otherwise, he says, we'd be stealing their soap and paper towels. So I feel like I'm honoring my father here as well.

> *She quickly let down her jar from her*
> *shoulder, and said, 'Drink, and I will give your camels drink also.'*
>
> GEN. 24:46

Day 115. Mr. Berkowitz—the man who inspected my wardrobe for mixed fibers—is still calling. He wants to meet up and pray with me, but I've been busy with my own Biblical duties and my own prayers, so I've been dodging his calls.

This morning, he leaves me a message at 8:30 a.m.

"Hello, Arnold," he says. (He calls me by my real name Arnold; I must have told him once about it and it stuck). "It's Bill Berkowitz. It's very important that you call me back."

I get nervous. Very important? That sounds bad. Maybe he's got a kidney stone and needs help getting to Mount Sinai hospital. I called him—it turns out he's going to be in my neighborhood, and wants to pray with me at my apartment. Well, how can I refuse a house call?

Mr. Berkowitz arrives a couple of hours later, and he's as disheveled and kindly as ever. He comes bearing gifts—books and candles for the Sabbath.

"Can I get you anything?"

"A cup of water, please," he says. "Oh, and it has to be bottled water, please."

Oh yes. I'd heard of this. Two rabbis in Brooklyn had made a contro-versial ruling declaring New York City tap water non-kosher. They said it contained tiny multi-cellular organisms that could qualify as shellfish. Which is why, if you want to make a lot of money, you should open a Poland Spring concession in Crown Heights.

I look in the fridge. We have bottles of Dasani—but Julie refills them from the faucet. Tap water in Dasani clothing.

"Can I offer you anything else?" I ask. "Maybe Juice? Soda?"

"No. Water."

Here I face a dilemma. The poor guy had schlepped several miles from Washington Heights in a thick black coat and black hat. No doubt he's parched. And the Bible tells me to ease my fellow man's suffering.

So I decide: What he doesn't know won't hurt him. And most rabbis say the tap water is fine to drink. Everyone will be happier.

I pour him a cup from the bottle.

"Thanks," says Mr. Berkowitz, as he lifts the cup to his lips, then puts it down to tell me something about the Sabbath. I'm not sure what he said. I'm too busy staring at that cup. He does it again, like the clueless husband in a forties noir film who keeps almost-but-not-quite sipping the poisoned milk.

Finally, before he can actually drink, I lunge.

"You know what? I think this may be refilled with tap water."

Mr. Berkowitz is grateful. He puts the cup on the table gingerly, like it's filled with hydrochloric acid.

I just couldn't do it. What if, in the off chance, Mr. Berkowitz is right? What if the water would have tainted his soul? I couldn't take the risk, even if his body will suffer.

> *So Abraham rose early in the morning, saddled his ass, and took two*
> *of his young men with him, and his son Isaac;*
>
> GENESIS 22:3.

Mr. Berkowitz says it'd be good for me to get a minute-by-minute guide to the properly devout day. So he starts at the beginning: I should wake up early—just like Abraham woke up early on the day he was to sacrifice Isaac.

"Abraham didn't say, 'Hey God, it's 5 o'clock in the morning. You sure you want me to get up so early?' Abraham got up early."

After that, there are many rituals to be done: You must wash impurities off your hands. Recite several prayers. Bind the commandments to your hand and forehead. Go to the synagogue to worship. Mr. Berkowitz tells me he loves going to synagogue; it's not an obligation, it's a gift. I'm jealous, I want that kind of hunger for spirituality.

He hates being late to prayer, so he lays out all of his religious gear the night before—his prayer shawl, his fringes, etc.

"It's like a fireman," he says. "The fireman has his hat, jacket and boots on a peg, so when there's a fire, he doesn't have to think. Everything is set up."

He once again stresses the importance of being punctual to services.

"If it means I have to run with my shoelaces untied, then I will."

Mr. Berkowitz pauses, decides he's gone too far.

"Well, I don't do that. That's an exaggeration. But I like to be on time. I don't want to run like a madman. I walk briskly."

Speaking of shoes, Mr. Berkowitz tells me that you don't just put them on any old way. There's a proper procedure. You put on your right shoe. Then your left shoe. Then you tie your left shoe. Then you go back and tie your right shoe.

Why that order? Mr. Berkowitz doesn't know.

"That's what the rabbis tell us to do. I don't have to think about it. It saves me a lot of thinking. It allows me to concentrate on more important things."

If this were on TiVo, I would have rewound to make sure he said what I think he said. How much thinking could that possibly save? Do I really waste a lot of brainpower deciding the order in which I should slip on my Rockports? It seems like some serious religious micromanagement. I didn't want to say this to the sweet and no-doubt-thirsty Mr. Berkowitz, who was onto the next topic, but at the time, I thought: Crazy.

In retrospect, though, I'm starting to think maybe it's not really that insane after all. My dad always talked about how his hero Albert Einstein owned seven identical suits—so that he wouldn't waste any neuronal activity on choosing what to wear. Similar idea.

In fact, it's part of a bigger theme I've been mulling over: Freedom from choice.

I'd always been taught to fetishize freedom of choice. It's the American way. It's why I went to Brown University, where they don't have any requirements and you can go through all four years writing papers about the importance of Christian Slater's oeuvre.

But more and more I'm starting to see the beauty in a more rigid framework. The structure, the stable architecture of religion.

My brother-in-law Eric—now getting his doctorate in psychology—likes to lecture me about an experiment at a grocery store by researchers from Columbia and Stanford. They set up two tables offering free tastes—one had six flavors of jam, the other had 24 flavors of jam. Oddly, more people bought jams from the table with six flavors. The conclusion was that the other table was just too overwhelming, too many options.

The Bible takes away a lot of those jam jars. What should I do on Friday night? Stay at home with the family. Should I waste my time reading about Cameron Diaz's love life? No. Should I give to the homeless guy on 77th? Yes. Should I be stricter with Jasper? Yes. There's something relieving and paradoxically liberating about surrendering yourself to a minimal-choice lifestyle, especially as our choices multiply like cable channels.

I recently heard a rabbi give a talk on Moses, and how, in a weird sense, he was a slave even after his release from bondage. He was a slave to goodness. He had no choice but to do the right thing.

There's a Jewish book that restricts choice even more—far more—than the Bible itself. It's a massive work from the 16th century called The Set Table—or Shulchan Aruch in Hebrew. It's an amazing book—it gives practical instruction on everything you can think of: eating, sleeping, praying, bathing, sex. Some Orthodox Jews follow a lot of The Set Table's guidelines, but it'd be darn near impossible to follow every rule. There are thousands of them. One stipulates that when going to the bathroom, you should face north or south but not east or west.

Most of the Set Table's rules are post-Biblical. The Scriptures don't get into shoe-donning procedures per se. But the Bible still has plenty of laws to keep me busy—some that I like (the Sabbath) and some I don't (monthly wife-avoidance). The key questions seems to be: How do you choose which choice-restricting rules to follow in the first place? I don't know. It's like an Escher drawing. It hurts my brain.

Mr. Berkowitz, by the way, finished his lesson and the prayers, and left about an hour later. As he was leaving, he reminded me to prepare for Sabbath by reciting a little ditty:

> *"A Shabbas well spent*
> *Brings a week of content."*

I agree with the sentiment, if not the grammar.

> *I the LORD your God am a jealous God, visiting the iniquity of the fathers*
> *upon the children to the third and the fourth generation of those who hate me.*
>
> DEUTERONOMY 5:9

Day 117. My son Jasper has finally improved his vocabulary, but not in the way I was hoping. And I'm the one to blame.

Perhaps I can explain what happened via a quick Biblical story: In Genesis 12, Abraham moved to Egypt with his beautiful wife Sarah to escape a famine. Sarah was so stunning, Abraham feared the Egyptians would kill him and steal Sarah for themselves. So Abraham lied. He said that his wife Sarah was his sister. Abraham took the deception so far that the Pharaoh, thinking Sarah was single, married her. And when the Pharaoh found out that he'd been deceived, he was—somewhat justifiably, I think—furious, and ejected Abraham from the land.

Abraham and Sarah eventually conceived a son named Isaac. When he's grown, Isaac and his wife Rebecca move to the land of the Philistines to avoid a famine. And what does Isaac do? He pretends Rebecca is his sister. He doesn't want the Philistines to kill him and steal Rebecca.

This is a big recurring theme in the Bible: The children mimic the parents' behavior, even the flaws, perhaps especially the flaws. (One other example: Rebecca played favorites with her son Jacob; Jacob played favorites with his son Joseph).

I've always known that parents influence their kids. It's not an obscure concept. But it didn't sink in on a gut level until I saw Jasper aping our words and deeds.

I first noticed it when he adopted one of Julie's more endearing habits. After Julie takes a sip of a drink, she'll often let out a satisfied 'ahhh,' like she's secretly taping a Sprite commercial. Now Jasper is doing it. He'll polish off his watered-down apple juice, plunk the sippy cup on the table and exhale noisily.

But with me, it has taken a darker turn. A few days ago, Jasper's Elmo plate slipped out of my grasp, scattering cubes of cantaloupe all over the kitchen. I shouted a four-letter-word that is a synonym for the Biblical verb 'to know.' (I'd type it here, but I think that'd be breaking the rules again). Apparently, Jasper was paying close attention. He has now decided this is a great word. It has replaced the perfectly acceptable 'uh-oh' as the go-to exclamation.

When I've seen kids cursing on TV or in the movies, it's kind of adorable. When my two-year-old niece said the S-word? I chuckled. But when my own kid squeaks out swear words in his high-pitched voice, it's not funny at all. I immediately picture him fifteen years down the road with a syringe sticking out of his arm in some train station bathroom.

In Deuteronomy 5:9, the Bible says "I the LORD your God am a jealous God, visiting the iniquity of the fathers upon the children to the third and the fourth generation of those who hate me." I used to find this an appalling sentence. Why should God punish my grandson for my sins? It seemed outrageously un-American. What about everyone being entitled to a clean moral slate? And yes, if you interpret this as a threat that God will smite your child with leprosy when you worship a carved idol, then absolutely, it's cruel.

But I've come to appreciate it. The trick is, you have to see the passage as a warning that your moral failings will affect your kids' ability to make the right choices. If you beat your son, he'll be more likely to beat his son. If you get angry at cantaloupe-related mishaps, your son will too. What better deterrent could there be to bad behavior?

It had even more resonance in Biblical times. As Jack Miles points out in God: A Biography, ancient Israelites didn't have the clearly-formed concept of immortality of the soul, as we do now. You achieved immortality through your children and children's children, who were physical extensions of you. The basic building block of society was the family, not the individual.

With no afterlife, God dispensed justice to a family—a person's actions reverberate through his descendants' lives. The most extreme ex-

ample: When Adam and Eve disobeyed God and ate the fruit of knowledge, the family of humanity has been paying ever since.

I can't say why for sure—maybe the Bible has seeped into my brain,
maybe there's an inevitable mental shift that accompanies parenthood—
but I've edged away from extreme individualism. My worldview is more
interconnected, more tribal.

> *Ask now, and see, can a man bear a child?*
>
> JEREMIAH 30:6

Day 120. On this brisk December morning, Julie and I make a trek to the
fertility clinic on the east side. They've been steeping two of Julie's eggs
in a test tube for five days. The doctors are implanting both, in the hope
that one will stick.

Man, does it feel unnatural. Surgical caps, antibacterial lotion, gur-
neys, charts. This is about as far from Adam and Eve as you can get.

They wheel Julie out a few minutes later. And it is done. She is, God
willing, pregnant. For reasons I still don't understand, Julie has to lie in a
hospital bed with a full bladder for about half an hour.

"Distract me please!" says Julie. "Talk about anything."

I start in on a Biblical story about Tamar.

"Anything but that."

Okay. But it's a good story, a relevant story—and a profoundly
strange story. Julie, feel free to skip this section, but here goes:

Tamar's tale is found in the Book of Genesis. Tamar was married to
a man named Er, son of Judah. Er died before they could have kids.
There was a custom in Biblical times—as bizarre as it sounds now—that
a widow who has no children stays within the family: She must marry
the brother of her dead husband. It's called 'levirate marriage.' So
Tamar married Er's younger brother, Onan. Onan too died. Tamar was
understandably distraught. But her father-in-law Judah told Tamar not
to worry—she could marry his youngest son, Shela. But Judah failed to
follow through. Tamar was left without a husband.

Tamar was desperate to get pregnant. So she came up with a plan:
She put on a veil, disguised herself as a prostitute, and intercepted her

father-in-law Judah as he was on his way to shear his sheep. The unsuspecting Judah slept with Tamar, and then gave her his staff and personal seal as a IOU for payment. The plan worked. She got pregnant.

Judah, unaware he had been duped, found out his widowed daughter-in-law was with child, and accused her of loose morals. He wanted her burned to death. So Tamar showed him his staff and personal seal. Now he understood. He was the father of her child. He backed down and repented. Tamar had twin sons by Judah. They were named Zarah and Peretz. And here's an interesting twist: Peretz eventually became the ancestor of that remarkable leader of ancient Israel, King David.

When I first read this, it was too outlandish to have any meaning for me. A woman having sex with her father-in-law? In a prostitute disguise? But after rereading it four times, I've wrung a powerful moral out of it. And that is this: Even great things can be born from ethically murky origins. Even an illicit, deceit-filled union can lead to someone like King David.

So . . .perhaps in vitro fertilization is the same. It's ethically complicated, but maybe our child will be great. Or maybe I'm justifying like crazy here.

In the end, I do end up distracting Julie by finding some common ground. We play a name-a-movie-with-a-Biblical-title game.

I will never forget thy precepts; for by them thou hast given me life.

PSALMS 119:93

Day 123. It's New Year's eve, and Julie and I pull our rental car into the driveway of our friends' house in New Jersey. We'll be staying there for a three-day weekend.

After hellos and avoided hugs, I lug our suitcase upstairs to the guest room, heave it onto the bed, unzip it—and immediately realize my mistake. I forgot to bring my ram's horn. It's back in my closet in New York. Damn. I won't be able to blow a horn on January 1, the start of the new month.

I try to argue with myself that, well, January 1 isn't the Hebrew calendar, so maybe it's not really a new Biblical month. Doesn't help. I feel surprisingly anxious and off-kilter, like I'm back in high school and forgot to study for a big physics exam. I take it out on Julie by picking a fight with her about the volume of Jasper's baby monitor.

The truth is, I've began to get really rigorous with my rituals. I hate missing my daily routine—the praying, the binding, more praying, the tassels, the white clothes, the praying again. Why? Perhaps because these rituals dovetail beautifully with my own obsessive-compulsive disorder.

Thanks to my OCD, I'm prone to weird little rituals, like touching the shower head four times after turning off the faucet. Or opening my jaw into a yawn-like position whenever I look in the mirror. Or making sure never to start a conversation with the word "you" because I saw an Eight is Enough episode when I was 11 in which an estranged father's first words to his son were "You doing all right?" and the relationship went sour after that—probably not because the father started his sentence with 'you,' but you never know.

I've been doing my own rituals less and less frequently, as the Bible rituals take over more and more of my time. And why not? People have been doing these Bible rituals for thousands of years. They're time-tested. Why should I try to invent my own ceremonies, when my heritage provides me with a book full of them. Mr. Berkowitz doesn't waste his days concocting his very own rituals; he takes them off the rack.

At least in this way, I'm preprogrammed for Biblical living. Religion—especially ritual-heavy religions like Judaism and high-church Christianity—have three key OCD traits.

First, the repetition (every day the same prayers, every week the same candle-lightings). Second, the fascination with taxonomy—everything in its proper category: Good or evil, holy or profane. And third, especially in Judaism, the fixation on purity and impurity (the equivalent of my constant hand-washing). I'm drawn to all three.

Of course, I'm not the first to make this connection. Freud, a Jew who, as a child, regularly attended Catholic mass with his Czech nanny, believed that religion was the "universal obsessional neurosis of humanity."

If so, I think it can be a healthy neurosis. I'm more open to the chukim nowadays—those inexplicable commandments such as the wearing of tassels on the corners of your clothing. Without realizing it, I had been practicing my own self-generated chukim for years. How long had I wasted turning on and off the radio because I needed the final word to be a noun? Compared to my radio ritual, strapping commandments to my forehead looks positively rational. Instead of compulsively repeating the list of my freshman year classes—French, math, biology, etc. (don't ask), I compulsively repeat certain passages from the Bible that I am mandated to remember. Like that God gave us the commandments. And that God brought us out of Israel. And gave us the Sabbath. And that God instructed us to blow a horn at the start of every month.

Month Five: January

*Do not pay attention to every word people say, or you may hear
your servant cursing you. For you know in your heart
that many times you yourself have cursed others.*
—ECCLESIASTES 7:21–22 (NIRV)

Day 124. January 2. We're back in New York. I'm not supposed to make
New Year's resolutions—probably a pagan ritual—but if I did, here's
what it would be: I have to start thickening my skin. It's right there in the
Ecclesiastes: Don't pay attention to everything everyone says about you;
you know you've talked badly about other people too.

Today, I was reading the Amazon.com reviews for my encyclopedia
book (I know, not Biblical) and I ran across one that was very strange.
The reviewer said she looked at my author photo and discovered that I'm
not really that ugly. In fact, I'm kind of "normal-looking." Which I guess
is sort of flattering. Normal-looking.

But she didn't mean it as flattery. She said that I'm normal-looking
enough that I have no excuse to be socially awkward, neurotic or beset
with an inferiority complex. So I should shut my normal-looking trap
and stop complaining. This is the most backhanded compliment I've
ever received. It sunk me into a bad mood for three hours. The Bible is
right: I have to toughen up.

And I must, absolutely must, stop self-Googling. It's a horrible habit
that I still haven't kicked in my Biblical year. I found one blogger in Sin-
gapore who got my book for a birthday present, though he seemed more
excited about the another present, a T-shirt that read "I'm looking for
treasure, Can I see your Chest." I've done image searches on myself, and
found an outtake from an appearance on C-Span's Book TV where the
website froze on a particularly unflattering moment that makes me re-

semble Sean Penn in I Am Sam.

This is all very un-Biblical, very vain. I should think instead on the well-being of my family and my neighbors—and on God.

I should be more like Noah. It took Noah decades to build his ark. Can you imagine the mockery he must have received from doubting neighbors? If Noah were alive today, he wouldn't be wasting his time checking out what blogs said about him. He's be down at Home Depot buying more lumber. Starting today, I'm going to be like Noah. No checking the blogs.

You shall teach them diligently to your children

DUETERONOMY 6:7

Day 126. There's one upside to my son not talking a lot—I don't have to figure out what to tell him about God yet. Because I don't know what to say yet.

The subject came up at dinner tonight with our friends Jessica and Peter, up from Washington D.C. for a visit. Here's how Jessica answered the question when their daughter asked her about God.

"I told her God is in the wind, in the trees, He's in the rocks, He's everywhere."

Her husband Peter looks dismayed.

"Well, maybe not everywhere," says Peter.

"Yes, everywhere," says Jessica.

"God's in that cement mixer?"

"Yes," she says.

"In the forklift?"

"Yes, why not?" says Jessica.

Peter shakes his head. "You've got to draw the line somewhere."

But I know what Jessica is saying. In the past couple of weeks, I've taken if not a leap of faith—then a cautious, test-with-one-toe baby-step of faith. I'm not sure why. I think it's that the three-times-a-day prayers are working their mojo.

The point is, I don't see the world as a collection of soulless quarks and neutrinos. At times—not all the time, but sometimes—the entire world takes on a glow of sacredness, like someone has flipped on a unfathomably huge halogen lamp and made the universe softer, fuller, less menacing.

I spend a lot of time marveling. I haven't stared at a forklift yet, but I'll marvel at the way rain serpentines down a car window. Or I'll marvel at the way my reflection is distorted in a bowl. I feel like I just took my first bong hit. I feel like Wes Bentley rhapsodizing about that dancing plastic bag in American Beauty.

I've noticed I sometimes walk around with a lighter step, almost an ice-skating-like glide, because the ground feels hallowed. All of the ground, even the ground outside the pizzeria near my apartment building.

All well and good, right? The only thing is, this is not the God of the Israelites. This is not the God of the Hebrew Scriptures. That God is an interactive God. He rewards people and punishes them. He argues with them, negotiates with them, forgives them, occasionally smites them. The God of the Hebrew Scriptures has human emotions—love and anger.

My God doesn't. My God is impersonal. My God is the God of Spinoza. Or the God of Paul Tillich, the Protestant theologian who believed God was "Essence." Or the God of the Jedi knights. It's a powerful but vague all-pervading force, some slightly more sophisticated version of pantheism. The official term is panentheism—divineness in Being. I don't even know if my God can be said to have a grand plan. Can I keep edging toward the true Biblical God? I'm not sure.

And the LORD said to me, 'Arise, go on your journey'

DEUTERONOMY 10:11

Day 127. Before I buy my tickets to Israel, I want to make sure my ex-uncle Gil will be there. I get his phone number from an Orthodox friend of mine in Israel, which was surprisingly easy. And I call.

My plan is to make it a stealth mission. I won't reveal that I'm his former nephew. That's not lying, right? That's just omission of information. If he doesn't know I'm an ex-relative, he can't think that I'm giving him tacit approval, the family's big fear.

I dial the 14 digits. The phone rings.

My heart is thumping. I haven't been that nervous since I called Julie for our first date

"Hello?"

I don't know what I expected—a booming voice speaking Aramaic?—but his pitch was a regular old mid-range American.

"Is Gil there?"

"Speaking."

"Yes, well, I'm a writer, and I'm writing a book about trying to live by the Bible, and I'm coming to Israel, and—"

"What's your name?"

Part of me was hoping I could just be known as The Writer. So what do I do now? Should I give him a fake name? That would be lying. Well, maybe he won't know my name. I've never met him, and I have a different last name from his ex-wife.

"My name is A.J. Jacobs"

"Oh! You're related to my daughters."

Well there goes that theory. We set a date for me to come to his house for dinner. I'm tense enough about breaking the family taboo that it takes me three hours to go to sleep.

You shall write them on the doorposts of your house

DEUTERONOMY 6:9

Day 128. I've devoted lots of time to both my physical appearance and my soul. But I feel I haven't sufficiently Bibli-fied my house. The only thing I've done is to strip our apartment of those images that verge on idolatry, even if it's of the celebrity kind: The poster of Ray Charles at the Monterey Jazz Festival, the half-dozen photos of Julie standing next to celebrities she accosted at events or on the street. (Julie with a reluctant Willem Dafoe, Julie with a skeptical Tupac Shakur, etc.)

Today, as instructed in Deuteronomy, I'm going to write a section of the Bible on our doorpost. I tell Julie, who has two stern commandments of her own.

1. Do not, under any circumstances, let Jasper see you write on the doorpost. We've been battling his tendency toward crayon abuse. This would not help.

2. Please, please do it in pencil. "I don't want to get a call from the co-op board about this. I don't want to have to pay for a painter."

I promise.

When he came down from Mount Sinai, Moses commanded the Israelites to write God's words on their doorposts and their gates. It's the origin of the mezuzah—the diagonal box that we (and most other Jews) have nailed at the entrance to their homes.

The tradition has been to delegate the writing of the mezuzah to an officially-sanctioned scribe. It all comes prepackaged. But the Bible's literal wording—and presumably what some Israelites did back in ancient times—says that we should write on our doorframes ourselves.

But what to write? Moses says "these words which I command you." I briefly considered trying to squeeze in hundreds of commandments in tiny font, but settled on the famous 10—they appear in the Bible right before the doorpost passage. (Incidentally, traditional mezuzahs instead go with the famous prayer known as the Shema: "Hear, O Israel! The LORD is our God. The LORD is One!)."

So I get out my Number 2 Officemate pencil, make sure Jasper is safely distracted by Legos, prop open the front door, and start slowly, very slowly, writing God's words on the avocado-colored doorframe. It takes an hour. All the while I am inhaling the mysterious odor that always wafts from apartment 5R (I think they have an illegal albacore cannery in there), taking a break between every commandment to shake out my wrist and elbow, and being vigilant not to make a stray loop or spike.

At first, I feel absurd. Like a Biblical version of Bart Simpson at the chalkboard. Absurd and nervous—am I committing an egregious sin by ignoring the centuries-old tradition? Orthodox Jews might say so. Probably would say so. There are an astounding 4649 instructions that go into creating a certified mezuzah. You must write with a quill taken from a kosher bird, like a goose or turkey. It must have 22 lines. And on and on. By comparison, I am winging it.

But after about half an hour, I sink into a quasi-trance. I haven't done any monk-like handwritten copying in years—not since the invention of digital cut-and-paste, anyway. But there's something to it. You are forced to linger over every letter, every cadence. You absorb the text. It's the difference walking to town and taking the bus—you can't help but notice things.

> I notice the minimalist beauty of Commandments 6–8:
> "You shall not kill.
> You shall not commit adultery.
> You shall not steal."

And I notice the syncopated rhythm of the list of those banned from working on the Sabbath.

"You, or your son, or your daughter, your manservant, or your maidservant, or your cattle, or the sojourner who is within your gates."

I think about how every word that I am writing has launched a thousand debates. Even something as straightforward as: You shall not kill.

This is widely regarded as a mistranslation. The Old Testament features plenty of God-sanctioned killing—from capital punishment of blasphemers to the annihilation of enemies. The actual commandment is more like: You shall not murder.

Nothing is free from dispute, even the number "ten." Depending on how you parse the language, you could argue that it's actually the Thirteen Commandments. "You shall not make for yourself a graven image" is one commandment. "You shall not bow down to them" is another. But those two are generally lumped together.

They are deceptively simple, those Ten Commandments.

Do not go as a gossiper amongst your people"
LEVITICUS 19:16 (JPS)

Day 129. I keep thinking back to Amos, the harmonica-playing Amish man, and how he answered most questions with a monosyllable or a nod. And that's if you were lucky. Sometimes he just stared over your shoulder until the silence got so unbearable you asked another question.

I'm no Amos, but I feel myself drifting in his direction. Guard your tongue, I tell myself. Ration those words. Just nod your head and smile and don't get provoked when they say "Hey Chatterbox over there!" as my coworkers did at a recent Esquire dinner at an Italian restaurant.

I feel I have to clam up. It's the best way to battle the overwhelming urge to spew Biblically-banned negative language. The pastor out to pasture Elton Richards gave me a good metaphor on this topic: think of negative speech as verbal pollution. And that's what I've been doing: Visualizing insults and gossip as a dark cloud, maybe one with some sulfur dioxide. Once you've belched it out, you can't take it back. As grandma said, if don't have anything nice to say, don't say anything at all.

The interesting thing is, the less often I vocalize my negative thoughts, the fewer negative thoughts I have to vocalize. My theory is, my thoughts are lazy. They say to themselves, Well, we'll never make it out into the world, so why even bother? It's more powerful than repression. The thoughts don't even form enough to require being repressed.

Yes, the sales guy at the Biblical bookstore sold me a hardcover copy of What Would Jesus Eat when, as I found out today, there's a paperback version that costs $10 less. But I refuse to complain about him to Julie. Maybe he didn't know, or maybe he thought I'd prefer a good durable cover for posterity. I refuse to let that toxic cloud gather in my brain. It's a purifying feeling, the verbal equivalent of wearing white clothes.

Tonight, over dinner with Julie, I was in fine no-negative speech form. My wife's job is all about creating fun; she works for a company that organizes scavenger hunts—they do corporate events, public events, bar mitzvahs—but apparently her day had not been fun at all.

She had this client who insisted on doing an outdoor event. Julie told her it would be much better to do the scavenger hunt indoors this time of year, but the client said no. And of course, the day turned out to be ear-numbingly cold. And now the client is freaking out and demanding a refund.

"She is such a pain in the ass," says Julie

"It's a difficult situation."

I don't know this woman. Technically, I shouldn't say harmful speech about her.

"I told her three times to do the hunt indoors, and she refused to listen," says Julie.

"Maybe next time will be better."

"I hope to God there won't be a next time."

"Sounds like she has some pluses and minuses, just like everyone."

"What?"

"Everyone has their good and bad sides."

"What does that mean? Everyone has their good and bad sides."

"Well, it sounds like there was an unfortunate lack of communication."

"There was no freakin' lack of communication. I told her to do it and she ignored me."

Julie paused.

"Why aren't you supporting me? "

"I am. But I don't want to say anything negative. It's gossip. Lashon hora."

"Well, you sound like a creepy child psychologist."

I'm jolted. But she's right. I do sound absurd. I faced one of the many cases where two Biblical commandments butted heads. The commandment to refrain from gossip, and the commandment to treat my wife as I would have her treat me. I chose the wrong one. I should have broken the ban against negative speech. Even absolutism must have exceptions.

I will multiply your descendants as the stars of heaven and
as the sand which is on the seashore

GENESIS 22:17

Day 132. It's been 12 days since our visit to the clinic, and Julie and I just got the call from the nurse. She should have some news. Julie takes it on the black cordless in our living room.

"Uh-huh. Uh-huh."

Julie smiles. Gives me the thumbs' up.

She's pregnant! Yes!

She gives another thumbs' up, this time with an overly-clenched smile.

"Okay. Yeah. Thanks."

Julie clicks off the phone. She's not just pregnant—she's really pregnant. Her hormone levels show that she's probably carrying twins. The doctor put in two fertilized eggs, and they both appear to have stuck.

Huh. Twins.

I knew there was a higher chance of twins with IVF, but still. That's hard to process.

I always felt ambivalent about taking the be fruitful and multiply commandment too far. The world is in the midst of a scary Malthusian population boom—I had figured two kids would be about right for me.

Julie and I sit on the couch together, stunned silent for a minute.

"Two for one deal," she says flatly. "Double the fun."

I guess compared to biblical families—Jacob had 12 kids, David had at least 20—three isn't too bad. Be thankful, I remind myself. Be thankful.

Offer to God a sacrifice of thanksgiving
And pay your vows to the Most High

PSALMS 50:14

Day 133. Twins are, to use religious language, a mixed blessing. But they are a blessing nonetheless.

Two kids. It's no doubt the biggest news I've gotten all year, and I decide that I need to express my gratitude somehow. I need to do more than just clasp my hands and utter thanks with my lips. If I really want to be Biblical, I should sacrifice something.

So today in Union Square. I put some olives and dates on a platform of stones and left them there as an offering to God. I said a prayer and walked away. I don't know what I was hoping for—a vision, a bolt of lightning—but whatever it was, I didn't get it. Instead, I got to feel like I'd just spent $15.46 at the grocery store contributing to New York's rat problem

It was a letdown—especially after my previous experience with sacrifice. That one was profound, enlightening and deeply disturbing.

Let me rewind a few months.

When I first read the Bible, it became clear that sacrifice isn't a weird footnote in the Hebrew Scriptures—it's central to it. The biblical rules for sacrifice go on for pages, and are staggeringly complex. I've since read them dozens of times, and still don't have a handle on them.

I have, however, figured out three things.

1. Animal sacrifice is preferable to other types of sacrifice, including fruit, grain and incense sacrifices, which are seen as B-level offerings.

2. The ancient Israelites sacrificed an impressively wide range of species: oxen, doves, she-goats, he-goats, turtledoves, pigeons, lambs and so on.

3. They sacrificed often, very often. Sins, death, birth, holidays—all required sacrifices at the Temple. After reading the sacrifice section of the Bible, you start to wonder how there was any time left to reap or sow or beget or anything else ancient Israelites had to do.

Luckily for me—and more luckily for the animals—practically no Bible followers sacrifice animals anymore. Sacrifices were allowed only at the Temple in Jerusalem, and the Romans destroyed the Second Temple in about 70 CE. So maybe that's my loophole. Perfectly understandable.

And yet, animal sacrifice is such a huge part of the Bible, I feel I have to experience it somehow. Which won't be easy. Being a city boy, I've never killed anything larger than a waterbug.

Over lunch one day, my adviser, the history teacher Eddy Portnoy, told me that there is still one ritual that borders on animal sacrifice. The ritual is called Kaparot, and it's practiced by some ultra-Orthodox Jews once a year—on the night before Yom Kippur. The idea is that you buy a live chicken, hold it over your head, say a blessing, and have the bird slaughtered in front of you. The chicken is then donated to the poor.

Kaparot is not in the Bible. The earliest mentions of the ritual are in ninth century literature from what is now Iraq. But it's the closest thing I'll find to legal sacrifice in the tri-state area, so on a drizzly night back in October, I hop the subway to Crown Heights, Brooklyn.

I know I am getting close by the smell. As I walk from the subway station, the smell segues from the traditional New York City garbage-and-car-exhaust odor to a startling Arkansas-poultry-farm odor.

I arrive a few blocks later later. I'll say this: There wasn't much of a chance I'd walk by without noticing. Hundreds of Orthodox Jews mill around in their black hats and long black coats and prayer books, all soggy from the light drizzle.

The black hats are outnumbered only by chickens. Chickens in cages, chickens on the street, chickens tucked under arms. It could be a Lithuanian town in 1805—minus the ever-present cell phones and digital cameras.

My guide is Rabbi Epstein, a round-faced Hasid originally from Tennessee. We meet on a predetermined corner.

We start by talking about our beards—common ground.

"Do you do any trimming?" I ask.

No trimming allowed," Epstein says.

"But you can try to clean it up a bit," says his friend, another rabbi. With that, the other rabbi grabbed his beard and did a quick roll-and-tuck-under-the-chin. Real sleight of hand, Ricky Jay stuff. But it made his beard half a foot shorter.

The atmosphere is oddly festive, like a Jewish Mardi Gras. We have to talk loudly to be heard over the clucking and squawking and flapping. And just in case the scene needed to be more surreal, Rabbi Epstein has a noticeable Southern accent, so his Hebrew words are filtered through a Garth Brooks twang.

I ask about the sacrifice part of the ritual.

"Kaparot is definitely not a sacrifice," says Epstein, kindly but firmly. "You can only sacrifice at the Temple, and the Temple does not exist anymore."

"How is it different?"

"The chicken does not die for our sins. It reminds us what could or should be happening to us because we are sinners."

"But isn't it in the same ballpark as the original scapegoat?" I ask.

I was referring to an ancient Biblical ritual in which, on Yom Kippur, the Israelites, transferred their sins to a goat and ran it over a cliff. It's the origin of the word 'scapegoat.'

"Maybe," he says reluctantly. "But it's very different. The sins aren't in the chicken. It's to arouse within us the knowledge that 'there but for the Grace of God go I.'"

I try to keep an open mind, but I am having trouble.

"I've gotta tell you," I say. "I feel bad for these chickens."

Epstein shakes his head. "No, it's kosher slaughter. These butchers use the sharpest knives. It's like a paper cut. You know how paper cuts don't hurt for awhile after you get them? This doesn't hurt."

The crowd is thick. Kids with boxes ask for donations for charity. Friends snap photos of each other holding up chickens. We bump into Rabbi Shmuley Boteach—he's the third most famous Orthodox Jew, right after Joe Lieberman and reggae rocker Matisyahu. Boteach wrote the book Kosher Sex and, for a brief moment, was Michael Jackson's spiritual adviser, appearing next to him at press conferences. Boteach has a Treo clipped to his belt, a TLC show in development (which has since aired), and is alarmingly media-savvy.

"We've had documentary crews here before. And if you show this alone, out of context, it seems barbaric and irrational."

Rabbi Boteach is right. I know I'll be committing the same sin, since I can't devote my entire book to explaining ultra-Orthodox rituals, it will, by necessity, seem out of context.

"Is it any more irrational than a lot of things in our culture?" he asks. "Is it more irrational than Botox? Or more irrational than transubstantiation?"

Again, maybe he's got a point: In my admittedly brief encounters with the Hasidim, I've found them to be a lot more reasonable than I imagined. The ones I've met have been, for the most part, bright and friendly. And they have a fascinating self-awareness. Early on, Rabbi Epstein told me he took his kids to Colonial Williamsburg.

And one of his kids asked him, "Do people still live like this?"

And Rabbi Epstein told him, "No one lives like they did in the 18th century. Well, except for in Crown Heights."

So they aren't wackjobs. Well, let me qualify that. Most of them aren't wackjobs. There are exceptions.

Case in point: The short Hasidic Jew wandering among the chickens with a sandwich board over his black coat. The sandwich board has a huge photo of Rabbi Menachem M. Schneerson, the leader of the Lubavitchers, the huge Brooklyn-based Hasidic movement.

"The Rebbe is coming soon!" he says in an Israeli accent.

"I thought Rabbi Schneerson died a few years ago."

"Well, we interpret it as dying, but he's not dead. He's going to come back and there will be the Messianic age."

This guy had drunk the kosher Kool-Aid.

"What does that mean? What will the Messianic age look like?" I ask.

"'Money will grow on trees. And clothing will also grow on trees. And the sand will be like candy. Everything will be provided for, so all we have to do is study Torah all day."

What an amazingly detailed vision. I expected some vague generalizations, not beaches of Skittles and orchards of chinos. As for the activities, I already study the Bible all day, so this wasn't too enticing.

"Have you ever studied anything but religion?" I ask.

"I had a little math and science when I was a kid, but not much. When I'm done with religion, I'll study other topics." He smiles.

"But you'll never be done with religion, right?"

"I'm not done yet."

Man do I hate that insular thinking. It makes me think of my distant ancestor—the rabbi named Vilna Gaon. He railed against that mindset, saying an understanding of the Bible required a broad education, including the study of math, astronomy, geography, botany, zoology and philosophy.

I find Rabbi Epstein again. Enough procrastinating. It's time for me to actually do this ritual. I pay $10 to a man behind a table, and am directed to the open back of a huge truck. It's packed with chickens fluttering in coops.

"One male," says Epstein. Men get male chickens, he explains, women get females, and pregnant women get one of each to cover all contingencies.

The truck guy hands me my chicken—white-feathered, red-beaked, very much alive.

"Hold it under the wings," says Epstein. He takes the chicken and demonstrates for me a full Nelson grip.

"Really? But—"

"It's comfortable for them, totally comfortable," he assures me.

The chicken squawks. I stroke him to calm him down.

Now here's the thing: I know the chicken I get at Ranch 1 did not die of natural causes. It did not drift off to eternal sleep in its old age surrounded by loved ones and grandchicks at a chicken hospice. It had its throat slit too. But modern society has done an excellent job of shielding me from this fact.

I look at the chicken again. Oh man. I have an awful epiphany: The chicken kind of looks like Jasper—the same big eyes, same cocked head, it all but says "Dada" (or actually, "A.J.").

You don't have to be Maimonides to see where this is going. I'm playing Abraham to the chicken's Isaac. And I don't have even a speck of the faith of Abraham. I feel nauseated and loosen my grip. The chicken flaps out of my hands and starts scampering down the street. Epstein scampers after it, scoops it up, and brings it back to me. I stroke the chicken's head again.

"Now wave it in a circle over your head."

This is one of the strangest parts of the kaparot ritual—you are supposed to gently twirl the bird three times in the air.

Epstein is holding the prayer book for me to read: "This is my exchange," I say. "This is my substitute, this is my expiation. This chicken shall go to its death and I shall proceed to a good, long life and peace." I was hoping I'd feel my sins flow out of me, but I don't. I'm too focused on holding the flapping chicken.

Next stop is the kosher slaughterers. There are three of them standing behind a counter on a raised platform, bringing to mind very violent pharmacists. They're wearing black garbage bags over their bodies to protect themselves from splattered blood. And my goodness, is there blood—it coats the ground, it spots the faces, it soaks the gloves. The smell of chicken blood is so strong, a girl in line is dry heaving. In the era of avian flu, can this be a good idea?

I give my chicken to the slaughterer. He takes it, flips it over, bends back the neck, and makes three quick saws with the knife. The chicken is dead, just like that..

The butcher tosses my chicken in an upside down red Con Ed traffic cone, which is where it will stay as the blood drains out of its body. My chicken will then be plucked and packaged and trucked to a poor family somewhere in Brooklyn.

I'm elbowed out of the way. I'm still in my city-boy stupor: My chicken was alive; now three knife strokes later, it's dead. Epstein is say-ing something, but I can't really focus. I'm too dazed.

As I said, I've started to look at life differently. When you're thanking God for every little joy—every meal, every time you wake up, every time you sip of water—you can't help but be more thankful for life itself, for the unlikely and miraculous fact that you exist at all.

What I mean is that I do admire the sentiment behind kaparot. I think it's good to be reminded that I could be scampering around the street one minute, and the next minute find myself gone from this world. That life is so absurdly precious and fleeting.

And yet, I don't admire the method. Perhaps if I grew up as a Hasid, it'd make more sense to me. But as Rabbi Boteach says, out of context, it just seems barbaric. If I ever do kaparot again, I'm going to do it like my aunt Kate. She practices a tamer—but still approved—version of ka-parot: instead of poultry, they wave money over the head.

On the way home, as I walk to the subway and the smell of chickens fade, I thank God that He discontinued the daily need for ritual slaugh-ter. I had enough trouble with a chicken. I'd hate to try a goat or ox.

And you shall not strip your vineyard bare, neither shall you gather
the fallen grapes . . .you shall leave them for the poor

LEVITICUS 19:10

Day 140. Our living room table is covered with four large terra cotta pots containing cucumber plants. Or at least scraggly, struggling versions of cucumber plants.

I've been trying to engage in some agriculture, seeing as so many Biblical laws involve farming. I bought cucumber seeds online (cucumber was eaten by the Hebrews when they were slaves in Egypt, along with melons, leeks and garlic) and planted them in soil. For good measure, I added a couple of dozen cinnamon-colored plant-food pellets that brought to mind that discussion of rabbit digestion at the Creation Mu-seum.

The cucumbers do grow—they each get to be the size of a Good & Plenty candy. And then they promptly die. I don't understand why. To date, I've grown and killed about 100 dozen tiny, prickly, inedible cucumbers.

My hope had been to leave cucumber 'gleanings. The idea of 'gleanings' is one of my favorites in the Bible. It goes like this: When you harvest your field, don't reap the entire field. Leave the corners unharvested so that the leftovers—the 'gleanings'—can be gathered by the poor.

It's a beautiful and compassionate rule. Plus, the commandment rewards people for doing a half-assed job, which I think is a nice notion. Part of the idea is that, ultimately, the land belongs to God, so you respect that and be sure to provide for God's children.

And it can lead to unexpected blessings. Consider this great, romantic story in the Old Testament's Book of Ruth: Ruth was an impoverished foreigner who had followed her mother-in-law Naomi to Israel. To survive, Ruth gathered gleanings of barley. One day, the rich owner of the land—a man named Boaz—spotted Ruth gleaning and was smitten. When she found out about his crush, she bathed herself, anointed herself, put on her finest clothes and sneaked into Boaz's room to "lie at his feet." (Some say the phrase is a euphemism for lying elsewhere). Boaz was startled but pleased. They were soon married—and it all started because of the command to glean.

In any case, how to apply this amazing notion of gleaning to my life, since the cucumber experiment is flopping. I suppose 'gleaning' could be generalized to mean 'give to the poor.' But I'm already doing that, thanks to tithing and other commands. Gleanings are a slightly different creature.

I decide to try to figure out how to update it. Which is hard. If I do a lax job on an Esquire article, it doesn't help the poor. It just means a copy editor has to fill in Scarlett Johansson's age and unsplit my infinitives.

But then I have this idea: What's the closest thing to harvesting in my life? Going to an ATM. What if I leave $20 in the machine whenever I took out $200? I do this twice, and it isn't bad. Though I got the queasy feeling that Ron Perelman was coming in after me, and that he'd use my $20 as Kleenex.

So I came up with a new plan: if I accidentally drop anything valuable on the street, I'll leave it there. It would be God's will. I would not gather it up.

Perhaps I psyched myself out: for several days, I don't drop a thing, not even so much as a nickel or clump of lint. But then, yesterday, I am pulling out my wallet on the corner of 81st and Columbus and a crumpled five-dollar bill falls out. I glance at it for a second, and keep walking.

"Excuse me sir!"

I turn around. A woman was holding up my bill.

"You dropped this!"

"Uh. That's okay," I say.

"It's yours. I saw it drop out of your pocket," she says.

I pause.

"No, it wasn't mine," I say, and kept walking. This lying has to stop.

> *Praise the LORD with the lyre,*
> *make melody to him with the harp of ten strings!*
> —PSALM 33:2

Day 143. My white garments have gotten a shade a darker, thanks to food stains and general urban pollution. But I still loving wearing them. They make me feel buoyant, like I'm floating a couple of feet above the sidewalk.

They're such a success, I decide that I should have an even more Biblical appearance, which is how I settle on following Psalm 33:2. This instructs us to praise the Lord on a harp of 10-strings.

Do 10-string harps even exist anymore, I wondered? Or would I have to make my own? Maybe I'll gain worldwide acclaim as the only living 10-string harpist.

One Google search later, I discovered I would not be the only 10-string harpist. Far from it. When will it sink in that there is no such thing as an obscure Bible verse?

Turns out there's a thriving underground world devoted to the Biblical instrument. You can buy 10-string harps on eBay. You can send a Christmas eCard featuring 10-string harp music (the harp is plucked by a computer-generated angel who looks like a winged Kate Hudson). You can read about how the Messianic Age will usher in 10-string harps that will miraculously expand the octave from eight notes to ten notes.

The Tiffany's of 10-string harps is an Indiana-based shop called Jubilee Harps. (Motto: "Home is where your harp is!") The website features audio samples of harp music, a photo gallery, accessories such as amplifiers and charcoal-gray harp cases, and promises of spiritual rewards: "Although not fully understood, people today are experiencing the healing powers of the harp. Just hold this harp close to your heart, rest your face on the side of its arm, and feel peace and serenity surround you."

I call to find out more. The co-owner Mary Woods gets on the phone; she tells me that she and her husband Rick have sold more than 1,000 of their handmade, wooden King David-inspired harps to clients in 18 countries.

They set up shop soon after Rick was downsized from his job as a scientist at Bristol-Myers Squibb. He made his first harp for a celebration at their church.

"It was late one night," Mary recalls, "And Rick got me to come out to his workshop, and I looked at the harp, and I couldn't quit crying. He thought I was mad because he spent three months in the workshop and all he had was this harp. But I went over and hugged it, and I couldn't quit crying."

At this point, two things happen: Mary starts choking up on the other end of the phone. And I start feeling like more of a voyeuristic schmuck than I have since this year began. Much has touched me in these months—the humility of the Amish, the joy of Hasidic dancing, the power of prayer—but I can't relate to Mary's passion for a Biblical harp. It's totally foreign to me. I thank her and hang up.

In the end, I did buy a 10-string harp online—a $40 one from a second-hand store, not the $800 version offered by Jubilee. Mine is made of coffee-colored wood and is about the size of a cafeteria tray. I play it twice a day, as instructed by the Psalms. I don't really know what I'm doing, but the good news is, it's hard to screw up too badly on a harp. A pluck here, a glissando there, and it sounds soothing.

I sometimes take it out for walks, which mostly inspires the cautious sideways glances I've become so accustomed to. I have had a couple notable reactions, though. When I strummed harp during a recent stroll on Columbus Avenue, a woman walking her dog offered me a dollar. Also, a white-haired man near Rockefeller Center started yelling at me. "A 10-string harp? The Bible actually says an eight-string harp, not a 10-string harp." He could have been playing with my mind, or he could have been your garden-variety crazy, hard to tell.

In the end, though, the harp isn't transporting me. I'm going to have to find another PIN code to spiritual transcendence.

These are the living things which you may eat among all the beasts that are on the earth.

LEVITICUS 11:2

Day 147. The Bible is filled with so many Thou Shalt Nots, that I've started to take advantage of anything that is allowed. Even if said allowed activity isn't so alluring. Which is how, today, I ended up eating a bug.

To start at the beginning: Before this project, I'd had just a little exposure to the Bible's food laws. When I was in college, I used to order kosher meals on airplanes because someone told me that they were better—the reasoning was that the airlines have to give the kosher meals special attention and can't throw them in the vat with everyone else's slop. Frankly, I found the meals no tastier than the airline's secular lasagna. So I stopped doing that. Which is probably good, since feigning piety to upgrade your lunch is ethically dubious.

My airline adventure wasn't a total waste. I did pick up the very basics of the Bible's dietary restrictions. Namely these rules, found in Leviticus:

—You shall eat no pork or bacon or any other pig meat (land creatures must have cloven hoofs and chew their cud to be edible)
—No shellfish (sea creatures must have both fins and scales to be edible; shrimp, clams and their cousins have neither)
—No blood

—No rabbits

—Certain birds—most of them birds of prey, such as eagles, vultures and buzzards—are off-limits.

Why the food taboos? The Bible itself doesn't give a reason. I'd always thought they developed as a primitive way to avoid trichinosis and other nasty diseases. But apparently, I was wrong. Most anthropologists now believe the food bans were all about separation. The Israelites wanted to keep themselves apart from other tribes like the pork-loving Philistines. They were marking their territory with menus.

Observant Jews follow the Bible's laws today. In fact, they follow a far more elaborate version of the laws, a system elaborated by the rabbis. The strictest kosher eater abides by hundreds of other rules, including ones about separating milk and meat that could take years to learn.

A handful of Christians keep the basic rules, including the evangelical author of a book I own called The Maker's Diet, who writes: "in an odd twist of logic, many religious Americans dismiss the Jewish dietary laws as outdated legalism, invalid for the modern era. Yet, they embrace the fundamental truths of the ten commandments as universal and timeless." This guy's is in the minority. Most Christians believe that Jesus' sacrifice freed Christians from the food laws.

Over the last few months, I've been trying to abide by the rules explicitly listed in the Bible (as opposed to the full rabbinical kosher laws). It's been an enormous challenge.

Granted, in some sense, I've gotten lucky. The laws align with my own preferences. I've never liked shellfish. Lobsters, for instance, remind me too much of something you'd kill with Raid. So it wasn't a hardship to give up the ocean's bottom-feeders. I don't eat much bacon, either; my cholesterol already hovers around the score of a professional bowler, and I don't need it to break 300.

The problem is, forbidden foods are hiding everywhere. Bacon lurks in salad dressings. Gelatin is sometimes derived from pig bones, so an argument can be made—and often is—that it's forbidden. And pig fat. That terrifies me. Typical is this recent exchange I had with a waitress at a midtown restaurant:

"Do you know if the pie crust is made with lard?"

"I don't think so, but I'll check."

"Thanks. I can't eat lard."

"Allergies?"

"No, Leviticus."

It's a conversation-stopper, that one. It's hard to trot out the Bible at a New York restaurant without sounding self-righteous or messianic. But the Proverbs say I must tell the truth, so I told the truth.

It's often pointed out that following religious food laws sharpens your discipline. The great 12th-century philosopher Maimonides says this is precisely their purpose: "[They] train us to master our appetites; to accustom us to restrain our desires; and to avoid considering the pleasure of eating and drinking as the goal of man's existence."

The thing is, I've been mastering my appetites since my cholesterol first bubbled up in my early twenties. For years, I've been eating Styrofoam-like fat-free cheese and scouring ingredient labels for the evil hydrogenated oil. It seems most people nowadays have some sort of food restriction, whether it's avoiding carbs, sugar or non-organic vegetables. One woman I know refuses to eat "nightshades," whatever they are.

So if self-regulation of our urges is the purpose, perhaps the Bible laws are no longer necessary. As a society, we've outgrown them. I told this idea to my Orthodox adviser Uri. He shook his head. "You can't know the mind of God," he said. "There may be benefits beyond what we know now or can imagine."

So I sucked it up and stuck with the laws, still hoping to trip over one of those elusive benefits. And maybe I did. It happened about three weeks ago. I was following one of the most obscure food taboos in the Bible. This one concerns forbidden fruit. According to Leviticus 19:23–25, you cannot eat fruit unless the tree that bears said fruit is at least five years old. If a tree is four years old or younger, its fruit is not for human consumption. (Some Orthodox Jews follow this, but say it only applies to fruit grown in Israel or that you grow yourself).

So I tried to find out the ages of all the fruits I ate by emailing and calling grocery stores and companies. This was not a success. I got a lot of terse responses like this one, from the corporate headquarters of

Polaner All Fruit spreads:

Mr. Jacobs,

Unfortunately there would not be any way for us to guarantee the age of the plants from which our suppliers pick the blackberries.

I was reduced to researching which kinds of fruits came from slow-bearing trees and which from fast-bearing. I learned that peach trees can bear fruit in two years. Too dangerous. Pear trees in four. Again, too risky. But cherry trees are, those are slowpokes. They take at least five to seven from planting to produce.

Cherries are safe. Not my favorite fruit, but they're safe, so they will be my fruit for the year. I went to Fairway supermarket, bought half-pound and began eating them out of the plastic bag on the walk home, spitting the seeds into garbage cans on the street corners.

Each cherry took about three seconds to eat. Three seconds to eat, but at least five years in the making. It seemed unfair to the hard-working cherry tree. The least I could do is devote my attention to the cherry in those three seconds, really appreciate the tartness of the skin and the faint crunching sound when I bite down. I guess it's called mindfulness. Or being in the moment, or making the mundane sacred. Whatever it is, I'm doing it more. Like the ridiculously extended thank you list for my hummus, the fruit taboo made me more aware of the whole cherry process, the seed, the soil, the five years of watering and waiting. That's the paradox—I thought religion would make me live with my head in the clouds, but as often as not, it grounds me in this world.

> *Of them you may eat: the locust according to its kind,*
>
> LEVITICUS 11:22

But anyway, back to the bugs. To really connect with my forefathers through my stomach, I decided the food taboos were only half the story. I'd have to do more. I'd have to eat the same foods Moses and Jesus did.

To help me with this, I bought the aforementioned The Maker's

Diet, a 320-page book by an evangelical nutritionist named Jordan Rubin. It's a helpful guide. The basic idea is a modified Mediterranean diet, which means our refrigerator is now packed with even more hummus, tahini and pita bread. At the suggestion of the Maker's Diet, I've also cut out all cow's milk. Cows in Biblical times were mainly used for dragging farm implements. The beverage of choice for Israelites was goat or sheep's milk.

I called around and, sure enough, I found a health food store in midtown that stocks fresh goat's milk from upstate New York. They stash a few half-gallon cartons in the fridge behind the massive display of vitamin B and echinacea.

Every morning I splash a little goat's milk on my oatmeal. It's not bad, really. It's like regular milk but thicker, the consistency of those overpriced blackberry Odwalla smoothies.

Also, I'm eating a lot of honey. Honey is one of the few certain pleasures in the Bible. It's the very description of the Promised Land—a place God says is "flowing with milk and honey," so my oatmeal gets a healthy dollop of honey.

(My aunt Marti—the vegan and animal rights activist—found out about my honey eating, and sent me a rebuking email. The subject header was "the bitter truth about honey." She listed all the ways the commercial honey industry mistreats bees. I won't reprint it here, but her description of artificial bee insemination was disturbingly graphic. She signed the note "Your eccentric aunt Marti.").

The Mediterranean cuisine is working out well. Maybe it's buried deep somewhere in my DNA, this love of chick peas and pita. It's my kind of Semitic food. Incidentally, I can't stand that other Jewish food—the Eastern European variety. I don't know why—a shrink would probably say it's because I have conflicted feelings about Judaism in general—but I can't eat it. The single most nauseating meal I've ever had was at a lower-east side Jewish restaurant called Sammy's Roumanian. This is a place where, instead of salt and pepper, the condiment of choice is liquefied chicken fat. They put a big bottle of thick yellow chicken fat—schmaltz is the official term—smack in the middle of the table, just in case your potato pancakes aren't quite sopping wet enough with grease already. I ate at Sammy's with a guy who, after a couple of vodkas, mistook the chicken fat for a complimentary bottle of orange juice, and downed several gulps before turning white and excusing himself for the bathroom.

Where was I? Oh yes, the bugs. Now this doesn't get much play in The Maker's Diet, but there was one other source of protein in Biblical times: Insects. Leviticus forbade the ancients from indiscriminate bug-eating, banning most insects with the rule: "All winged insects that go upon all fours are an abomination to you," which means no beetles, no mosquitoes, no bees, etc.

But Leviticus also says this: "Of them you may eat: the locust according to its kind, the bald locust according to its kind, the cricket according to its kind, and the grasshopper according to its kind . . ."

In other words, locusts, crickets and grasshoppers are fine. It's not clear from the Bible how often our forefathers actually them. Were they a popular meal? Or just in case of famine? The Bible's only other reference to bug-consumption comes in the story of John the Baptist, who was reported to have survived on locusts and wild honey (though even this is controversial; some say the word 'locust' here is a mistranslation, and he really ate carob pods).

Regardless, since the Bible diet contains so many restrictions, I figured I'd try to take advantage of this loophole. Maybe it'll make me feel manly and adventurous. It'll be Fear Factor, Old Testament style.

It isn't hard to find the bugs. The Internet is teeming with edible insects, or "microlivestock," as its called. There are chocolate wafers with ants mixed in. And beetle toffee bars. And larva cheddar cheese snacks

And plenty of crickets, which are apparently called "the other green meat" (high in protein, low in fat). The most promising supplier is named Fluker Farms, which describe theirs as "oven roasted to perfection and then covered with the finest chocolate available to create one truly unforgettable, exotic snack." Plus, you get an 'exclusive' I Ate a Bug Club button.

A few days later, I get a purple box with two-dozen individually-wrapped chocolate crickets. I'm going to need a fellow traveler on this one. I ask Julie, but she gives me another in a long line of overly enthusiastic "Thanks for asking! But I'm going to take a pass this time!"

So I take a couple of crickets along to dinner with my friend John. For my last book, John went to singles bars and tried to pick up women using facts from the encyclopedia about penguin mating rituals, so I figure he might be willing. He wasn't so sure.

"If I feel sick in the next couple of days, I'm going to blame you."

"Fair enough," I said.

"I'll think about it."

After we finish dinner at a downtown diner, I eat my cricket. Or at least I swallow it. I pop the cricket in my mouth, bite down twice, then chug water, ingesting it like a chestnut-sized pill. I tasted nothing.

I offer the other one to John.

"Come on. Just one."

"Fine," he says.

John unwraps his cricket and takes a bite, chewing slowly while looking at the ceiling, brow furrowed in thought.

"You like it?"

"A little crunchy," he says. "Hard to actually taste the cricket."

"I read it's supposed to be tangy. Is it tangy?"

"The chocolate is overpowering. But you do get a nice crispness."

He takes in the other half.

"It tastes like that candy bar Krackel. Same consistency."

A couple of day's later, I am at my grandfather's house boasting about my insect eating. Rick—my cousin who is a high school sophomore—isn't impressed.

"You eat insects all the time," he says. "There are insect parts in everything."

Rick has embraced entomology with a passion most kids reserve for baseball and illegally downloaded music. If E.O. Wilson had a poster, Rick would have it on his wall. So presumably he knew what he was talking about.

And he did. I found a tremendously disturbing FDA website that lists the "natural and unavoidable" amounts of insects for every kind of food.

A pizza slice can have up to two or more bugs per slice.

100 grams of drained mushrooms may contain 20 or more maggots.

And if you want oregano on your mushroom pizza, you'll be enjoying 1,250 or more insect fragments per 10 grams.

So I was violating the Bible rules even without intending to. Or maybe not. Depends on the interpretation. Orthodox Jews usually—but not always—reason that since they didn't have microscopes in Biblical times, then a bug must be visible with bare eyes to be forbidden.

Why would God weigh in on any insects at all, visible or not? Once again, my secular mind wanted to know the reason for the Lord's decrees. What's the logic? The Bible doesn't say—it's one of the unexplained laws.

But one book I read—the Bible As It Was by James Kugel—had a theory. It said that, in Biblical times, swarming locusts would often devour the crops and cause famines. The only way for the poor to survive was by eating the locusts themselves. So if the Bible didn't approve of locust-eating, the poorest Israelites would have died of starvation. This I like. More and more, I feel it's important to look at the Bible with an open heart. If you roll up your sleeves, even the oddest passages—and the one about edible bugs qualifies—can be seen as a sign of God's mercy and compassion.

> *If you chance to come upon a bird's nest . . .you shall not take*
> *the mother with the young.*
>
> DEUTERONOMY 22:6

Day 150. As a New Yorker, I'd generally avoided interacting with pigeons, much like I avoided dark alleys or the Jekyll & Hyde theme restaurant. But living Biblically makes you do some strange things.

Tonight, I got a voicemail from Mr. Berkowitz, the man who inspected my wardrobe for mixed fibers awhile back.

"Good evening, Mr. Arnold Jacobs. It's Bill Berkowitz of Washington Heights. There's a pigeon with an egg under her tonight, if you want to come over."

You bet I do.

You see, Mr. Berkowitz, in addition to shatnez, also specializes in another commandment. This one is likewise among the most obscure in the Bible. You won't find it on stone tablets in front of any federal courthouses.

The commandment says that if you find a mother bird sitting on her egg in a nest, you cannot take both mother and egg. You are only permitted to pocket the egg—and only on the condition you send away the mother so she can't see you doing it.

The Bible doesn't say why. Most commentators think it has to do with compassion—you don't want the mother to have to watch her offspring snatched up for the breakfast table. In fact, many rabbis have expanded the meaning of this commandment to forbid cruelty to all animals, not just expectant birds, which is a great thing. I'm glad mainstream Judaism stresses kindness to animals, despite the sacrificial past.

But the actual wording of Deuteronomy 22:6 is solely about eggs and nests, and it is this formulation that Mr. Berkowitz—along with others in his community—have taken to the literal limit.

He has set up two pigeon nests on his third-floor windowsill in his Northern Manhattan apartment. Whenever there's a newly-laid egg, he allows a faithful seeker to come over, pay $100 to charity, shoo the mother pigeon away, pick up the egg, hold it aloft, say a prayer, place it back in the nest (or, in some cases, eat it), and thereby check off this commandment as officially 'fulfilled'.

This I needed to do. In fact, I'd been waiting for several months for my egg, tempted by a half-dozen false alarms and missed opportunities. Tonight is the real thing.

I get to Mr. Berkowitz's apartment at 7:30, and he is all business. He has an appointment in a half-hour, so we are on a tight schedule. He gives me a quick orientation on how this commandment works.

"It must be a kosher bird," says Mr. Berkowitz.

Pigeons, interestingly, are kosher—they're related to the doves mentioned in the Bible.

"It has to be a wild bird, and the egg must be fertilized."

We're sitting at his dining room table, which is covered with half-open books and plastic cups. Mr. Berkowitz occasionally pauses in his speech to flip through his books. There's a colorful tome on kosher birds and a tablet-sized book on Jewish law. There's also a Hebrew manuscript devoted exclusively to the study of this single commandment, complete with diagrams of men climbing ladders, and photos of backlit eggs.

I express my concern that maybe the pigeons don't love the experience. Mr. Berkowitz shakes his head.

"Don't feel bad, because, first, God gave us this mitzvah And second, you ever eat an egg before?"

"Yeah."

"You feel badly about that? Your wife makes a scrambled egg, do you feel bad?" Mr. Berkowitz takes on a mock-petrified voice, "Oh no, don't do that! Not a scrambled egg!"

Speaking of which, most of Mr. Berkowitz's clients put the pigeon egg back in the nest—the option I've chosen. But some take them home for a hard-boiled snack.

"Have you tried it?" I ask.

"I once tasted it. I ate it raw."

"Raw? How'd it taste?'

"Tasted like a regular egg."

He shrugs his shoulders. No big deal.

The time for egg-gathering is at hand. He leads me into a dark room off the entrance hall and flips on his gray flashlight. It's a huge and powerful flashlight—the kind used for spelunking or locating fugitives in the woods—and more than bright enough to help me see the nests.

The nests are actually two white plastic boxes—originally olive boxes from the grocery—each with a pigeon and some shredded newspaper inside. Mine is on the right.

"You have to do something to send her away," says Mr. Berkowitz. "You can't just scream at her, 'fly away, birdie!' That won't work. It has to be a physical action."

I stamp my feet, wave my arms. Nothing. The pigeon—a big one, about the size of a football—clucks contentedly, enjoying the show.

"Open the window and reach in."

"Won't she fly into the room?"

"Don't worry about it."

I open the window and reach in. I'm wearing thick blue insulated ski gloves, official pigeon-shooing equipment provided by Mr. Berkowitz. Overcoming a lifelong of revulsion to pigeons, I nudge the bird with my index finger.

She flutters up and away.

I take off the glove, and pick up the egg. It's cream-colored and warm, about the size of a walnut. I hold it up for Mrs. Berkowitz to snap a photo.

Mr. Berkowitz tells me now is the time to ask for God for anything. "To have more children, make a million dollars a year, become a big scholar. Whatever you want."

In the outlying edges of Judaism (and I should stress that most Jews have never heard of the commandment, much less fulfilled it), the bird nest ritual has taken on mystical meaning, seen as a good luck, especially for infertile couples.

I make my wish for a safe delivery for our twins, and soon after, am shooed gently away from Mr. Berkowitz's apartment.

On the subway home, I'm euphoric. I just followed a rule that maybe five dozen people in America have followed. I'm one of the faithful elite.

But that feeling soon fades to worry. If there is a God, did I just please Him? Or did I maybe get Him angry? If His nest egg rule is meant to teach compassion, wouldn't it been more of a compassionate to not pester the pigeons with a high-wattage flashlight and a crazy dance?

You shall not round off the corner of your head

LEVITICUS 19:27 (JPS)

Day 153. A physical update on my/Jacob's appearance: The beard has gone wild. You can see only about 40 percent of my face nowadays. It's got its disadvantages, of course—my wife now will only kiss me after covering her face with her hands so that only her lips are exposed. But I try to look on the bright side. It's keeping me warm from the wintry New York winds, like a sweater for my cheeks. Plus, it's providing me a level of anonymity. Not that I've ever been mobbed on a subway plat-form by adoring fans. But if I happen to see my former boss on the street, it's nice to know I could stroll by unrecognized.

I've even started to get the occasional positive comment about my looks. The Italian woman who works at the corner deli said she feels more sacred around me, and is afraid to curse or gossip. And my co-worker Tom, whom I hadn't seen in months, said he was all ready to greet me with a one-liner about Mel Gibson's facial hair, then decided he couldn't make a joke because he felt almost reverential. Reverential, that's the word he used. I was on a high for two days afterward.

The beard is the most noticeable, but I'm making other changes to my appearance too. I'm pleased to report I got a new set of tassels. For the first few months, I tried the homemade approach: I attached four tassels from Tassels Without Hassles to my shirt with safety pins. But here was a case where I decided I didn't need to reinvent the wheel: Why not use the prefab tassels known as tzitzit and worn by Orthodox Jews? For about $20, you can get a towel-sized rectangular cloth with four clusters of meticulously-arranged white strings tied on each corner. The cloth has a hole in the middle, and you simply slip the whole thing over your head and wear it under your shirt.

If you're really hardcore, like I'm trying to be, you need to go further. The Bible says you must attach a blue string to your fringes (Numbers 15:38). For centuries, almost all Jews skipped the blue string because no one could figure out the exact shade of blue used in Biblical times. No more. Archaeologists in the last decade have discovered a type of mollusk that the ancient Israelites used for blue dye. The mollusk is still around and still capable of making blue. So for the first time in hundreds of years, a handful of ultra-Orthodox Jews are, once again, wearing four blue strings tied to their fringes. As am I.

And then there's my hairdo, which is starting to take on a personality of its own. The Bible has a lot to say about hair. In general—despite claims to the contrary that I read on a website for pious heavy metal rockers—the Bible comes down on the side of short hair for men.

Consider Absalom, the vain and nefarious prince whose flowing locks got tangled up in an oak tree during battle. They cost him his life. And in the New Testament, the Apostle Paul is even more to the point. He asks: "Does not nature itself teach you that for a man to wear long hair is degrading to him?" (1 Corinthians 11:14).

But what of Samson? Granted, he did lose his superhuman strength after Delilah gave him a haircut—but his is a special case. Samson was part of a holy sect called the Nazirites who took a vow to drink no wine, touch no dead bodies and cut no hair. He broke the vow. He paid the consequences.

I'm no Nazirite, which is why I've been getting monthly haircuts at the local barbershop. Of course, as with everything in my Biblical year, a haircut is not a simple matter. You want your hair mostly short, but a typical Number 4 buzz-cut is out of the question. Leviticus says you are forbidden to chop off the sides.

This led to some extreme micromanagement at the barbershop.

First, I requested for a male haircutter—purity issues. Then, after giving him elaborate pre-trim instructions, I periodically piped up:

"You won't cut the temples, right?"

"I won't cut the temples."

Two minutes later:

"You know not to cut the temples, right?"

"Yes, I know. No cutting the temples."

By the end, I think he was ready to slay me with the jawbone of an ass.

He did tell me he needed to clean up the hair on my neck.

"So you look religious, not dirty," he said. "No offense."

Most Biblical scholars believe the purpose of the uncut side locks was, as with the food laws, to distinguish the Israelites from the pagans. Apparently, the pagans cut and shaved the sides of their hair short, perhaps, says one commentator, to give it the shape of a 'celestial globe,' perhaps as some sort of mourning ritual.

But in Jewish tradition, the hair style has taken on moral significance as well. One man told me that if you pass by a harlot on the road, God will blow your side locks into your eyes to shield you. Another rabbi has said that one day, he will grab hold of them to pull his students out of hell.

The ultra-Orthodox twirl their side locks while praying or studying—resulting in those amazing curly-cue stalactites, frequently as long and thick as rolling pins. The Bible doesn't require this. So I've left my side locks untamed, leading to these odd hair formations that grow upwards and outwards, bringing to mind an ethnic Pippi Longstocking.

> *But to this day the LORD has not given you a mind to understand,*
> *or eyes to see, or ears to hear*
>
> DEUTERONOMY 29:4

Day 154. The more I research these side locks, the more confused I am about whether I've been properly following this commandment. The word 'payot' in Hebrew is often translated 'corners.' Do not cut the corners of your head.

What are the corners of the head? Not being a robot or cartoon sponge, my skull is reasonably ovoid. And if it is corners, shouldn't it four corners? So maybe I should grow sideburns, a rattail and a unicorn-type forelock. Could be interesting. But there's only so much I can subject my wife to. Payot is sometimes translated 'edge.' But this doesn't help much.

The Hasidic-style payot have been around for centuries, but what did they do in Biblical times? Can we ever know? I'm growing more and more skeptical that I'll ever hit Biblical bedrock and discover the original intent. The Bible's meaning is so frustratingly slippery.

Uri told me that the Bible has seventy faces. The ancient rabbis themselves don't even claim to have struck the bedrock. The Talmud—the huge Jewish book with commentaries on Biblical law—is far from black and white. As writer Judith Shulevitz puts it: "You cannot compare the Talmud to, say, the United States civil code, a series of prescriptions issued from Congress, or to Catholic doctrine, which comes directly from the pope. The Talmud is more like the minutes of religious study sessions, except that the hundreds of scholars involved in these sessions were enrolled in a seminar that went on for more than a millennium and touched on every conceivable aspect of life and ritual."

Even more exasperating: if I do get to the bedrock, it may be such strange bedrock that I won't be able to process it. In Karen Armstrong's excellent book A History of God, she says that the ancient Israelites weren't really monotheists. They believed in the existence of many Gods—Baal, El, and so on. It's just that Yahweh is the boss of all Gods. Hence the command "You shall have no other Gods before me." It doesn't say "You shall have no other Gods at all."

Could I ever hope to get into the skull of an ancient Israelite who believed in several gods? Do I want to?

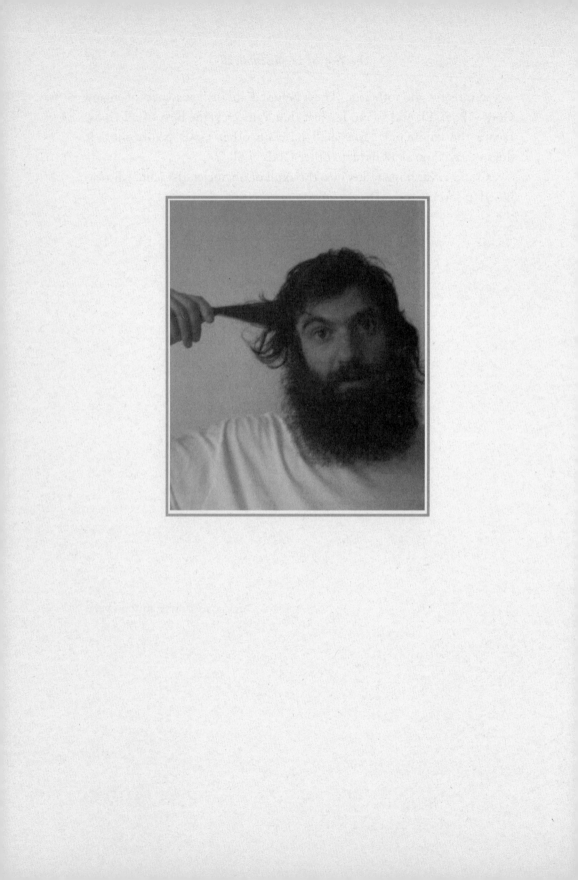

Month Six: February

You shall rise up before the grayheaded and honor the aged
LEV. 19:32 (NASB)

Day 156. I'm currently in Florida. Julie and I have made a trip to Boca Raton for the wedding of Julie's college friend. We got through airport security without a second glance, which made me both happy and slightly concerned about the screeners' competence.

It's the night before the ceremony, and we're at a strip-mall restaurant. It's 5 p.m., Jasper's mealtime. Florida. 5 p.m. dinner. As you can imagine, the average age approached that of a Genesis patriarch—maybe not Methuselah's 969 years, but perhaps Mahalalel, who saw 895 years.

The Bible has a lot to say about your elders. In fact, there's this one law that I keep meaning to abide by, but so far has gotten lost in the avalanche of other rules. It is Leviticus 19:32: we should not only respect our elders, but stand in their presence.

If there's a time to laser in on this rule, it is now. So as we wait for our pasta, I start standing up and sitting down. I pop up every time a gray-haired person enters the restaurant. Which was pretty much every 45 seconds. It looks like I'm playing a solitaire version of musical chairs.

"What are you doing?" asks Julie.

I tell her about Leviticus 19.

"It's very distracting."

I stand up and sit down.

"I thought you had a wedgie," Julie says.

I stand up and sit down.

"Are you going to do this for the rest of the year?"

"I'm going to try," I say. I know I'll fail—there's just too much to remember to follow in Biblical living—but I don't want to admit that yet.

There's a reason the Bible commands us to respect the elderly. According to scholars, the ancient Israelites lived a subsistence-level nomadic life, and the elderly—who couldn't do much heavy lifting—were seen as a liability.

The command seems disturbingly relevant today. After the ancient times, the elderly did have a few good centuries there. Victorian society especially seemed to respect those with white hair and jowls.

But now, we've reverted back to the elderly-as-liability model of Biblical times. This has become increasingly troublesome to me as I speed toward old age myself. I'm 38, which means I'm a few years from my first angioplasty, but—at least in the media business—it's considered ancient. I just hope the 26-year-old editors out there have mercy on me.

And I have pledged to have mercy on those even older than I. A week ago, when I volunteered at the soup kitchen, I sat next to this fellow volunteer, she must be in her 70s. And she complained . . .for half an hour straight. She was like the Fidel Castro of complainers—a never-ending stream of fault-finding. She spent five minutes alone on how the tree roots in her neighborhood make the sidewalk uneven. But instead of trying to stuff my ears, I tried to empathize. Yes, that must be hard. Uneven sidewalks. I never noticed it, but yes, someone could trip.

As Julie and I finish our dinner, we watch an old man get up from his table and shuffle off to the bathroom. He emerges a few minutes later and sits down at an empty table. It is a table two tables away from the table with his wife and kids. He sits there alone for several minutes, his head cocked, staring into the middle-distance. What's going on? Is he mad at his family? I didn't see them fighting. Why his banishment?

Suddenly, the daughter notices her father sitting two tables away.

"Dad!" she calls. "We're over here. Over here!" He looks over, suddenly remembering. He returns to the table, still somewhat dazed.

I turn to Julie. She looks like she's about to cry.

"The standing stuff I could do without. But I think it's good that you're honoring your elders. That's a good thing."

Let your eyes look directly forward,

and your gaze be straight before you.

PROVERBS 4:25

Day 157. My glasses broke today. Jasper grabbed the wire-rimmed frames and stretched out the temples, so the glasses keep slipping off my nose. I'm reduced to keeping my head tilted up at a 45-degree angle as we walk around Boca Raton. My neck is killing me.

Plus, I look arrogant; my nose stuck in the air all day. I wonder if I'm breaking a Biblical rule. I'm not sure. Maybe. In the Talmud, there's a ban against walking more than four cubits in a "jaunty, insolent, upright position," as one translator puts it. This is why you see some old Jewish men and women walk with such a stoop, their hands folded behind their backs. In America, land of Trump and self-esteem, humility isn't much of a virtue. But my ancestors wouldn't even stand up straight for fear of looking boastful.

I keep my chin in the air while watching the wedding the next day. It's a lovely, quiet, outdoor ceremony in a Japanese-style garden. You could barely hear the bride and groom, but it doesn't matter.

I try to not to think about the pro-polygamy parts of the Bible. That would be disrespectful to the event at hand. I try to focus instead on those parts of the Bible that say one wife per husband is a good ratio. In Genesis 2:24—a passage quoted by Jesus—we read about man and woman are not complete until they cleave to one another. They are two halves. Only together can they create a full being.

So you shall do with any lost thing of your brother's,
which he loses and you find

DEUTERONOMY 22:3

Day 161. On the flight back from Florida, I found the checkbook of a Fort Lauderdale woman in the seat pocket in front of me. The Bible says, if your neighbor loses an ox or a sheep—or any thing for that matter—you are to return it to him or her.

So I sent the checkbook back. I felt good, honorable. I'm not a hard-hearted New Yorker: I'm acting with random kindness.

And the beauty part is, it actually worked out to my benefit. She sent me a thank you note (fyi, the stationary had a cartoon of a fat guy wearing an "I'm too sexy for my shirt,"), and enclosed a Starbucks gift card.

The checkbook triumph gives me such a moral high, I use the card to pay for the latte of the guy behind me at Starbucks. I got the idea from a religious website devoted to kindness. Just tell the cashier that three bucks of the next guy's bill is on you.

I am opening out the door, when I hear him call.

"Scuse me," he says. He is about forty, squat, wearing biking shorts despite the chilly weather.

I turn around.

"Did you pay for my coffee?"

"Yes, I did."

"I really don't feel comfortable with that."

I pause. Huh. I didn't know what to do here. Did he think there must be a catch? Did he think I was hitting on him?

"Uh . . ." I say. Then I walk out very quickly out the door and don't look back till I am a block away.

Tell the people of Israel to bring you a red heifer without defect,
in which there is no blemish.

NUMBERS 19:2

Day 165. I finally got a call back from a Mississippi minister I've been trying to reach for weeks.

I want to talk to him about red heifers. The Bible's rule on red heifers makes my list of the Top Five Most Perplexing Commandments. It is found in Numbers 19, and it tells us to purify ourselves by finding red cow. And not just any red cow—it must be a perfect red cow, an unblemished one, and one that has never plowed a field. Once I do this, I have to sacrifice the cow, burn it, mix the ashes with water, and have the resulting blend sprinkled on me by someone holding some hyssop. Only then will I be spiritually clean.

So how do I find an unblemished red cow in Manhattan? Well, I don't. They don't exist here. They don't exist anywhere yet. But maybe soon.

In a handful of ranches across America, there are some people trying to breed just such an animal. The quest has created a bizarre alliance between ultra-fundamentalist Christians and a group of ultra-Orthodox Jews, both of whom see it as a key to the End Times.

The Jews need it because it will make them ritually pure from contact with dead people. Without that, they can't build the Third Temple in Jerusalem. Without the Third Temple, the Jewish Messiah will never come.

The ultra-fundamentalist Christians need it for the same reason. Sort of. To them, the Jewish Messiah will be the false Messiah, the anti-Christ. The true Christ will have an apocalyptic battle with the anti-Christ, which will bring on the 1,000-year reign of peace on earth. The Jews will convert to Christianity or be destroyed.

On and off for the past 20 years, cattle ranchers in Israel, Texas, Nebraska and Mississippi have been trying to breed the ultimate rust-colored cow. It's a lot tougher than it sounds. According to tradition, the cow must be at least three years old and cannot have a single non-red hair. One promising Israeli calf got believers excited a couple of years ago. But in the end, she sprouted white hairs.

The Mississippi minister who called me today is a man named Dean Hubbard, a Kia car salesman, who has been working on the red heifer project for years. He caught me on my cell phone as I was walking out of my building. But I was so eager to talk to him, I didn't want to call him back. I plopped down on a lobby chair and grilled him for an hour, nodding at my neighbors as they passed by.

Dean is hard not to like. He's got a big voice and a big laugh. Dean became a minister in 1974 after he was zapped by 4,600 volts of electricity during a mishap at a radio station. He says God meant for him and me to talk. God has blessed him so far in life. Even when his wife died a few years ago, he says God provided him with another.

"I prayed to God for a new wife. I prayed I don't want a big one. I want a small one—about 5 foot 3. I want her between 50 and 60 years old. I want her cute. And I said, I don't want to go far to find her. I want her to show up in my driveway. I gave God all these criteria. I prayed at 2 in the afternoon—because it says in the Bible that a man needs a female.

And at 7 p.m. that evening I walked to the end of my driveway to my mailbox, and there she was in a tennis skirt carrying a bunch of gardenias."

They are still happily married. And she's still small.

Hubbard works on the red heifer project with a born-again cattle rancher and preacher named Clyde Lott, also of Mississippi. About three years ago, Lott bred one they thought could be unblemished. But there was a problem.

"The thing about Mississippi is we have something called hoof and mouth disease," says Hubbard. "The thing about Israel is there's a coming war. We don't want the cows over there now."

So for safety, they shipped the cow off to Nebraska. Hubbard and Lott believe that the true, world-changing red heifer must be born in Israel, so they are waiting till the political situation calms down before exporting this—or any other—potential red mothers.

Their contact in Israel is a Massachusetts-born rabbi named Chaim Richman. Richman runs the Temple Institute, which is a remarkable place staffed by people who make my ex-uncle Gil look moderate. He and his colleagues are awaiting the establishment of the Third Temple and the restoration of animal sacrifices. They aren't just waiting, though. They're preparing. They have a museum in Jerusalem with dozens of vessels and vestments pre-approved for Temple use. If you want, you can browse the photos online. There's a three-pronged fork for turning over the roasting goats. There's a golden flask, a menorah cleaner and the sacred jewel-bedecked breastplate of the high priest. And so on.

I like Dean, but I'm no fan of his and Chaim Richman's project. It's not just that it's zany—I'm certainly not opposed to occasional zaniness—it's that it's potentially dangerous. If the red heifer arrives, it'll be seen by some as divine permission to build a Third Temple. Where would it go? On the Temple Mount, which is currently controlled by Muslims—home to their sacred Dome of the Rock. Then it really might be the end of the world.

Frankly, the apocalypse sections in the Bible leave me cold. It's one of the few topics in my Biblical year that I can't even begin to wrap my brain around. Not that I don't believe we could be living in the End

Times. I do. I think about it way too much. I worry about which lithium-deprived manic-depressive misfit will finally decide to use the nuclear bomb.

But I don't believe the Bible predicts how the world will finally be destroyed. The main apocalyptic text in the Bible is the Book of Revelation (not Revelations, as I always thought). The writing is poetic, vivid and terrifying. Killer horses with heads like lions and tails like serpents stampede across earth. People are thrown into lakes of fire. The sky opens up like a scroll being unfurled. If it weren't in the public domain, I could see Jerry Bruckheimer optioning it.

How to interpret this notoriously complex text?

A few fundamentalists go with the ultra-literal. In the very near future, just like Revelation says, seven angels will sound seven trumpets. The sun will go black and locusts will cover the earth. A red dragon with seven heads will try to attack the Messiah as a child, but God will save him.

A step down the literalism ladder are those who say that the main points of Revelation are true—the world will end in a battle between Christ and the anti-Christ—but some passages use symbolic language.

For instance: I was watching Pat Robertson's 700 Club—the fundamentalist version of The Today Show—and there was a news story about how the Israeli army is using nano-technology with the hopes of creating "killer bionic hornets". Robertson—actually, it was Robertson's son Gordon, sitting in for Pat—said this was fulfillment of Revelation prophecy. Specifically, the passage about deadly insects:

"And the sound of their wings was as the sound of chariots of many horses running to battle. And they had tails like unto scorpions, and there were stings in their tails: and their power was to hurt men five months."

There are endless examples of this kind of interpretation. The "mountains falling from the sky into the sea" refer to meteors, for instance.

So that's one side. At the other end of the spectrum are the religious moderates who say that no part of the Book of Revelation should be taken literally. And just as important: no part of the Book of Revelation should be taken as a Nostrodamus-like prediction of events in the hazy future. Instead, the Book of Revelation referred to things happening at the time it was written.

In this view, the book is an extended allegory about the persecution of the Christians by the Roman Empire. The seven-headed beast, for instance, is the city of Rome, a reference to the seven hills it was founded on. The elaborate symbolism was partly to avoid censorship, partly because it's a hallmark of a then-flourishing genre called 'apocalyptic literature.'

"To take Revelation literally is entirely missing the point," says Elton Richards, my pastor out to pasture. "It'd be liking taking Aesop's fables as literally true."

Their hearts are far from me . . .

Isaiah 29:13

Day 169. I've taken a step backward again, spiritually speaking. My faith is fragile. Little things jolt me back to pure agnosticism. All that talk of red heifers last week—that did it. As will a story about a suicide bomber, which reminds of religion's dark side. Or even a quote like the one from the philosopher interviewed in The New York Times in which he said that ethical monotheism is the single worst idea that humans have come up with.

If my spirituality could be charted like the Dow Jones, the general trend so far is a gradual rise, but there are many valleys, and I'm in a deep one now. It's making me lazy. I forget to put on my fringes and I tell myself, well, what's the big deal? I'll put them on tomorrow.

I'm still praying several times a day, but when I do, I'm saying the words with as much feeling as I give to a Taco Bell drive-thru order.

I often think of this verse in Isaiah where he lashes out against the Israelite hypocrites.

"Because this people draw near with their mouth
and honor me with their lips,
while their hearts are far from me,
and their fear of me is a commandment of men learned by rote."

That describes me right now.

I even find myself being skeptical of those times when my heart was near to God in the last few months. Perhaps it was an illusion. If I prayed to Zeus every day, would I start to feel a connection to Zeus? And what if I'm drawn to spirituality simply because I'm bored of the dry, dusty rational mindset that I've had these many years. I get bored easily. I can't sit through a sequel to a movie because I'm already bored of the characters. Maybe spirituality attracts me for its novelty factor.

> *O my son Absalom, my son, my son Absalom!*
>
> 2 SAMUEL 18:33

Day 172. Jasper has been suffering from what Julie calls, in honor of my project, a series of minor plagues. Rashes, colds, coughs. And today, he got hit with a bad one. He suffered a major fracture in his left leg.

I was at a meeting when it all went down, but apparently, he stepped on his toy truck the wrong way and snapped his thigh bone. He paused that terrible calm-before-the-storm pause, and then just let out a Category Five wail.

The doctor told us that Jasper must to be a invalid for at least the next six weeks. No playground, no sports, no playdates, no dancing, no walking. Just sitting. A baby Buddhist.

I can't tell you how depressed this makes me. So far, we've been lucky to avoid much time in the hospital with Jasper. And this will, God willing, eventually heal. But Jasper's stunned. He looks beaten for the first time in his life. He looks like Jack Nicholson after getting electroshock therapy in One Flew Over the Cuckoo's Nest.

I got a taste—just a little taste—of what King David meant when his rebellious son Absalom is killed.

> "And the king was deeply moved, and went up to the chamber over the gate, and wept; and as he went, he said, 'O my son Absalom, my son, my son Absalom! Would I had died instead of you, O Absalom, my son, my son!'"
>
> 2 SAMUEL 18:33

As I sit here with Jasper on my lap watching Dora's singing backpack on the TV—it's 2 a.m. and he won't sleep—I waste a lot of time retro-actively bargaining with God about Jasper's leg. It's a habit of mine, this fake bargaining. I say, God, let me break my leg instead of him. I would break both legs. I'd break both legs and both arms. Would I amputate my legs? I don't think so, God. But I'd amputate one toe. Okay, two toes. It's a macabre game, and a waste of God's time.

> *Do not say to your neighbor, "Go, and come back,*
> *And tomorrow I will give it"*
>
> PROVERBS 3:28

Day 177. I may have found a way to help my neighbor Nancy, the self-de-scribed 'kooky dog lady' who lives in apartment 5I. She knocked on my door today.

"Can I ask you a favor?" she says.

"Sure."

I could tell she hated this conversation already. I think she considers it an imposition to ask a waiter for the check, so asking me for a favor kills her.

"But I don't want you to do it because the Bible tells you to. I want you to do it because you want to."

"Okay," I say. "Sometimes I can't tell the difference anymore, but okay."

"I have a book idea."

"Yup."

I guess I should have said something else, because Nancy got skit-tish.

"I don't know." She turned to go away.

I finally squeezed it out of her: Nancy wants to write a book about her life in the sixties. About hanging with the classic rockers—Janis Joplin, Frank Zappa, and especially Jimi Hendrix. She was good friends with Jimi. She sketched him for the cover of one of his albums and col-laborated with him on still-unpublished poems.

"What were the poems about?"

"Hippie stuff. Clouds. Sky. Love. I'll give them to you when I'm done with the book."

"How much have you written?"

"Only fifteen hundred pages. I've got a ways to go."

She smiles. She says she'd always been resistant to writing about her rocker days, but, well, it's been a long time. And frankly, she needs the money.

I tell her I'd be happy to give whatever advice and/or referrals I can. I do want to help. Aside from a few blissful moments in the sixties, Nancy's life has been an unhappy one—an abusive mother, a rough marriage, inability to have kids, a fizzled career. She deserves something good. And if I help her, I will be "making a deposit of righteousness in God's bank," as I heard one preacher say.

But her question also nags me: Am I doing this just because of the Bible Project? Or would I be this eager to help her no matter what?

"In the end, people appreciate frankness more than flattery,"

PROVERBS 28:23. (TLB)

Day 179. I'm still wrestling with the no lying commandment. It's up there with 'no coveting' in the pantheon of difficult rules. But the Bible says to tell the truth, no matter what. People appreciate frankness. I've got to follow the lead of those Biblical heroes take enormous risks to tell the truth.

Consider the prophet Nathan, who confronted King David. It's one of the Bible's most dramatic tales. The background is that David had wronged his loyal soldier Uriah by sleeping with Uriah's wife Bathsheba while Uriah was away at war. David got Bathsheba pregnant. To try to cover up his act, he arranged for Uriah's murder.

So Nathan, one of the wisest people in the kingdom, told David a parable: There's a rich man and a poor man. The rich man has a vast herd of sheep. The poor man owns but one lamb. One day, the rich man gets a visitor. What should he feed him for dinner? The rich man decides to slaughter the poor man's only lamb and serve that for dinner.

When he heard the parable, King David had the reaction most people have: The rich man is a horrible person. He's greedy and pitiless.

At which point Nathan reveals to King David: You are the rich man. Nathan's point was, King David had everything—including eight wives—and still chose to steal Uriah's wife.

Nathan was taking a huge risk—criticizing the king to his face could have backfired. But in this case, the truth worked. King David realized the prophet was right. He had acted evilly.

As you might imagine, I'm not the Prophet Nathan. So far, my truth-telling hasn't laid bare the hypocrisies of great men. But I have managed to my slash my total production of white lies by one third.

Sometimes this works well, other times not so much. Consider tonight. Julie, Jasper and I go for a 5 p.m. dinner at Homer's, a greasy spoon tastefully decorated with a flat-screen TV playing nonstop Nickelodeon.

I'm busy cutting Jasper's hot dog while simultaneously making sure not to touch the skin myself, as it's unclean. At the next table, as at pretty much every other table, is a family. A dad in typical Upper West side khakis, a mom in a pony tail, a three-year-old girl busy with some Crayolas.

"Julie Schoenberg?" says the pony-tailed woman.

It's an acquaintance Julie hasn't seen since college. Hugs are exchanged, compliments toward babies are extended, spouses introduced, mutual friends discussed.

At the end of the meal, we get our check, and Julie's friend says: "We should all get together and have a playdate sometime."

"Absolutely," says Julie.

"Uh, I don't know," I say.

Julie's friend laughs nervously, not sure what to make of that.

Julie glares at me.

"You guys seem nice," I say. "But I don't really want new friends right now. So I think I'll take a pass."

A few weeks ago, I read a book called Radical Honesty about telling the truth in all situations. It talks about the scary thrill of total candor, the Six-Flags-worthy adrenalin rush. I felt that. I heard myself saying the words, but they seemed unreal, like I was in an Off-Broadway production.

Julie is not glaring at me anymore. She's too angry to look in my direction.

"It's just that I don't have enough time to see our old friends, so I don't want to overcommit," I say, shrugging. Hoping to take the edge off, I add: "Just being honest."

"Well, I'd love to see you," says Julie. "A.J. can stay home."

Julie's friend pushes her stroller out of Homer's, shooting a glance over her shoulder as she leaves.

> *And it shall be to you as a sign on your hand*
> *and as a memorial between your eyes*
>
> EXODUS 13:9

Day 180. Today marks the 26th time I've been asked whether I'm going to sacrifice Jasper during my Biblical year. No, I say politely, only Abraham was commanded to do that.

"No binding your son to a rock?" asked David, a friend of Julie's who has drifted slowly towards Orthodox Judaism over the years.

"No binding him."

David clearly knows his stuff: 'the binding' is what some Jewish scholars call Abraham's near-sacrifice of Isaac. Binding, I've noticed, is a huge theme in the Bible. Isaac's is the most famous, but there are plenty of other less violent examples. And those I am trying to do.

Last week, I scratched Deuteronomy 14:25 off my list: you shall bind money to your hand. This is one of the verses that my ex-uncle Gil took literally, and though most take it metaphorically (be careful with your money), I wanted to follow Gil, at least for a day.

When I woke up, I found a rubber band in Julie's desk and used it to strap a five dollar bill on top of my left knuckles. I went about my day— going to the grocery and to Starbucks. It felt like I was tempting fate. New York still has a sizeable crime rate, so this seemed about as clever as walking around Yellowstone with a salmon strapped to my hand. Luckily, despite lingering stares, no one tried to grab my exposed money.

There's another type of binding I've been doing every day. This one comes from Exodus 13:9. It tells us to bind the commandments to my wrist and forehead.

Since I began my year, I've been using this homespun method: I take two Xeroxed copies of the Ten Commandments, fold each to the size of a Polaroid photo, and, every morning, I tie one around my wrist with a white string, the other around my head.

It's been startlingly effective. Just try forgetting about the word of God when it's right in front of your eyeballs, obscuring a chunk of your view. Sometimes I imagine the commandments sinking through my skin and going straight to my brain like some sort of holy nicotine patch. If you look really closely, Thou shalt not steal is branded somewhere on my frontal lobe.

Even after I take off the string for the day (usually at about noon), I still have indentations on my hand and head for hours afterward.

So in that sense, my binding feels good, righteous. But lately, my daily binding has also become tinged with guilt. I feel a tug from my ancestors or conscience or God, that maybe now is the time to try it the traditional Jewish way to bind the commandments to my wrist and forehead. I should try to wrap tefillin.

I had a passing familiarity with the Jewish prayer straps (they're usually called tefillin, but sometimes they're known as phylacteries). When I was 14, on an El-Al flight to Israel, I saw the ritual for the first time: a group of Orthodox Jews stood in aisle with leather boxes on their heads that looked like jeweler's loupes. They wrapped straps, they bounced their heads back and forth, they chanted. It was mystifying and a bit frightening.

My only other brush with tefillin was a book I was sent when I was an editor at Esquire. It was by Leonard Nimoy—Star Trek's Spock himself—who, as it turns out, is also a photographer and a quasi-religious Jew. His book contained racy black-and-white photography of half-nude women wrapped in tefillin, a sort of Mapplethorpe-meets-Talmud motif. (Brief but relevant sidenote: You know Spock's famous split-fingered 'live-long-and-prosper' salute? It's actually a sacred hand signal used by the Jewish priestly class, the Kohanim).

Tefillin have been around a very long time—they found a pair near the Dead Sea in Israel dating to right before the time of Christ. And some believe that Jesus himself put on tefillin every day, though he did criticize the bulky versions worn by the Pharisees.

But what about the origins of tefillin? What did they do in the beginning? In the time of Moses? No one's sure. Biblical scholar Oded Borowski—author of Daily Life in Biblical Times—told me it might have been much more primitive, perhaps a string with a scroll. Others say that perhaps nothing was worn at all: The passage is originally meant metaphorically.

However it started, tefillin has evolved into an enormously intricate ritual. There are dozens of rules, right on down to a ban on passing gas while wearing them.

I would be needing some help. I ask Uri, one of my Orthodox advisers, to be my tefillin-wrapping tutor. He invites me to his house on the Upper West Side. It's late in the afternoon—ideally, tefillin should be wrapped early in the morning, but it's still acceptable to do it now.

Uri welcomes me with a handshake, goes to his closet and takes out a small blue velvet pouch. Inside are two black leather boxes, each with tiny scrolls of scripture inside and leather straps attached.

"Are you right-handed or left-handed?" asks Uri.

"Right."

"Okay, then give me your left arm."

I stick my arm out, palm up, and Uri places the black box on my bicep.

As prescribed by custom, I wrap the band around my arm seven times starting above the elbow and ending at the wrist. Well, actually, I do it five times and then ran out of arm. So I start over, with Uri's help, which wasn't easy for him, as it required him to do reverse wrapping.

"It's like tying a tie on someone else," he says.

He finally wraps it the proper seven times. He points to a part in the prayer book and I read: "Blessed is the Name of His glorious kingdom for ever and ever."

The tefillin is tight, creating six little lumps of forearm. The experience isn't frightening or odd, as I'd imagined. It was more . . .comforting. The wrapped arm reminds me of getting my blood pressure taken, so my unconscious logic probably went like this:

Getting my blood pressure taken is good for me

This feels like I'm getting my blood pressure taken.

Therefore it must be good for me.

Or maybe it's that that it reminds me of getting swaddled. I used to envy Jasper whenever I rolled him into a human burrito in his swaddling blanket. Perhaps this was God swaddling me.

Or maybe it's something about connecting with my father's father. My aunt had recently told me that my grandfather used to wrap tefillin. Which startled me. I knew he was more religious than most of my secular family. But wrapping tefillin? That's seriously religious. And if he did it, you know his dad did it. and so on back for hundreds of years.

As Uri helps me unwind the straps from my arm and head, I feel relief. Not just that I hadn't totally messed up the ritual. But relief that, after trying to do DIY religion for months, I'd finally done it the approved way. The Vilna Gaon would be happy.

It didn't send me into the mystical trance that I seek, but it was far more moving than I thought it'd be. As strange as the ritual is, it also has beauty. As I walk home, I feel my red heifer-inspired skepticism ebb away.

Moses finished writing the words of this law in a book, to the very end

DEUTERONOMY 31:24

Day 181. My Esquire boss just sent me a final version of the article I wrote about the Wikipedia—the online collaborative encyclopedia. I like the Wikipedia, though I do so with much guilt, since it's the enemy of my beloved Britannica.

In any case, I've decided—and my aunt Kate would kill me if she heard this—that the Wikipedia and the Bible have a lot in common. Hardcore believers say that the Bible emerged from God's oven like a fully-baked cake. Or, to be precise, several fully-baked pieces. Moses transcribed the first five books. King David wrote the Psalms. The Gospel of St. Luke was written solely by St. Luke. Every book of the Bible was written by a single author who transcribed God's words.

The alternative is called the Documentary Hypothesis. This says that the Bible has many, many authors and editors. The First five books of Moses didn't come from Moses alone; it's a patchwork from four anonymous writers—they've been named J, P, E, and D. The writers each have their own linguistic quirks and theological passions. P, for instance, short for "Priest", was fascinated by the laws. He wrote the sections on food and sex prohibitions in Leviticus, for instance.

The passages have been chopped and pieced together by various editors. In short, the hypothesis says The Bible has evolved. Like humans themselves. Like a Wikipedia entry.

I believe the Documentary Hypothesis. And as with creationism and evolution, I just can't see myself ever embracing the alternative. I'm too in awe of archaeology and secular historical scholarship to reject it. I'm too attached to the idea that everything has untidy origins.

The challenge is finding meaning, guidance and sacredness in the Bible even if I don't believe God sat behind His big oak desk in heaHEAheaven and dictated the words verbatim to a bunch of flawless secretaries. Or maybe the fundamentalists are right and this is impossible.

For the company of the godless is barren

JOB 15:34

Day 182. I was on the subway today, sitting a few seats down from a Buddhist monk. He looked at me, with my white raiment and bushy beard, I looked at him with his orange robes, and we exchanged a knowing nod and smile.

It was a great moment. I felt like I've been let through the velvet rope at a holy nightclub.

Here, at the halfway mark of my journey, I've had an unexpected mental shift. I feel closer to the ultra-religious New Yorkers than I do the secular. The guy with the fish on his bumper sticker. The black man with the kufi. The Hasidim with their swinging fringes. These are my compatriots. They think about God and faith and prayer all the time, just like I do.

Yes, there's still a difference between me and my alter-ego Jacob—but Jacob is gaining strength. In fact, he's often the dominant one, quizzically observing my secular self. Jacob looks at the world and says Secular people are the freaks, not religious people. How can you NOT think about the Big Questions all the time? How can you put so much energy into caring about earthly matters like basketball games or Esquire's sell-through rates or the divorce proceedings of TV actresses?

I'm still aware of the Bible's crazy parts. I haven't forgotten about the red heifer. But I find myself drawn to look for the Bible's good parts—or at least put the insane parts in context. Yes, it's crazy that I have to grow a huge beard. But if you think about it, it's actually a humane hairstyle. You're not supposed to shave the corners—the payot—the same word used when God tells us to leave the corners of the field unharvested. As with the side locks and the crickets, maybe the beard teaches us to remember the less fortunate.

Last week, as part of my equal time policy, I read Mark Twain's Letters From The Earth. It's both very funny and wildly sacrilegious. At one point, Twain says he doesn't understand why the Bible so despises those who piss against a wall. He's referring to this verse in the King James Bible:

> *"And it came to pass, when he began to reign, as soon as he sat on his throne, that he slew all the house of Baasha: he left him not one that pisseth against a wall, neither of his kinsfolks, nor of his friends." (I Kings 16:11)*

Twain writes: "A person could piss against a tree, he could piss on his mother, he could piss his own breeches and get off, but he must not piss against the wall—that would be going quite too far."

Yet, I knew from my research that "piss against the wall" was an idiom for an adult man, since men would go behind a wall to get a modicum of privacy. Not quite as nonsensical. I want to stick up for the Bible, maybe insert a footnote in Twain's book.

Today, a friend of mine who knows of my Biblical quest sent me a funny email. It's the third time I've gotten this email since I started. Depending on the version, it's either an open letter to conservative Jewish radio host Dr. Laura or else one to a strict evangelical minister. It first started circulating a few years ago, and inspired a scene on the West Wing in which President Bartlett dresses down a barely-disguised fictional version of Dr. Laura.

The email thanks Dr. Laura/the minister for reminding us the Bible condemns homosexuality (Leviticus 18:22). But the writer has some questions.

Should he stone his mother for working on Saturday?

If he sells his daughter into slavery, as sanctioned in Exodus, what would be a good price for her be?

He wants to burn a bull in sacrifice, but what should he do about his pesky, complaining neighbors?

The Bible says we can't touch the corpse of a dead pig. So he should avoid directly touching a football. But can he play football if he wears gloves?

The first time I read this email, I thought: Excellent. What a great critique of those who follow the Bible literally, but haphazardly. It imagines a world of Biblical literalism free from picking and choosing—the world I'm trying to create.

And now, here it is again, for the third time. As always, I was amused, and agreed with the gay rights thesis. But here's the odd thing: I also got a little defensive. I wanted to send the author a note. Yes, the mixing fibers sounds berserk, but maybe the emailer should talk to Mr. Berkowitz about the glory of following things we can't explain.

Also, I know from my encyclopedia-reading days, a football is not made of pigskin anymore. NFL footballs are made of regular old cow hide. And my son's football is some sort of plastic. The email commits the same fallacy that it satirizes—it overliteralizes the word 'pigskin.'

The email did make me think twice about touching pig carcasses. I don't have any pigskin clothes, so that's good. But to be really safe, I'm avoiding playing cards, because they're often made of gelatin, which can be made of pigs. So even if poker didn't lead to greed and coveting, it would be off limits for me.

Month Seven: March

He who winks his eyes plans perverse things
PROVERBS 16:30

Day 184. Julie's dad is visiting from Florida. We're out to dinner at a Chinese restaurant. It's proving to be a trying experience, mostly because her dad—a former software salesman—is indulging his weakness for particularly excruciating puns.

I can't even remember how it came up, but over entrees he punned on the word 'olive' and the first letter of the Hebrew alphabet 'aleph.'

Then he looked at me and winked.

"You know, the Bible is anti-winking," I say.

"Really? What's the origin of that?"

"Not sure."

"Well, when you get down to it, the Bible is all about the prophet motive."

I purse my lips and nod. A little part of me dies.

"Proph-et," he says. "Like the Prophet Elijah."

"I got it."

The Bible's anti-winking bias (there are at least four warnings against winkers) is one of the least-studied scriptural motifs around. I found negligible literature on the topic. But it does seem wise and ahead of its time, the wink being perhaps the world's creepiest gesture, with the winker coercing the winkee into being a part of his little cabal. If the Bible condemned people who call me 'captain' . . . well, a man can dream.

The LORD has made everything for its purpose

PROVERBS 16:4

Day 185. I blew my shofar on the first of the month, and frankly, I'm feeling much better about my skills. Mr. Berkowitz gave me a few pointers—including holding it between your fingers like a giant cigarette—and the shofar has begun to sound respectable. I'm no Miles Davis, but I can hit a couple of clear notes.

Today, we have an appointment at Mount Sinai to get a sonogram. Julie is dreading it. It's not so much a fear of hospitals. It's a fear that we'll find out the twins' genders—and that they'll both be boys. She's wanted a daughter from Day One.

"We'll be fine," I say. "There's a 75 percent chance we'll have at least one girl. My guess is two."

An hour later, the Italian-accented nurse is sliding the microphone-like sonogram gadget over Julie's stomach. She stops on the right side.

"Okay, Baby A is a boy. That's very clear. Baby A is a boy."

Julie starts laughing nervously. She's muttering "Please be a girl Baby B, please be a girl."

The nurse is digging the gadget into the left side.

"And I'm sorry," the nurse says.

At which point, my stomach drops, my pulse triples. What? What's wrong?

"I'm sorry to say that you have two boys. Baby B is a boy."

I'm relieved. For a moment, I thought there was something seriously wrong with Baby B. But the only thing wrong is that he has a Y chromosome.

Julie isn't relieved. Her face crinkles. She starts crying, then sobbing. My relief fades to mild depression.

"I know it's stupid," says Julie. She's caught her breath now. "I'm mad at myself for being so upset. But it's just the finality of it. I'll never have a girl. That's it."

It's true. I love Jasper—but three boys? That's far too much testosterone for a two bedroom New York apartment. That's a future filled with hundreds of lacrosse games and countless hours discussing vehicle parts.

The doctor—a stout fiftyish man—comes in. He sees Julie's wet cheeks.

"I used to do a lot of sex change operations," he chuckles. "I could do one for you guys."

Julie and I don't even so much as smile. This doesn't deter him.

"You know, Daniel is a nice name. A strong name. Dan. Daniel and the lion's den." The doctor's name is Daniel, you see.

Daniel puts some petroleum jelly on Julie's stomach for the sonogram. "Yesterday I used grape. This is raspberry." The guy is relentless.

After the sonogram, Julie and I go out to lunch. We barely talk.

I've got to focus on being thankful. Maybe this is God's will.

"Maybe it's not so bad. Think about My Three Sons," I say. "They seemed happy."

"That doesn't help me," says Julie. "The mother was dead."

We sit silently for another couple of minutes.

"You know what my spiritual adviser Uri would say?"

"What?"

"What seems terrible at first may turn out to be a great thing. You can't predict."

Uri had been talking to me about this to me the other day. We were discussing the Biblical story of Esther. This is the story of a pagan king who went on a kingdom-wide search to find a new queen for himself. He set it up as a beauty pageant, and a surprisingly carnal one. Each contestant would be primped for an entire year—six months with oil of myrrh, six months with perfumes and spices—then be sent in to sleep with the king. The winner—the one the king loved 'above all the women'—was a Jewish exile named Esther. The king crowned her his queen. This mixed marriage would have been viewed with horror by the Jews of the day. But here's the twist: It turned out to be the best thing that could have happened. Because Esther ended up convincing the king to spare the Jews, against the wishes of his evil adviser Haman. Bad can lead to good. We don't know the greater plan.

"I agree with that intellectually," Julie says. "But right now, it's a little hard to swallow."

Yeah. It's not helping me much either.

My mouth is filled with thy praise
And with thy glory all day long.

PSALM 71:8

Day 186. Speaking of Uri, he gave me a stern talking-to today. I was over at his house on the Upper West Side. We sit on a couch in his living room—a room dominated by books. There's a huge set of shelves stuffed with books and pamphlets on whatever Biblical topic you can think of, even the obscure ones like polygamy and sacrifice.

"I love saying prayers of thanksgiving," I said, "because it makes me more grateful for life. But I still have trouble with the prayers where you're glorifying God . . ."

"You're on thin ice there," he said.

He told me: Stop looking at the Bible as a self-help book.

That is the way I view it a lot of the time. I ask myself: How can religion make me more joyous? How can it give my life more meaning? How can it help me raise my son so he won't end up an embezzler or scam artist?

But religion is more than that. It's about serving God.

Uri tells me this story:

Two men do their daily prayers while at work. One spends 20 minutes in his office behind a closed door, and afterwards feels refreshed and uplifted, like he just had a therapy session. The other squeezes a five-minute prayer in between phone calls and does the prayers super-fast in a supply closet.

Who has done the better thing?

"The first," I say.

"No," says Uri. "The second."

The second guy was doing it only for God. He was sacrificing his time. There was no benefit to himself.

I think: That's interesting. Prayers are a good way to teach me the concept of sacrificing my time for the higher good. I'll become a more selfless person. A better person.

And then I realize: I'm back to self-help again. I can't escape it.

I will ask you a question; hide nothing from me.

JEREMIAH 38:14

Day 198. Tuesday morning March 17, I wake up early to make my pilgrimage to the Holy Land. That is if I can get through El Al airline security at Newark.

The security woman—a feisty, olive-skinned Israeli woman who looks like Julia Louis-Dreyfus—grills me but good. I don't fit her into any of her categories—a beard, but not the traditional black hat or coat? So commenced 45 minutes of questions.

"What was your mother's maiden name?"

"Kheel."

"Why do you have such a big beard?"

"I'm writing a book about the Bible, and [here a one-minute summary of my premise]"

"Hmm. Did you celebrate Purim?'

"Technically, it's not mandated by the Bible proper, so no."

"What does the 'J-R' at the end of your name stand for?"

"Junior."

"Why are you a Junior if you're Jewish?"

"My parents weren't so observant."

"Did you have a bar mitzvah?"

"Uh, no."

By the end, my mouth is dry, my palms are damp and I felt like I have just had been on worst first date in history—but for some reason, she lets me board.

Go up to a land flowing with milk and honey

EXODUS 33:3

Day 199. The plane touches down in Tel Aviv, and I hop on the one-hour shuttle bus to Jerusalem with a couple of Scandinavian tourists.

I'm a mess. I'm jetlagged and energized at the same time. And above all, I'm jittery. I'm jittery about meeting Gil. I'm jittery about trying to wrap my brain around this unfathomably historic place in a mere week-long stay. I'm jittery about Jerusalem Syndrome (The bona-fide psychological disorder in which tourists become delusional during their stay in Israel end up wandering the streets in a white gown and spouting moralizing sermons. Among the symptoms: 'the need to scream, shout or sing out loud psalms, verses from the Bible, religious hymns or spirituals." I doubt I'll fall prey to it—I'm too self-controlled—but you never know). And, as I have been since 9/11, I'm jittery about terrorism.

After I check in at the hotel, I meet a friend of a friend—a curly-haired 26-year-old TV producer named Miri—who has agreed to show me around. We go to a café of her choosing, a laid-back place with couches and patterned pillows. I eat pastries and pick her brain about what I should see.

As we leave, she takes me around to the side window of the café.

"I didn't want to show you this before we ate, but do you see this plaque?"

I nod. It's a bronze plaque engraved with a flame and a half-dozen names.

"This is to memorialize the people who died in a terrorist attack here a couple of years ago."

My shoulders tense up. She anticipates my question before I ask it.

"It's not out of the ordinary," she says. "Pretty much all the cafes in this neighborhood have been bombed at one point or another."

She wasn't blasé, but she wasn't overly dramatic either. It's a fact of Jerusalem life; she talked about it with the same tone you'd hear a Los Angelino talking about earthquakes or Alaskans talk about the blizzards. If you love Israel as she does, she tells me, you live with it.

The Lord is my shepherd

PSALM 23:1

Day 200. The next morning, I head off to the Negev desert. That's where I want to go first.

Chronologically, it appears earlier in the Bible than Jerusalem—it's the arid land where Abraham and Isaac once pitched their tents. I'm also hoping it'll get me into the Biblical mindset. I'd been reading about these patriarchs for months. Now I'm going to walk the ground they walked.

I rent a small car from Hertz, get hooked up with a translator by Miri, and we set off at 10 a.m. with two cups of strong Israeli coffee. The landscape gets sparser and sparser. The wind picks up. The street names become more Biblical—Jacob Street and Abraham Street. And then, a couple of hours later, we arrive.

The Negev is an extraordinary place. Step out of your car and look around, and you can visualize what it was like to live in Biblical times. Well, you could if you removed the yellow-and-black camel crossing signs. And the cigarette cases littering the roadside, and the omnipresent electrical wires with weird orange balls on them to keep birds from flying into them.

Over the last three millennia, the desert has become a bit cluttered. But it's still as Biblical a landscape as we have on this earth: dunes that stretch to the horizon, fine sand that coats your mouth whenever there's a gust of wind.

Unfortunately, aside from the view, the trip is turning out to be a bit of a letdown. The best we can muster is a visit to a Bedouin Museum, which had a faux Bedouin tent that felt too sterile and orderly, like an ancient room at the Ramada Inn.

We are actually heading back to Jerusalem when we spot the thing that will save us. On the right side of a twisty, empty road: A flock of sheep. And a shepherd.

As even the most casual Bible reader knows, sheep and shepherding imagery pervades the Scriptures. The 23rd Psalm talks about the Lord as shepherd. Exodus compares the Israelites to a flock of sheep. Jesus is the lamb of God. Plus, most of the patriarchs were shepherds at one time: Jacob, Moses, King David.

So lambs have been very much on my mind. (My strangest lamb sighting before this: At a Judaica store on the west side, there was a kids' video of a Passover dinner with Dom DeLuise, Shari Lewis, and the sock-puppet Lamb Chop, which must have been disturbing for Lamb Chop, seeing as lamb shank is a Seder staple). But here, finally, was the real thing.

The shepherd is a Bedouin man in his twenties wearing a red sweater and an orange jacket. He is shy and quiet, but in keeping with Middle

Eastern hospitality, he invites me to tend with him.

We stand side by side, watching the sheep graze. I expected shepherding to be a silent occupation, but it's not. The sound of 200 sheep chomping grass is surprisingly noisy. And that's not to mention the constant b-a-a-a-ing. And lambs do say just that: "B-a-a-a-a-a." It reminds me of how Julie sneezes; she lets out an "Ah-choo!" as if she's reading from a script.

The shepherd does not have a flute or harp or staff (the hook-shaped instrument). But he does have a rod. He carries a black rubber tube that looks like it might have once been part of a tractor.

I ask through the translator: "What do you do with the rod?"

"It's just for appearance," he admits.

I love that. Even shepherds are concerned with superficial things.

I ask him a few other questions.

"How long have you been doing this?"

"Two years."

"Is the black sheep really rebellious?"

"No, it acts the same way as the white sheep."

"Do you like being a shepherd?"

"Yes, very much."

And then the conversation dies. Which is a relief to him, and okay by me. We just stroll along silently, listening to the chomping and b-a-a-aing.

My mind is uncluttered, settled, still. At least for a few minutes, the separation between me and my Biblical alter-ego Jacob dissolves. Theoretically, if God is everywhere, then he should be just as present in a New York forklift as he is in an Israeli sheep pasture. But what can I say? Maybe I lack vision, but the idea of God is just easier to sense out here, away from the beeping of backing-up trucks and the sight of gym posters.

Occasionally, one of the sheep strays too far away. The shepherd teaches me to chuck a rock near it to get it to return to the flock. It's the method that's been in use since the days of King David, which is how David was so adept at embedding a rock in Goliath's forehead.

Perhaps the biggest revelation from my afternoon of shepherding is this: It's astoundingly good for your confidence. I have minimal management skills, but even I could handle a couple of hundred sheep. Because in addition to "ba-a-a-ing," sheep fulfill another stereotype: They are sheepish. A loud "Hey" or a tossed stone, and the sheep fall right into place. Everyone can be a Jack Welch on the pasture. You can see why shepherding was the ideal first job for patriarchs. There's a reason Moses led sheep before leading the Israelites out of bondage.

> *It is not good that the man should be alone*
>
> GENESIS 2:18

Day 201. If the desert is relatively empty (not counting the accumulating 21st-century detritus), then Jerusalem is the most packed place I've ever been. Every square inch seems drenched with people, history and religion.

This afternoon, as I was walking along some twisty cobblestone streets of the Old City, I turned a corner and witnessed what has to be the highest density of spiritual devoutness on planet earth. The scene was this:

Dozens of brown-robed, hooded Franciscan friars are slowly, solemnly walking the stations of the cross. They are singing Ave Maria, accompanied by a single-speaker boombox strapped over the right shoulder of one friar. Another friar is swinging a miniature umbrella in the exact same way that altar boys swing incense lamps.

Then, slicing through the crowd of friars comes a family of Orthodox Jews. The father—his head topped by a brown fur cap the size of a manhole cover—leads the way, with eight Hasidic children trailing behind in single file. And, at that same moment, mingling with the Ave Maria, comes the Muslim call to prayer over a tinny loudspeaker. An Arab man with a fez edges past the Hasidic Jew. All three Abrahamic faiths intersecting on the same street.

It's an astounding sight. And it makes me feel more alone than I've felt since Project Bible began.

Here I am, a stranger in a strange land, away from my wife and child, in a city where everyone belongs to his or her own gated spiritual community.

It drives home a disturbing point: My quest is a paradoxical one. I'm trying to fly solo on a route that was specifically designed for a crowd. As one of my spiritual advisers, David Bossman, a religion professor at Seton Hall University, told me:

"The people of the Bible were groupies. You did what the group does, you observed the customs of your group. Only the crazy Europeans came up with the idea of individualism. So what you're doing is a modern phenomenon."

I've loved that crazy European individualism all my life. To use author Robert Putnam's phrase, I bowl alone, and I've always preferred it that way. It gives me more control, or at least the illusion of it. It's made me resistant to joining anything. No frats, no Rotary clubs, not even the Kiss Army when I was a kid.

This year, I've tried to worship alone and find meaning alone. The solitary approach has its advantages—I like trying to figure it out myself. I like reading the holy words unfiltered by layers of interpretation. But going it alone also has limits, and big ones. I miss out on the feeling of belonging, which is a key part of religion. I experienced this most keenly once before—during the biblical holidays of Yom Kippur and Rosh Hashanah back in October. I tried to do them alone—I fasted. I ate sweets. I sent portions to the poor. But I was doing it cluelessly and by myself, and it felt empty. I couldn't even bring myself to write a chapter on them, because I failed to wring anything approaching the proper level of meaning from them. And many of my more profound experiences have come when I've joined a group, even momentarily, whether that group be huge (the Hasidic dance party) or small (Amos, Julie and I singing 'Amazing Grace').

Maybe I have to dial back my fetishizing of individualism. It'd be a good thing to do. the age of radical individualism is waning anyway. My guess is, the world is going the way of the Wikipedia. Everything will be collaborative. My next book will have 258 co-authors.

You shall surely tithe all the produce

DEUTERONOMY 14:22 (NASB)

Day 204. Before I left for Israel, my adviser Uri had given me a list of commandments that—according to traditional Judaism—can only be fulfilled in the homeland. Many involved sacrificing animals. But one was relatively nonviolent: tithing fruit.

Today, I spend a couple of shekels for an orange at an Israeli farmer's market. Outside the fruit market, I meet a man named David. He is a portly guy in a Gilligan-style hat who is reading passages aloud from the Bible. I can't remember the exact passage, but I know it involved the word 'harlotry.' His audience consists of me and a tall guy in ripped jeans.

David seems like a good candidate.

"I want to give you 10 percent of my fruit," I say. "I need to give it to my fellow man on the street."

"Oh, you're tithing?" David knew all about this, and thought this was a good idea. "Problem is," he says. "I don't eat oranges. Give it to Lev here." He motions at the tall guy.

Lev is unsure.

"Come on!" says David. "He can't eat the orange unless you take a tenth of it."

"Fine," says Lev.

So I peel the orange and, with my index finger, dug out two sections.

"Here you go!"

Lev recoils. Understandable, actually. I wouldn't take a manhandled orange slice from a stranger.

"Take it!" urges David.

Lev thinks about it.

"How about I take the 90 percent and you take the 10 percent."

He's not kidding. I agree and keep the small chunk for myself. It's true, what they say. Everything's a negotiation in the Middle East.

But a Samaritan, as he journeyed, came to where he was; and when he saw
him, he had compassion,

LUKE 10:33

The next day, I climb into a small Israeli cab to go visit a Samaritan. Before my project, I figured I'd have to climb into a time machine to visit a Samaritan. I assumed they had gone the way of the Hittites and Canaanites and other long-lost Biblical tribes. But no, the Samaritans are still around 21 centuries later.

The Samaritans get a couple of brief mentions in the Hebrew Scriptures, but they are far more famous for their role in Jesus' parable. When Jesus is asked by a Pharisee 'who is my neighbor,' he answers:

A man was going down from Jerusalem to Jericho, and he fell among robbers, who stripped him and beat him, and departed, leaving him half dead.

Now by chance a priest was going down that road; and when he saw him he passed by on the other side.

So likewise a Levite, when he came to the place and saw him, passed by on the other side. But a Samaritan, as he journeyed, came to where he was; and when he saw him, he had compassion, and went to him and bound up his wounds, pouring on oil and wine; then he set him on his own beast and brought him to an inn, and took care of him.

It's a powerful story—all the more powerful when you understand the historical context. The Judeans and the Samaritans hated each other, so the idea of a Samaritan helping this man deliberately shocking, like a modern-day Hezbollah fighter tending to an Israeli soldier.

The Samaritans are particularly relevant to my quest because they lean towards Biblical literalism. They disregard the interpretations of the rabbis in mainstream Judaism and place great—if not exclusive—emphasis on the Bible itself.

So I called Benyamin Tsedaka, the community's unofficial spokesman—he edits the Samaritan newspaper—and he has invited me to his home outside Tel Aviv. He's waiting in his front yard when the cab pulls up.

"Tell me your name again?" asks Benyamin.

"It's A.J."

"Ah. Like C.J. on Baywatch."

This took me aback. I knew that, at one time, Baywatch was beamed to all of earth's seven continents, but it was still a bit startling. Here was a member of the Samaritans, the most ancient surviving Biblical tribe, and the first words out of his mouth are about TV's top-heavy harlot

Pamela Anderson?

"I think that is a good ice-breaker," says Benyamin. He laughs.

"Yes, a good ice breaker," I agree.

Benyamin, 62, has gray hair combed straight back, a neatly trimmed white moustache and a thick accent. He's wearing a gray skirt down to his ankles, the traditional Samaritan dress for the Sabbath, which he has kept on in my honor. His apartment feels clean, modern; it somehow reminds me of a middle eastern version of my late grandmother's condo in Century Village. As with everyone I've visited so far, Benyamin offers food and drink moments after I enter his door. He brings out a pot of tea and a plate of Samaritan cookies that look like madeleines, but taste more spicy than sweet.

We wander around his apartment, looking at the gallery of Samaritan photos on his wall. I stop at a photo of a group of Samaritans gathered on top of a mountain. The men are wearing white suits and white fezzes.

"That's the entire Samaritan community in 1914. One hundred forty six people."

The current population has grown to all of 700 Samaritans, he says. Which is still an astounding statistic. Seven hundred people. His whole ethnic group could be comfortably seated in a high school auditorium.

Think of it this way: Benyamin tells me about how a Samaritan mother gave birth to severely premature twins. They survived—but if they had died, Benyamin said, it would have been the equivalent of "wiping out your Kansas City."

The 700 remaining Samaritans either live near Benyamin—in a city called Holon—or in the West Bank. Neither Israeli nor Palestinian, they feel slightly out of place in modern-day Israel, trying to remain friendly with both sides. As Benyamin puts it, "We dodge the political raindrops."

They weren't always such a minority. The Samaritans—who trace their descent to ancient Samaria, which was in Northern Israel—reached a peak in the fourth century with more than a million followers. They were wiped out in the centuries that followed by Romans, Ottomans and the plague. Benyamin and his fellow Samaritans believe they are one of the lost tribes of Israel, upholding the true Biblical tradition.

"Should we take a walk?" asks Benyamin.

We step outside and into the Samaritan enclave—a quiet little maze of backstreets. We see no one except for a half-dozen teenagers playing soccer and a neighbor out for a late-night errand. Benyamin points out that each house has a stone tablet with a Biblical passage written on it next to its door.

About three blocks from Benyamin's house, we arrive at the Samaritan temple—a squat structure—which is closed for night. But inside, says Benyamin, is the Samaritan Bible.

It's a fascinating thing, the Samaritan Bible. Because it's almost exactly like the Judeo-Christian Bible—with one key difference. The Ten Commandments aren't the Ten we know. Instead, one of the commandments is to build an altar on Mount Gerizim, which is located on the West Bank. To the Samaritans, Mount Gerizim is the most sacred place in the world, the one where Noah beached his ark, where Abraham nearly sacrificed his son.

To this day, it is the place for their annual lamb sacrifice. Yes, unlike the Jews, the Samaritans still practice animal sacrifice. Every year on their Passover, the head of each Samaritan household slits the throat of a sheep. Then all the sheep—about 40 of them—are skinned, put on stakes and roasted over pits for eating.

"It's a beautiful ceremony," says Benyamin. "The smell is delicious. It's next week—you should come."

I had enough trouble with the chickens.

"I'll be back in New York, I'm afraid."

We get back to the house, Benyamin introduces me to his wife, a short-haired woman who, frankly, doesn't seem in the mood to chat with me. She nods her head, and that's about it.

Benyamin's wife was a convert from Judaism. Apparently, there are a few Jewish women who convert, but not too many. As one commentator points out, the Samaritans' super-strict menstruation laws are a hard sell.

"In the Torah, a woman in her period has to be departed," says Benyamin. So there is a special room in the house. "My wife has her own TV and small refrigerator. It's like a hotel room."

Can she come out?

"Yes, and we can talk, but not face to face, because of the saliva. And we do talk. Mostly about my cooking."

Benyamin has to cook the meals, since his wife cannot touch the food. Benyamin tries to put a positive spin on it: It's a vacation for the women from household chores.

"Fifty years ago, there was a special tent for the women. And I believe it was the happiest tent in the camp."

I still have trouble accepting the menstrual laws, whether Jewish or Samaritan.

Before I leave, I ask the obvious question: What do the Samaritans think about the parable of Good Samaritan? Well, not surprisingly: They don't object. They like it. There was even a Good Samaritan coffee shop in the West Bank.

Benyamin tells me he has given Jesus' parable a lot of thought, and has his own take on it:

It was autobiographical. Benyamin believes that the wounded man is meant to represent Jesus himself. And Jesus chose to have a Samaritan rescue him because he'd had a good experience in Samaria. When Jesus fled the Pharisees and passed through Samaria, the locals treated him kindly and gave him water (John 4).

On the cabride back to the hotel, I can't stop thinking about the Samaritan Bible. So similar, but so different too. What if history had taken a left turn? What if the Samaritan Torah had become the standard, and millions of Semitic faithful flooded to Mount Gerizim every year to sacrifice lambs, except for a few hundred people called the Jews who worshiped at an obscure site known as the Western Wall?

> *I give thanks to thee, O Lord my God, with my whole heart,*
> *and I will glorify thy name for ever.*
>
> PSALM 86:12

Day 207. I can't stop thinking about the two praying guys in Uri's story—the one who emerges refreshed and the one who emerges more harried than before. Sometimes I'm the first guy, sometimes the second.

Today I'm taking a rest from a walk on a set of stairs near the Jaffa

Gate. Or maybe near Lion's Gate. I'm not sure. Frankly, I'm lost. But I'm resting here on the stone steps, which are cool and shaded and have a bumpy surface that makes it look like a Rice Krispie treat.

I have my head bowed, and my eyes closed. I'm trying to pray, but my mind is wandering. I can't settle it down. It wanders over to an Esquire article I just wrote. It wasn't half-bad, I think to myself. I liked that turn of phrase in the first paragraph.

And then I am hit with a realization. And hit is the right word—it felt like a punch to my stomach. Here I am being prideful about creating an article in a mid-sized American magazine. But God—if He exists—he created the world. He created flamingos and supernovas and geysers and beetles and the stones for these steps I'm sitting on.

"Praise the Lord," I say out loud.

I'd always found the praising God parts of the Bible and my prayer books awkward. The sentences about the All-Powerful, All-Mighty, All-Knowing, the Host of Hosts, He who has Greatness beyond our Comprehension. I'm not used to talking like that. It's so over the top. I'm used to understatement and hedging and irony. And why would God need to be praised in the first place? God shouldn't be insecure. He's the ultimate being.

Now I'm starting to see why. It's not for him. It's for us. It takes you out of yourself and your prideful little brain.

Therefore the people of Israel shall keep the Sabbath

Exodus 31:16

Day 208. As I ambled to a café near the hotel for a bagel, I realize something: walking around Jerusalem in my Biblical persona is at once freeing and vaguely disappointing.

In New York—even though it's home to the Naked Cowboy and Gene Shalit—I'm still unusual enough to stand out. But in Israel, I'm just one of the messianic crowd. A guy with strange outfits and unusual facial hair? Big deal. Seen three dozen today. Jerusalem is like the Galapagos Islands of religion—you can't open your eyes without spotting an exotic creature.

Speaking of which, it's Friday. The day I'm finally going to meet him, the most exotic creature of my family, the official black sheep, the man who gave me the germ of the idea for this book: Guru Gil.

When I called up Guru Gil a couple of weeks ago, he said he wanted to meet me at the Western Wall, the holiest site for Jews in Jerusalem. He's there every day.

I get there on a drizzly, chilly Friday afternoon. It's an amazing place: dozens of mostly Orthodox Jews chanting and swaying, their fringes swinging, some so deep in ecstatic prayer they are clenching their fists and shuddering. It's impossible not to be moved by the combined kilowatts of faith.

Gil is nowhere to be found. When I ask his whereabouts, I discover that my family isn't the only one with mixed feelings about Gil. An Orthodox man from the Netherlands tells me that he and Gil no longer speak. What's the feud about? He won't say. But whatever Gil did, he did "these things AGAIN and AGAIN and AGAIN!"

Finally, I spot Gil. I recognize him from the many, many photos on the cover of his book. He's walking down the steps, his long beard forked in half by a headwind, a big white tuft blowing over each shoulder.

"Gil? It's A.J. Jacobs."

"You're A.J? You look so religious," he says, eyeing my beard. "I was expecting something else."

"Well, it's not as long as yours."

"You'll get there," says Gil.

He's smaller than I thought. Somehow, in my mind, thanks to years of family legends, he had grown into a Paul Bunyan-esque super-Jew. But in real life, he's far south of six feet. And with the beard, he looks his 60 years.

I tell him I'm in the middle of reading his book.

"In the middle of it? Well, you're the first person to ever put it down."

I can't tell if he's joking or if he's actually offended.

He grabs a chair and a prayer book and we sit down to worship next to the 60-foot wall. It turns out that this is Gil's second trip to the wall today. Every day, he wakes up at 1:45 a.m., takes a ritual bath, then arrives at the wall at 3 a.m. He stays there for a few hours, wrapping tefillin—the leather prayer straps—on willing tourists, then goes home for study, only to return in the afternoon. If you think, as I did, 1:45 a.m.

is an ungodly hour, you'd be wrong. At least according to Gil, the most
spiritual time of day is midnight to eight.

After an hour or so of prayers, we head back to Gil's apartment for
Shabbat dinner. His guests arrive a few minutes later.

"Come in and sit down," he says sternly. "You're late."

Gil's dinner is quasi-famous, a minor tourist attraction for students
and seekers. Tonight we've got a couple of Russian yeshiva students, a
pair of rabbi's daughters from Jersey, an Orthodox shrink and his wife,
and this spaced-out Berkeley dude in a rainbow-colored yarmulke. Gil
warned the Berkeley dude not to hit on the rabbi's daughters or "I'll
break both your legs."

"Hello?" shouts Gil, after we're seated. "Shut up! Earth to people!
Earth to people!"

We stop chattering. Time for the ground rules.

"Whoever asks the most questions gets the biggest dessert. But they
have to be good questions. They can't be 'What's for dessert.'"

Gil runs the dinner like he's still head of his yurt cult in upstate New
York. Though nowadays he talks. And during two minutes of the intro-
ductory prayers, no one else does—or else you have to go wash your
hands, as required by Orthodox custom.

He looks at the Berkeley dude.

"Are you going to talk?"

"Uh..no."

"You just did. Go wash your hands."

The Berkeley dude is already walking on eggshells. He was the first
one there, and made the mistake of touching his cutlery prematurely,
prompting Gil to snap "Stop with the plates, stop with the spoon, knock
it off!"

Not wanting to make eye contact, I glance at the surroundings. The
dining room table takes up most of the floor space. The walls are filled
with photos of rabbis—as well as a shot of Gil playing a . . . 10-string
harp. Yes, one alarmingly like mine. Gil tells me later he designed the
harp himself. "I based the notes on the sounds of a Hawaiian waterfall,"
he says.

One of Gil's big themes is that everything has a reason. Julie has the
same point of view, but Gil takes it to the extreme: Absolutely nothing is

an accident. A few years ago, he tells us, he got bird droppings on his tefillin. He was devastated. "I thought, God hates me! He hates my prayers. All these years I've been trying to please him, this is how he feels about me." He took the tefillin to an expert, and it turns out one of the parchments was upside down. God didn't hate him—He was just letting him know.

Each of the Bible's laws has a reason too. A perfectly rational explanation.

"I thought some of them we don't know the reason for," I say.

"Whoever told you that wasn't a deep person," says Gil.

And the little rules are just as important as the big ones.

"If you were in medical school to study brain surgery, would you want to follow all the rules? Or just the 'main ones?'" says Gil.

The rabbi's daughter has a question:

"Why is it important for a guy to have a beard?"

"Because Abraham had a beard."

"He also had two wives," replies the rabbi's daughter.

"I beg your pardon. One was a concubine."

"Solomon had 700 wives," I pipe up.

"Shut up," says Gil. "In those days you could. But since it was going to be forbidden later, Jacob was buried with Rachel, not his other wives."

The rabbi's daughter isn't satisfied. Gil tries again:

"If you see a guy with a long beard, you know he's not a warrior. There's no way. You can't fight with one of these things. The first they'd do is grab your beard. It's a handle on your head."

That is one I hadn't heard. Gil takes a big swig of his red wine, about half of which dribbles into his beard. He gets up to clear the first course, a vegetable soup. The chatter at the table devolves to who-we-know-in-common. Gil comes back. He is not well-pleased.

"Only holy topics!"

"But what is holy?" says one of the Russians. "Every topic can be holy."

This guy had given Gil some lip earlier in the night—he kept asking to sing a Russian song—and now Gil has had enough.

"You have no idea how hot things can get around here," Gil thunders. "One time, I had a guy from a yeshiva sitting right over there, and he was giving me a hard time. And I said,

'Look, I have two black belts in judo.'

And you know what the guy says?

'Oh yeah? I know martial arts too.'

So I jump up and grab him in a chokehold and he turns blue in the face and goes 'ahhhggghghh'. And I let go, and from then on, he was the sweetest guest I ever had.

Don't . . .push . . .the . . .buttons, kid. Okay?"

The Russian says nothing.

I decide Gil's shtick is part bully, part Vaudeville, part charismatic leader. He's an ultra-religious Donald Trump, and this is his board room. Maybe because I'm ex-family, I never get fully shellacked. He doesn't call me "klutz" or "idiot," as he does the others. The most I got is a "Bozo!" when I washed my hands wrong.

I can see how he was a cult leader. You can't take your eyes off of him. When he's telling a story, he'll jump out of his wicker chair to preach an important point. He'll laugh for no apparent reason—during prayers, he just started giggling, his face reddening, apparently filled with the joy of God. He also weeps. He was talking about a rabbi he knew, stopped mid-sentence, looked away, and cried for a good minute, as the rest of us silently contemplated our wine glasses.

He talks about his days as a cult leader only occasionally. At one point, he grouses about the burden of having 40 servants. "You know what I said every day? God get them out of here! What a pain in the tuchus to have to tell 40 people what to do."

When he finds out that one of the girls speaks American Sign Language, he boasts of the sign language he invented as a cult leader—and how it swept New York in the 1970s.

"I found a lot of my signs were the same as deaf sign language. Like the word 'understand.'"

Gil puts two of his fingers on his palm.

"You just did the sign for 'toast,'" says the girl.

Gil shrugs.

"Well, it wasn't the most important thing I invented in my life."

At about 9 p.m., Gil says it's nearing his bedtime, so we say the final prayers, and pass around a cup of water for hand-washing. At least the men did. When the shrink's wife tries to, Gil explodes.

"Ahhhhhhh! Ahhhh!! No woman will wash hands at my table!!!"

Gil is not a feminist. He calms down, tries to soften it.

"No foxy woman anyway. A short, fat woman, yes."

I look at the shrink's wife, a fiftyish woman who resembles Seinfeld's sitcom mother. She isn't in the traditional sense foxy.

"Why not women?" she asks.

"Because you'll give this guy bad dreams!" says Gil.

He points at me. I smile weakly.

After the handwashing incident, I get ready to go. Gil grabs my hand, looks me in the eyes and says "I love you." Oh man, my family would have a heart attack if they heard that one. How to respond?

"Uh . . . thanks for dinner!" I say.

As I walked down the cobblestone streets of the Old City, I remembered that Gil, when he first met my aunt Kate at a party, said those same words: "I love you." I can understand my grandfather's alarm. I sure wouldn't want my daughter marrying the Guru Gil of the 21st century.

Granted, he didn't end up strangling that Russian. In fact, he seems to me more of a religious clown than a felon. And I even agreed with a couple of his teachings. This one seemed kind of wise: "Whenever you're sad, things aren't working out for you, look around, see if there's someone else in trouble, go and help them. And I promise you I promise you I promise you, your problems will be solved."

But overall, what I found offensive and subtly dangerous about Gil was that he claimed to have all the answers. As he reminded me several times. "I'm glad you found me," he said. "Because I have all the answers." And later: "If you have an questions, call Gil. Others will lead you astray."

He's a spokesman for the arrogant side of religion. My favorite parts of the Bible are the ones that take the complete opposite tack, that admit that we don't know everything, that stress the mystery of God and the universe. Like Ecclesiastes says:

For who knows what is good for man while he lives the few days of his vain life, which he passes like a shadow? For who can tell man what will be after him under the sun?

Month Eight: April

Let my people go

Day 216. I've been home for a week. Julie's still recovering from her stint as a solo mom, and I'm still trying to decompress from Israel.

Israel was so intense, I need a week of as little activity as possible. I've been spending a lot of time slack-jawed on the couch watching Scripture-themed movies. Julie ordered me Charlton Heston's The Ten Commandments on Netflix. Man, I hadn't remembered it being quite so gloriously cheesy as it is. God sounds like Darth Vader. The seductive, bare-midriffed Egyptian dancers look like they strayed off the set of Elvis' Clambake. And director Cecille B Demille is the most un-humble man in the world. Just in case there was any question of who is responsible for this masterpiece, he fills the screen with DIRECTED BY CECIL B. DEMILLE in 8,000-point font. He gets higher billing than God.

It's a nice break from ruminating about Israel. Because Israel has got me tied up in knots. On the good side, it can humble you. Even physically it humbles you. The vastness of the desert humbles you. The height of the Wailing Wall humbles you. The echoing interior of the Church of the Holy Sepulchre humbles you. And the history. All those millions of seekers who have walked the exact same cobblestone streets asking the exact same questions—it's hard not to feel like you're part of something much larger than yourself.

But Israel can also be dangerous. It can bring out the fundamentalist in all of us. It can bring out everyone's inner Guru Gil. It can nurture your self-righteous side. I saw this even as I took the cab back from Newark Airport. I looked at the pedestrians yammering away on their cell phones, no doubt speaking evil tongue and coveting. Ugh. I'm not like that, I tell myself. I'm so much more Biblical than these people. These secular losers. Which, I know, is a completely un-Biblical way to think.

You shall not harden your heart or shut your hand against your poor brother,

DEUTERONOMY 15:7

Day 219. One unavoidable side effect of Biblical living: You think a lot about your forefathers. In my case, I find myself fascinated with my father's father.

My grandfather—who died when I was in high school—wore a gray fedora and lived by the Hudson river in an apartment with a plastic-covered couch. I remember him being perhaps the gentlest man I've ever met, a man who spoke so quietly you'd have to lean forward to hear.

And I remember him giving money away. Whenever we'd go for a walk—which usually meant we were either traveling to or returning from moo shoo chicken at Szechwan Palace—we'd inevitably pass a homeless person, and my grandfather would inevitably fish a couple of quarters out of his pocket. No doubt it was a reaction to his past. He grew up in a tenement on the Lower East Side. He'd never tell you, but his stepmother—a woman straight out of Grimm's—kept a lock on the icebox so that my grandfather wouldn't try to sneak an extra slice of bread.

I'm waiting on the subway platform for the downtown B train, trying not to get annoyed that express trains kept whooshing by while the local was MIA. About twenty feet away, I spot a woman in an Adidas T-shirt and blue jeans. She is working the platform, going from commuter to commuter asking for change.

She is making absolutely no headway. These people have perfected the art of ignoring the homeless. Their body language is very clear: "I am unable look up for even a second because I am so deeply involved in observing this discarded Tropicana pineapple juice carton on the track." It's heartbreaking.

The homeless woman does her best—she stares at them, open-palmed for a good half-minute, then moves on. She comes to me. I am

Biblically obligated to give, so I take out my wallet and hand her a dollar. She takes the money and smiles. I feel good.

And then she throws open her arms for a hug. I wasn't expecting that. As a germaphobe, I've never been a hugger. More of a polite nodder. And with my Biblical living, I've become even leerier of hugs, seeing as the Hebrew Scriptures caution against touching women. But what am I going to do? Be a callous schmuck? I hug her.

At which point she goes for a kiss. I swivel my head in time so she missed my lips and got my cheek.

She steps back and looks at me.

"Did you just take advantage of me?"

I laugh nervously. "No."

"I think you took advantage of me. I think you made a pass at me."

More nervous laughter from me.

"I'm going to report you!" she says, her voice rising. She isn't smiling. She just glowers at me as I sputter denials and apologies for any misunderstanding.

By this time, most of the commuters have stopped reading their papers to check out this grabby, hirsute, fringe-wearing pervert.

"I'm going to report you," she repeats.

The C train comes. It's not the train I needed, but close enough for me. "Sorry, I have to go."

As I sit down, I look out the window nervously to see if the Adidas woman is following me. She isn't. She is, instead, cracking up—having a good, stomach-clutching laugh. She'd been playing me. She'd honed in on a lanky guy with a beard, and decided to spice up her day. Can't blame her for that. Maybe it was an even better gift than the dollar.

A false balance is an abomination to the LORD,
but a just weight is his delight.

PROVERBS 11:1

Day 220. Julie is feeling slightly better about the impending three-sons situation. Part of her problem had been that the male/female ratio in our house will be 4:1 She'd be outnumbered. She'll be the One Who Doesn't

Belong.

As self-prescribed therapy, she's made a big list of sons who treat their mothers well. And conversely, another big list of sons who have terrible relationships with their dads. She consults this list often. This doesn't seem quite Biblical. But I'm not about to stop her. In fact, I decide to throw in a couple of dysfunctional father-son Bible stories to help her cause.

"Absalom led a rebellion against his father King David," I tell her.

"Okay," she says.

"And you know Reuben?"

"The firstborn son of Jacob," she says. (Julie's favorite musical is Joseph and the Amazing Technicolor Dreamcoat).

"Well, he slept with his father's concubine. He repented—in fact, he's the first person in the Bible to repent. But he still got punished. He still lost his birthright."

By the way, I can't tell you the number of people who try to console us by telling her that, with our three boys, we start our own team. They never say what kind of team. Three-man bobsled? Curling? The options seem somewhat limited.

Julie's also feeling better because she's been able to avoid getting too huge, at least so far. Her legs, arms and face look remarkably unbloated. Her stomach, though, is hard to ignore. It looks like she ate a wrecking ball for breakfast.

She's off to the OBGYN's office for a checkup this morning..

"I hate the scale there," she says. "It's always two pounds heavier than the one at the gym. Plus, the nurse rushes me. I never have time to take off my sneakers before getting weighed."

I nod. I decide not to tell Julie, since I know I'd be met with an eye roll, but she's hit on an important Biblical theme: inaccurate scales. I'm guessing the scales in question measured barley and spelt, not wives in their second trimester, but regardless, the issue gets a lot of play.

How much? The law of fair weights and measures appears an impressive six times in the Bible. By way of comparison, the passages often used to condemn homosexuality: also six.

The laws about weights and measures are generally given a wide interpretation; the Bible is demanding fair business practices. Which does seem like a good idea. But if frequency of mentions counts for anything, I should probably be focusing my wrath on improperly calibrated truck weigh stations.

Wine is a mocker, strong drink a brawler, and whoever is led astray by it is not wise.

PROVERBS 20:1

Thou dost cause . . .wine to gladden the heart of man.

PSALM 104:15

Day 221. I'm in the kitchen drinking a glass of red wine as Julie microwaves some pizza. Julie tells me she wants me to give up alcohol for her third trimester.

"It'll be a sign of solidarity," she says. "Paul did it when Lisa was pregnant."

I make a note to have a discussion with our friend Paul.

"And isn't there something in the Bible about not drinking?"

I tell her it's complicated.

After a couple of minutes of back-and-forth, Julie revealed her true motivation: She thinks a few weeks of abstemiousness would help shrink my gut.

"Look at that stomach," she says. "How many months are you? Four? Five? You having twins too?"

Okay, okay, very good.

And yet, there must be a better way to shed pounds. I'm no wine enthusiast—despite the bizarre and inexplicable fact that I edited the wine page at Esquire for a few months (it mostly involved spellchecking words like gewürztraminer)—but I do like an occasional glass.

Before I started living biblically, I had feared that I'd be forced into a year of sobriety. After all, I knew the puritans banned booze. And certain fundamentalist Christians think of booze as up there with adultery, idol worship and South Park. Some even argue that the "wine" drunk in the Bible is not wine at all, but actually grape juice. This was the think-

ing of a temperance advocate named Thomas Welch who tried to sell
"unfermented wine" in the late 19th century for communion services. He
failed. At least until he changed the name to grape juice and marketed it
to the secular.

The truth is, Biblical wine is wine. But is it a good thing or a bad
thing? In some passages, wine seems like a gift from God. In other passages, it's portrayed as a wicked toxin: "[wine] bites like a serpent, and
stings like an adder. Your eyes will see strange things, and your mind
utter perverse things. You will be like one who lies down in the midst of
the sea, like one who lies on the top of a mast. (Proverbs 23:32–34).

To clear things up, I found the expert of all experts, a conservative
Christian oenophile who goes by the pen name of Dr. Bacchus (a forbidden Greek God, curiously enough). Dr. Bacchus has made an astoundingly exhaustive study of every alcohol reference in Scripture Bible—all
247 of them. I quote his findings here:

On the negative side, there are 17 warnings against abusing alcohol,
19 examples of people abusing alcohol, 3 references to selecting leaders,
and one verse advocating abstinence if drinking will cause a brother to
stumble. Total negative references: 40, or 16%.

On the positive side, there are 59 references to the commonly accepted practice of drinking wine (and strong drink) with meals, 27 references to the abundance of wine as an example of God's blessing, 20
references to the loss of wine and strong drink as an example of God's
curse, 25 references to the use of wine in offerings and sacrifices, 9 references to wine being used as a gift, and 5 metaphorical references to wine
as a basis for a favorable comparison. Total positive references: 145, or
59%.

Neutral references make up the remaining 25 percent.

If I could add one observation to Dr. Bacchus' study: There is also
one reference to medicinal alcohol: "No longer drink only water, but use
a little wine for the sake of your stomach and your frequent ailments (1
Timothy 5:23)

It comes down to the battle between the Bible's gusto for life, and the
Bible's wariness of excess. Between its Epicureanism and Puritanism.
You can find both themes in the Scriptures. The Epicurean side is best
seen in Ecclesiastes:

"There is nothing better for a man than that he should eat and drink, and find enjoyment in his toil. This also, I saw, is from the hand of God."

The key seems to be to enjoy wine as one of the many great things that God has provided us. But don't enjoy it too much. Use what Anheuser-Busch public service announcements call "Responsible drinking."

Otherwise, bad things happen. For instance, there's the remarkable story of what happened when Lot—the one who fled Sodom—drank too much. Lot had escaped to a cave with his two daughters—his wife, as you know, had been turned into a pillar of salt. The daughters, thinking all other men in the world had died, got their father very, very drunk—and slept with him. Both got pregnant. Their incestuous offspring founded two nations—Moab and Amon—which became enemies of Israel.

Too much wine is an abomination. But a glass or two? That seems fine. I show Julie the results of Dr. Bacchus' wine study. I said I'd be willing to water down the wine a bit, since most scholars think Biblical wine had a lower alcohol content.

Incidentally, I just did an Internet search for marijuana and the Bible. As I suspected, someone has figured out a way to make the Bible seem in favor of pot-smoking. Not only does the website equalirghts4all quote Genesis 1:29 ("Behold, I have given you every herb bearing seed which is upon the face of all the earth. . . .To you it will be for meat"), but it claims Moses' holy anointing oil contained a high concentration of THC. This, as my high school hero Jeff Spicoli used to say, seems totally bogus.

You shall eat nothing leavened; in all your dwellings
you shall eat unleavened bread.

EXODUS 12:20

Day 226. It's April 12—perhaps the most famous Biblical holiday of them all: Passover. If you're even remotely Jewish, you know it as the religiously-themed, spring-time version of Thanksgiving. And if you're Christian, you probably know it, at the very least, as the meal that Jesus was eating at the Last Supper.

Secular as my family was, even I have been to a handful of Passover dinners, mostly at my dad's cousin's house in Long Island. We'd tell an abbreviated story of the Jews flight from Egypt, eat our matzoh and then talk about movies. They were lovely meals, but Biblically literal? Not so much. To give you an idea: We recited the Nine Plagues. The Tenth One—the killing of Egypt's first-born—was left out for being too harsh. Which seems like leaving that unpleasant throwing-herself-in-front-of-the-train business out of Anna Karenina.

This year, I wanted an uncensored Passover. I wanted to tell the whole story of the exodus. More, though, I wanted to try to recreate that very first Passover as much as I could. Today's Seders—even the strict ones—bear little resemblance to that original meal. Which I discovered is may be a good thing.

My attempted Biblical Seder took place at our apartment. My parents and parents-in-law show up around 5 p.m. I greet them in my in my Biblically-mandated outfit. Exodus says to eat with your "loins girded"—I wore a belt around a white robe. "Your sandals on your feet"—Tevas. "And your staff in your hand"—my maplewood Walden Walking stick.

We sit down and I pass around a plate of unleavened bread. I had made this myself—no store-bought matzoh for me. That very first unleavened bread, the Bible says, was cooked by the Israelites as they wandered out of Egypt. They didn't have time to put the bread on stones, so they put it on their backs and let the sun harden it.

I decided to do the same. That morning, I had taken some kosher flour, added water, made a hubcap-sized pancake, slipped it into a plastic Ziploc bag, and slapped the whole mixture on my back. I walked, hunched over, a few blocks to the hardware store, bought some C batteries for Julie, and came back. Maybe the dough was too well-camouflaged by my white shirt, because the guy at the hardware store didn't bat an eye.

The plate returns to me untouched. No one has taken a piece.

"I had it in a plastic bag," I say. "It's not like I sweated on it."

They shook their heads. Not surprising, I guess. "More for me." It wasn't bad, kind of chewy, what I imagine pizza dough tastes like after

30 seconds in the toaster oven.

As I am eating the matzoh, I lose control of the table. I am supposed to be the leader, the one telling the great story of the Exodus, but already the topic of conversation has devolved to a discussion of the prices at local parking lots.

I think back to my ex-uncle Gil, and how he screamed "ONLY HOLY TOPICS!" I wish I had his maniacal charisma.

Instead, I go to fetch the lamb from the kitchen. The ancient Israelites ate the sacrificed lamb—all of it, from head to feet. (Today, many Jews don't eat lamb on Passover, as it can't be sacrificed properly without the Temple). The closest I could get to this original meal was a 15-pound hunk of kosher lamb I bought at an Upper West Side butcher, and which I somehow conned my mother-in-law into roasting it.

The lamb at that first Passover was key, because it provided the blood that saved a nation. God ordered the Israelites to paint the lamb's blood on the doorposts—the secret sign so that the Angel of Death would know to skip over their houses.

That's another thing, lamb's blood. I needed to do something about that. After several phone calls, I had determined that selling lamb's blood in the U.S. is illegal. Which was a relief. I didn't really want a bucket of blood in the fridge—to Dahmeresque. Instead, I improvised by using the lamb juice from the saucepan, which at least contains some blood. And as for painting it on my doorpost? The paintbrush, says the Bible, should be made of hyssop, a minty herb. I discovered an online store Blessed Herbs—founded by Martha Volchok, "herbalist and mother of four homeschooled children"—and ordered a bag that looked alarmingly like something I would buy in senior year of high school from a guy named Boo on 68th Street.

"If anyone wants to watch me paint the doorpost, come with me now," I announce.

Most everyone stays at the table, but Julie comes along to supervise, and my nieces follow out of curiosity. I go into the building hallway and carefully dab lamb juice on the sides and top of our doorframe, leaving brownish stains and a couple of stray hyssop leaves. Julie isn't happy about the stains, but was more worried about our neighbor Nancy's dog.

"He's going to go berserk when he smells the blood."

Back at the table, I take out my ex-girlfriend's Bible and read a section from Exodus. I figure this is better than trying to summarize the story myself. I read for about three minutes, starting with this passage:

"Afterward Moses and Aaron went to Pharaoh and said, 'Thus says the LORD, the God of Israel, 'Let my people go, that they may hold a feast to me in the wilderness.'""

I close my Bible and let the story sink in. "Does anyone else have anything they want to say?" I ask.

My dad reads the section. He has brought a packet of photocopied handwritten pages. They are a collection of childhood memories that his mother—my grandmother—had written before she died. My dad read the section with her memories of family Seders in the 1920s.

"Before the Seders my mother would buy a very large live carp and bring it home (how, I don't know). She put it into the bathtub to swim until it was time to prepare the gefilte fish we all relished so much. We kids loved watching it swim, but it was so big it could barely (and sometimes not at all) negotiate a turn at the end of the tub. We all took our showers downstairs until after the fish was removed.."

She wrote about how the kids would file up and down the stairs carrying the kosher-for-Passover dishes, "all of us like ants, trip after trip, one after the other." And about how uncle Oscar once at a dozen hard-boiled eggs on a dare. About how, when the Seder dragged on, the prayers went "express, no local stops."

Her writing is vivid, fresh. The references to the customs are no longer confusing and foreign. The whole thing felt familiar.

My Biblical rituals—the doorpainting and sandal-wearing—were interesting on an intellectual level, but frankly I wasn't as moved as I hoped I might be. I didn't feel like I have been swept back to the time of the Pharaohs.

But this writing from my grandmother—that did sweep me back. Perhaps to make a ritual resonate, I can't skip directly from my stain-resistant dinner table in New York to a desert in 1000 B.C.E. I need some links in between. I need my grandmother and her memories of the leviathan-sized carp of Hinsdale Street in Brooklyn.

Do not boast about tomorrow

PROVERBS 27:1

Day 230. Here's a sample from a phone conversation I just had with my wife. I was at the Esquire office for a meeting.

"What time are you coming home?" Julie asks.

"Six o'clock, God willing."

"Also, John Munzer left a message on the answering machine."

"Thanks. I'll call him back, God willing."

"See you soon."

"God willing."

It's not an atypical sample. For the last month, I've been saying "God willing" at least 80 times a day.

Both the Old and New Testaments say this is a good idea. The Proverbs advise us:

"Do not boast about tomorrow, for you do not know what a day may bring forth."

In the New Testament, James 4:13–15 says: "Do not say 'Today or tomorrow we will go to such and such a city," but "Instead you ought to say, 'If the Lord wills, we shall live and do this or that.'" (NKJV)

It has become a reflex. Every time I use the future tense, I try to tag on those two words: "God willing." My mother hates it. She told me I sound like someone who sends in videos to Al Jazeera. And I know my verbal tic comes off as weird in secular settings.

But I find it a profound reminder of the murky instability of the future. Yes, I hope to return home at 6 p.m., but God or fate might have other plans. This, in turn, makes me value the present even more. As James 4:14 says, "For what is your life? It is even a vapor that appears for a little time and then vanishes away." (WEB)

I've got to try to squeeze all I can out of that vapor.

When her time to give birth was at hand, there were twins in her womb.

GENESIS 38:27

Day 232 Julie and I spend the morning at the doctor's office to get another sonogram. Julie lifts her shirt and the boys pop up on the little monitor.

They're starting to look human now. They both have the oversized skull of a bobbleheaded doll or talk show host, perched on a tiny body with reptilian limbs.

You can see them move—they wiggle and jostle and . . .um . . .smack one another.

"Did you see that?" Julie says.

"I saw it."

The boy fetus on the right had given the boy fetus on the left jab to the head. Actually, more of an uppercut. He just took his olive-pit-sized fist and thrust it directly into the ovarian wall, stretching it till it cuffed his brother in the face.

"You think it was intentional?" asks Julie.

"I don't know. Could have been a spasm. Though it did kind of look intentional."

"Oh man. These next few years are going to be hard."

Of course, being Bible-obsessed as I am, my mind goes straight to the scripture's most famous twins, Jacob and Esau—who also waged war in utero. A far more serious war.

> The children struggled within [Rebecca]
> And she said, 'If it is thus, why do I live?
> So she went to inquire of the LORD.
> And the LORD said to her,
> 'Two nations are in your womb,
> and two peoples born of you, shall be divided."
>
> GENESIS 25:22–23

I've been thinking a lot about Jacob and Esau lately. (The real Jacob, not my Biblical alter-ego). The brothers are relevant—almost eerily relevant—not just to my family life, but also to my quest for Biblical truth.

The story of Jacob and Esau provides a classic example of the gap between, on the one hand, what the Bible literally says, and, on the other, the centuries-old layers of interpretation that have built up around those words.

If you read the Bible cold, as if you'd been raised on one of Jupiter's moons, you would, I'd wager, have this reaction:

Jacob is a conniving scoundrel. And Esau, though maybe not a Mensa member, got a raw deal.

But the tradition—at least the more conservative tradition—says just the opposite:

Jacob is a righteous man. And Esau, if not totally evil, is certainly depraved and impetuous and untrustworthy.

How does this work?

Consider the story of the swapped birthright. Esau, the older brother, owned the birthright—a privilege that Jacob coveted. The Bible says:

> *Once when Jacob was boiling pottage, Esau came in from the field, and he was famished.*
> *And Esau said to Jacob, "Let me eat some of that red pottage, for I am famished!" . . .*
> *Jacob said, "First sell me your birthright."*
> *Esau said, "I am about to die; of what use is a birthright to me?"*
> *Jacob said, "Swear to me first." So he swore to him, and sold his birthright to Jacob."*
>
> GENESIS 25:29–33

My first thought on reading this was: What kind of demented brother is Jacob? Why wouldn't he just ladle out a bowl of red pottage for his starving sibling instead of blackmailing the poor guy?

But the tradition has a different read: Esau wasn't really about to die—he was just hungry. He's a slave to his urges, pure id, and an exaggerator to boot. He'd do anything for a snack, including selling the sacred birthright; he showed no respect for what God has given him.

Just a few pages later, Jacob dupes his brother again. This time, their father Isaac, who is blind and on his deathbed, wants to give a blessing to his eldest son. He sends for Esau. But Jacob—at his mother's urging—disguises himself as Esau, putting a goatskin over his arms and neck to mimic his brother's hairiness. Jacob announces himself as Esau. Isaac checks by feeling the faux hairy arm, and proceeds to give Jacob the blessing. Again, a first-time Bible reader might think Jacob a rascal for fooling his dad. But the tradition says that Esau deserved it.

You have to remember that Jacob is a patriarch, one of the original fathers of God's people, so Biblical interpreters had all the reason in the world to put a positive spin on his exploits.

Esau wasn't a patriarch. Well, not of righteous people, anyway: in the rabbinic tradition, Esau spawns an evil race—either the Romans or the Edomites, depending on the source (both were frequent enemies of the Israelites).

Even when Esau seems to act with nobility and forgiveness, the tradition doesn't buy it. Take Jacob and Esau's reconciliation. The two brothers—estranged for twenty years—finally meet up in the desert.

The Bible says:

> "Esau ran to greet [Jacob], and embraced him, and fell on
> his neck and kissed him, and they wept."
>
> GENESIS 33:4

Sounds innocent enough. But my friend Nathaniel Deutsch, who teaches religion at Stanford University, told me about a fascinating Midrash—a Jewish legend—about what really happened. The Midrash says that Esau's 'kiss' was not a kiss at all, but actually an attempt to bite Jacob on the neck. And not a love bite, mind you, a malevolent bite. Jacob, being a man of God, was saved when his neck miraculously turned to marble.

I'm not immune to the interpretative tradition. Now that I read the Bible again with the rabbinically-tinted lenses, I can agree that Esau sold his birthright too quickly. He needed to engage in more long-range thinking.

And Jacob is surely the smarter of the two—and a homebody like me—so maybe it's a good thing he tricked the doltish Esau to become the patriarch.

Still, I don't want to whitewash Jacob. I love the complexity of the patriarchs, that their flaws are as numerous as the stars in the sky, and, in some cases, come close to eclipsing their righteousness. And I am awed by the profound and extraordinary fact that the entire Judeo-Christian heritage hinged on a bowl of soup.

You shall not join hands with a wicked man

EXODUS 23:1

Day 233. I hate the nonsensical, bacteria-laden custom of shaking hands. And the Bible project—with its many purity laws—has given me an excellent excuse for avoiding shaking hands with women. Now I have figured out something beautiful: I can expand my prohibition to the rest of the population too.

The Bible says not to join hands with a wicked man. And what are the chances of a man being wicked? Remarkably high, especially with the strict standards I'm employing nowadays. So I find it's best to keep my hands in the pockets of my white pants, and just nod politely.

To be fair, the 'join hands' command occurs in relation to conspiring to give false evidence. So maybe it doesn't apply all the time. Which is why I've come up with a backup excuse.

The Bible's female impurity laws are more famous, but there are, in fact, corresponding laws of male impurity. Men don't get off scot free.

Leviticus says that a man shall be unclean for a day after his 'emission' (as the New American Bible calls it) and must take a bath to purify himself. In the 20th century, the male impurity laws are rarely observed, even by the strictest of the strict. The reason given is that such laws only applied in the era of now-destroyed Jerusalem Temples. But if I'm trying to recreate Biblical life, I should probably pay heed to the male laws.

My male friends usually assume that I'm evading the handshake because of germs. Since I'm Biblically required to tell the truth, I say

"No, not germs."

And then I explain. Which somehow turns out to be even more awkward then discussing the monthly cycles with women. Men don't like talking about their emissions.

"Well, I haven't in a week," said John. "Not that it's any of your business."

I've learned that men of my vintage aren't having a whole lot of sex. I think I'm hanging out with too many new fathers.

I like the male purity laws, and not just because they allow me to stay in my antiseptic bubble. I like them because they make the female impurity laws seem much more palatable. It's not only women who experience a miniature loss of life and must be avoided. Men do too. The Bible has its moments of egalitarianism.

Honor your father and your mother

EXODUS 20:12

Day 234. I feel like I've been dishonoring my father and mother by even embarking on this quest in the first place. They wanted me to write a book about something safer, like taking a year of dancing lessons. Worse, I still haven't told them about my visit to Gil.

Tonight, Julie and I are going over to my parents house, and I plan to make a conscious effort to be more honorable. Honoring your parents is not one of the inexplicable 'chukim.' It's eminently rational, perhaps even more so in Biblical times.

If you were a nomad—as many ancient Israelites were—the aging parents would be burdensome. They couldn't help with the heavy lifting or nailing down tent pegs. The temptation must have been to leave them behind. But you couldn't. Because God commanded us to honor them.

I've read objections to this commandment. The problem is the absolute nature of it. What if your parents don't deserve honor? Should Stalin's daughter honor him?

It's a hard question, and I don't have an answer. But in my case, my parents do deserve honor. Despite the embarrassingly early curfew they gave me in high school, despite the daily guilt trips about not seeing us enough, despite the quibbles, they've been, on balance, good parents. Just last week, I figured out something about my dad. I realized that he checks my Amazon.com page every day, and if there's a bad review up there, he clicks on the "Not helpful" box. It makes me want to hug him—if we weren't both so repressed.

I don't treat them nearly well enough. I honor them only in a lip-service way. I call them every weekend, but I spend the 20 minutes playing hearts on my Macintosh or cleaning the closet while tossing out the occasional "mm-hmmm." I delete without reading my mom's emailed jokes about vacuous blondes or wacky etymology. And when I do reply to her emails, I often do the I'm-so-important-I-don't-have-time-to-capitalize-or-punctuate thing.

So in this Biblical year, I've been trying to reform. I've been trying to capitalize my emails to my mom. And to actually to listen to what they say during our weekly calls. Listening is a key theme in the Bible. Or, in Hebrew, 'shema.' The Shema—a passage from Deuteronomy that begins "Hear, O Israel"—is considered the most important prayer in Judaism.

Tonight, it's dinner and a DVD. They chose Gods and Generals, a civil war movie that opened to wide apathy a few years ago. The title smacks of polytheism to me, but I don't object, and we settle into our respective chairs to watch it.

About 45 minutes in, during another musket loading scene, I look over and noticed my mom asleep in her chair. And not just light dozing. We're talking mouth-agape, head-slumped-on-the-chest deep slumber.

I nudge Julie. At this point, I am planning to whisper something clever along the lines of "Looks like my mom is really enjoying the movie." Or perhaps I would have gone with a sight gag—an impression of my mom with her jaw slack. But I stop myself. This isn't good-natured jesting. It has a tinge of mockery to it. And the Fifth commandment kicked in. So I just smile vacantly at Julie, who then goes back to watching Jeff Daniels.

I realize I nearly committed a major Biblical sin. Or at least a G-rated version of one.

Consider this story from Genesis: After the floodwaters had receded, Noah planted a vineyard, grew some grapes and made wine. One day he drank too much and passed out in his tent, naked. Noah's bare body was spotted by his son Ham, who then told his brothers about it—we assume in a disrespectfully jovial manner. For this, Ham would pay. Or more precisely, Ham's son Canaan would pay. Noah thundered: "Cursed be Canaan; a slave of slaves shall he be to his brothers."

What exactly was Ham's sin? Perhaps seeing his father's nakedness. Or maybe Ham did more than just look: Some believe that Ham perpetrated something X-rated on his dad, though this isn't stated in the text itself. To me, perhaps the biggest offense was that Noah was asleep. We're never more defenseless and vulnerable than when we're asleep. If you mock a napping person, you might as well be putting a stumbling block before the blind (to use another Biblical phrase).

So as difficult as it was to restrain myself from teasing my mother, it's best that I did.

When I get home, I check in on Jasper, who is sleeping as soundly as a drunken Noah. He is in my favorite sleeping position: on his knees, kowtowing before some invisible Chinese magistrate. I watch him for a good three minutes, smiling like an idiot the whole time.

> *When you make your neighbor a loan of any sort,*
> *you shall not go into his house to fetch his pledge.*
>
> DEUTERONOMY 24:10

Day 236. The writing on our doorpost is starting to attract more attention. The building manager—a tall Russian guy with a goatee—knocked on our door today. He told me I have to paint over it. Someone has complained. I ask him if I can wait a few months, till my year ends.

"Why so long?" he says.

"Well, I'm—"

"What is the writing, anyway?"

"It's the Ten Commandments. From the Bible."

"The Bible? Oh, religious?"

He puts his hands up and backs away. He looks flustered, like he just stepped on my cat or trieed to hit on my wife.

"Leave it there, leave it there."

It certainly wasn't our neighbor Nancy who was doing the complaining. I ran into her in the hall while she was walking her dog.

"I love the writing," she says. "I was thinking of doing it to my door."

Excellent! My first disciple.

"Anytime," I say. "I'll write it for you myself."

"Okay, I may take you up on that."

She pauses.

"You know what? Wait here."

Nancy vanishes into her apartment and emerges with a blue paperback.

"I'm not very religious," she says. "But I like this book. It's The Pirkei Avot: Values of Our Fathers."

She flips to a page with a passage highlighted in yellow.

She reads: "'In a world of no humanity, strive to be human.' That's my motto for living in New York."

That's good wisdom. It may not be from the Bible itself, but it's good.

"Here, take it." Nancy says. Before I can say no, she's shoved it into my hands and is on her way into the apartment.

"How's your Hendrix proposal?" I ask, before she shuts the door.

"Just a few thousand more pages and I'll be done."

You shall remember that you were a slave in Egypt

DEUTERONOMY 16:12

Day 238. I got an unexpected email today. It arrived in my inbox at 1:07 p.m. from a guy named Kevin Roose. "Allow me to introduce myself. I'm an eighteen-year old native Ohioan in the middle of my first year at Brown."

Kevin went on to explain that he's going to be working at a café in New York this summer, but he wants to be a writer, and he noticed I went to Brown as well, and . . .would I be willing to take him on as a part-time personal intern?

This was an unusual request in several respects. First, there's the fact that he wants to be a writer in this day and age, since it seems about as pragmatic as getting into Betamax sales. Second, that he took the initiative to email me. I don't inspire many groupies. I still have a special place in my heart for my one and only rabid fan—the guy who took off his sweatshirt at a Texas signing to reveal passages of my book scrawled on his T-shirt in magic marker. Other than that, I'm not in the market for bodyguards.

I write back saying to Kevin saying I'd hire him sight unseen on one condition: That I could call him my 'slave.' Now this might seem flip, and maybe it is, but slavery is a huge part of the Hebrew Bible, and I'd been struggling to figure out a way to include it in my Biblical year. The closest thing to legal slavery in modern America? An unpaid internship. And here it was. Heaven-sent.

Kevin accepted.

His internship was still a few months off. Which is fine by me, because it'll give me plenty of time to figure out Biblical slavery. There are some interesting rules. Like:

—You can beat your slave as hard as you want—as long as he survives two days post-beating. (Exodus 21:21)

—But you can't kill a slave with a rod, or else you'll be punished (Exodus 21:20)

—You also can't pluck out the slave's eye, or else you have to set him free. Likewise, you can't knock out his tooth or you set him free. (Exodus 21:26, 27)

—If the slave was born to the Hebrew race, then, regardless of his eye and tooth situation, he gets his freedom after six years. If he opts to refuse his freedom, you must put him against a doorpost and drill a hole in his ear with an awl (Exodus 21:6)

As much as I can't wait for Kevin to take over my Kinko's duties, the existence of slavery in the Bible is bewildering. It points to a bigger puzzle. Namely: Judaism, as practiced today, when practiced at its best, is a compassionate religion, just as Christianity, when practiced at its best, is a compassionate religion. Compassionate Judaism fights for the oppressed, encourages generosity, et cetera.

But if you read the Hebrew Bible literally, it's often not compassionate at all. Huge chunks of it seem downright barbaric. You've got slavery. An eye for an eye. Capital punishment for everything from adultery to checking your horoscope. God-approved genocide against the Canaanites. And sexism—the girl's consecration price is three shekels to a boy's five shekels, making her 60 percent as valuable.

So how to reconcile modern Judaism with the realities of the Bible? In my journey, I've heard three main approaches.

1. Ancient Israel was, in fact, barbaric. It was sexist, racist and violent. Judaism has simply evolved past that.

2. Ancient Israel was not barbaric at all. Quite the opposite. It was compassionate, even by today's standards. You'll hear this view from some hardcore traditionalists. Consider slavery, they say. Biblical slaves were not treated like slaves in antebellum Georgia. They had a much better life. One Orthodox Jew I know—who happens to be smart, funny and sane—compared the Biblical slaves' status to that of English butlers. It wasn't a bad job at all. The Scripture's many slavery laws were there to protect them.

3. Ancient Israel was barbaric by our standards—but it was morally evolved compared to other societies of the time. Yes, there was cruel slavery. But at least there were limits, including setting Hebrew slaves free after six years.

An eye for an eye did mean just that. But it's better than a head for an eye, which is what other Middle Eastern societies were doing; it's a way to limit the cycle of violence. And sure, there was capital punishment, but for far fewer crimes than in the Code of Hammurabi over in Mesopotamia.

From what I can tell, this Option Number 3 seems the most accurate. Or actually, Option-Number-3-with-a-slight-tweak seems most accurate. The writers of the Bible were reformers. As one rabbi told me, the Bible is a "minority report." The society portrayed by the Biblical stories was probably more advanced than true Israelite society.

Now, there is an Option Number 4, but it doesn't really tackle the issue directly. It's more of an elegant look-over-here! decoy.

One of my spiritual advisers, Julie Galambush, a professor of religion at William and Mary, explained this tactic to me: You simply act as if the Bible doesn't say what it says. There's a passage in Deuteronomy that says the Israelites should offer peace before attacking a city outside the land of Israel. If the city accepts, you take the residents as your slaves. If the city rejects your offer, you kill all the males and make everyone else slaves. For cities inside the land, you don't even offer peace. You just kill everyone: men, women, children, cattle—"save nothing that breathes." Pretty shocking stuff. But when talking about this in the Midrash, the rabbis completely ignore the blood-letting. Instead, they focus on the part in which the Israelites offer peace. They say, Look! The passage is all about compassion (I'm paraphrasing). "It's clear the rabbis have moral objections to this passage," professor Galambush says. "So they pretend it says something they do believe in—peace—rather than something they object to. You can't underestimate the radicalness of the rabbis.

My slave Kevin seems like a nice guy, so I'll probably take Option Number 4 on those passages that allow me to give him a beat-down.

Give ear, O LORD, to my prayer

PSALM 86:6

Day 239. Jasper got out of his cast a couple of weeks ago. But the medical traumas never end. Today he tripped today while dancing a bit too enthusiastically to the Wiggles masterpiece "Fruit Salad." I watch him as he falls face forward and smacks his forehead hard against the door-frame. It makes a horrible sound, a crack like a line drive off the wall at Shea Stadium.

I pick him up. He is crying by now. I inspect his forehead—a small bump.

"Should we get you some ice?"

He just keeps wailing, open-mouthed.

I look at the bump again. It is bigger. Scarily bigger. It had become a bump you'd see on Fred Flintstone's head after he got hit by a rock at the quarry. It looked like a golf ball had been sewn into Jasper's skin.

I run into our bedroom to show Julie—who was still sleeping. We call the doctor, who tells us that if he starts vomiting, bring him to the

ER. Otherwise, just ice it down, and expect him to have a black eye tomorrow. Toddler's foreheads apparently distort like that.

It's a horrible moment—and also, a milestone of sorts. My first reaction, as I was running to show Julie, was to pray to God for Jasper to be okay. It was like reflex praying. Unplanned, unforced.

Can . . .the leopard change his spots?

JEREMIAH 13:23

Day 240. A Spiritual update: I'm all over the place. My belief in God changes by the hour. I have three phases, about evenly split throughout the day. As I type this, I'm in Phase Two. But that could change by the time I finish the next paragraph.

First, there's the comfortable old position: agnosticism. I haven't erased that totally, and it especially pops up whenever I read about religious extremism.

The second phase is all about a newfound reverence for life. Life isn't just a series of molecular reactions. There's a divine spark in there. The official term is vitalism. I'd always thought of vitalism as a 19th century relic—in the same category as leeches and phrenology. But now I'm a believer, at least sometimes.

The third phase, the highest level, is when I believe in something more specific, a God who cares, who pays attention to my life, who loves. Why wouldn't there be a God? It makes just as much sense as having no God. Otherwise, existence itself is just too random.

It's an amazing feeling. For instance, my Hollywood dreams are in meltdown mode. My previous book—the one about the encyclopedia—was optioned for a movie. But now the director won't email me back. And when I call his assistant, she always tells me to hold, then returns to report—surprise!—he's not there right now but I am welcome to leave a message. Hmmm. I wonder: could he be breaking the commandment not to lie?

It's annoying—but things happen for a reason, right? It wasn't meant to be. Perhaps something better will come out of it. Maybe James

Cameron will call me out of the blue and tell me that encyclopedias have replaced shipwrecks as his new obsession.

Julie always told me things happen for a reason. To which I would reply, Sure, things happen for a reason. Certain chemical reactions take place in people's brains and they cause those people to move their mouths and arms. That's the reason. But, I thought, there's no greater purpose. Now I sometimes think Julie's right. There is a reason. There has to be. Otherwise, it's all too absurd. The world can't be that Dadaist.

It's certainly a healthier way to look at life. I feel better when I see the world this way.

I ask Elton Richards, the pastor out to pasture. Maybe I should commit myself to believing in God for the simple reason that it will make my life better.

"You could," he says. "But it feels a little too calculated for me."

It smacks of Pascal's wager. This was devised by Blaise Pascal, the 18th century French mathematician. He said we should believe in God because the cost is minimal, but the potential benefit of heaven is huge. Believe in God just to avoid hell. Pretty cynical, really. Or to use a more recent metaphor, maybe it's the Matrix wager. Am I taking a blue pill just because it's an happier worldview?

"I think you should believe for a more organic reason," says Elton. "If you're going to believe at all."

He who pursues righteousness and kindness will find life and honor

PROVERBS 21:21

Day 241. I've been trying to be as compassionate as possible. Often, this requires energy and planning—going to the homeless shelter, for instance.

But today, God or fate gave me a big juicy softball: an old lady asked me to help her across the street. Never in my 38 years has an old lady asked me to help her across the street. I didn't think those things happened anymore. I thought it was just an expression, like kittens getting stuck in trees.

But after lunch, outside the Jewish Theological Seminary, where I was meeting a friend, this kindly old octogenarian woman tells me she is worried about making it across Broadway's six lanes alone, and could I maybe help.

I'd be glad to. Though actually ecstatic is a better world. She locks her arm in mine—I figure she's safely past the age when I can't touch her—and we walk across, me holding my right hand out in a stern stop-traffic position, which was totally unnecessary, since the cars were safely stopped at the red light.

I am so happy about the situation, I stay with her for another several blocks, which oddly enough, doesn't creep her out.

> *Be glad in the LORD, and rejoice, O righteous,*
> *and shout for joy, all you upright in heart!*
>
> PSALM 32:11

Day 241, afternoon. Mr. Berkowitz is over to pray again today. I can only say "no" to him so many times. He's giving me one of his kind-but-stern lectures.

"You have to say a prayer in the morning," says Mr. Berkowitz.

"Right," I say.

"You have to say a prayer over bread,"

"Right."

"Did you say the prayers over bread today, Arnold?"

"Right."

"Arnold, I asked you a question. Are you paying attention?"

I was busted. I had tuned out. Mr. Berkowitz was frustrated; not angry, but frustrated.

"Yes, yes, I said the prayers over bread."

"Okay," he says.

Then, it's onto learning the Hebrew alphabet.

"Aleph, bet, dalet."

"No, aleph, bet, gimel."

"Aleph, bet, gimel, dalet.."

It's a time-consuming visit—a 90-minute chunk out of my day. But in the end, I'm glad he came over, because Mr. Berkowitz said two things that struck me as astoundingly wise.

The first was about how much he loves doing the commandments. "To me, going to pray is like going to do a $100,000 deal," he said.

This is a mindset I'm trying to adopt. I shouldn't look at the Bible as a collection of pesky tasks on my To-do list. I have to look forward to the commandments. I have to love them.

And in a few cases—just a handful, really—I'm starting to. Like with the Sabbath. I used to orient my week around Monday, the start of the secular workweek. Now, it's the Sabbath. Everything leads up to the Sabbath. On Friday morning, I start prepping for it like I'm going on a big date. I make a big pot of coffee so I don't have cook on the Sabbath. I pile my research books in a corner.

And when the sun sets, I flip off my computer and get to work not working. Because resting is, paradoxically, difficult. The writer Judith Shulevitz talks about how avoiding business requires much effort. She's right. You can't talk about work, you can't even think about work. A notion about Esquire will creep into my brain—I have to write that article on weddings for Thursday—and I'll squash it down. Another will pop up. It's like mental whack-a-mole. By the end of Saturday, as the sun finally sets, I feel as if I've done something strenuous but healthy, like a run through Central Park. I feel good, like I deserved the endorphin rush the Sabbath gave me. And then I start to look forward to next week's Sabbath.

The second thing Mr. Berkowitz says is this: "It's a different way of looking at the world. Your life isn't about rights. It's about responsibilities." It's the Biblical version of that famous quote from our first Catholic president: "ask not what your country can do for you, ask what you can do for your country.' It's a good way to think. It's not my natural mindset, far from it, but I'm giving it a shot.

Consider speech. As a journalist—even though I spent most of my career as a frivolous entertainment journalist—I've been obsessed with my right to free speech. If I was an absolutist in any sense, then it was as a zealot for the First Amendment. Journalists should be allowed to say whatever they want. It's our right. The American way. Take no prisoners. But now, I'm trying to balance that mindset with my responsibility not to engage in evil tongue, or the written equivalent. In my article on tuxedos, do I really need to make a cheap joke at David Arquette's expense? Does it make the world a better place? It hurts a little, but I leave my article free from Arquette mentions.

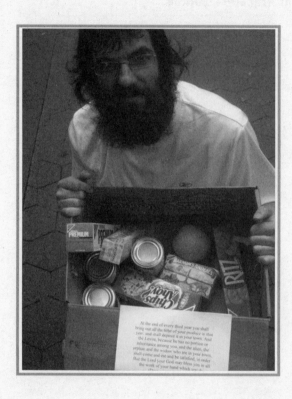

Month Nine: May

In the beginning was the Word

JOHN 1:1

Day 244. Today is the first day of my New Testament life. I'm as nervous as I've been since the start of this experiment, more nervous than even the first day, more nervous than when I called up Guru Gil.

On the one hand, I can't wait to dive in. It should be a massive education. Before this year, I knew only the very basics of the New Testament and Christianity. Well, the basics plus the random facts that I still remember from the encyclopedia (e.g. some early Christians believed the creation of the world was equivalent to conception, and it occurred on March 25, lending symbolic weight to Jesus' birth nine months later on December 25). But I want more in-depth knowledge. So this will be good for me.

Plus, it feels timely. It's hard to argue with the fact that the New Testament holds more sway in America today than the Old. Or to be more precise, the Christian literal interpretation of the Bible holds more sway than the Jewish method of exegesis. I don't buy that we're on the verge of a theocracy, but certainly evangelical Christianity—both conservative and liberal forms—have massive impact on our lives.

On the other hand, I'm freaked out. I've already been overwhelmed by the complexity of my own tradition, and now I'm going to venture into even more foreign territory. I told Julie I had a stress headache.

"You don't have to do it, you know," said Julie.

"If I don't, I'll only be telling half the story," I said.

"But it's a big half."

True. But like Nachson, I'm going to wade into the water and see what happens. Before I do, though, I have to wrestle with a bunch of Big Issues.

The first Big Issue is this: If I'm going to switch my focus to the New Testament, should I keep following all the rules of the Hebrew Bible? In other words, should I keep my beard and fringes? Or should I break out the Mach 3 and order shrimp fajitas?

After asking this question to pretty much every Christian expert I meet, I've come to this definitive conclusion: I don't know.

You can find a small group—a very small group—of Christians who say that every single Old Testament rule should still be followed by everyone. The ultra-legalist camp. They quote these words from Jesus found in Matthew 5:17:

"Think not that I have come to abolish the law and the prophets; I have come not to abolish them but to fulfill them. For truly, I say to you, till heaven and earth pass away, not an iota, not a dot, will pass from the law until all is accomplished."

Jesus is God, but he affirms that the laws of the ancient Israelites still stand.

On the other end of the spectrum are those Christians who say that Jesus overrode all rules in the Old Testament. He created a new covenant. His death was the ultimate sacrifice, so there's no need for animal sacrifice—or, for that matter, any other Old Testament laws. Even the famous Ten commandments are rendered unnecessary by Jesus.

Consider Matthew 22, in which Jesus is asked by a lawyer what is the great commandment of the law.

Jesus responds: "You shall love the Lord your God with all your heart, and with all your soul, and with all your mind.

This is the great and first commandment.

And a second is like it, You shall love your neighbor as yourself."

Some Christians say all the other eight commandments flow from those two. You love your neighbor, so you don't lie to him. You love your neighbor, so you don't steal from him. The Old Testament is important historically, but as a moral guidebook, it has been superseded.

And there's the vast middle ground. Most Christians I met draw a distinction between a) moral laws and b) ritual laws. The moral laws are the ones such as those found in the Ten commandments—no killing, no coveting, etc. Those we still need to follow. Ritual laws are the ones about avoiding bacon and not wearing clothes of mixed fibers. Jesus made those laws obsolete.

What does obsolete mean? Is it a sin to keep a beard and avoid shellfish? Or is it just unnecessary, like wearing sunscreen indoors? Ask 10 people and, once again, you'll get 10 different answers. But most seem to say, go ahead, wear that sunscreen. It won't hurt. You need to accept Jesus, but you don't need to shave the beard.

Which is a relief. I want to keep the beard. I'm not ready to give up my rituals. That would feel like I ran 17 miles of a marathon. So unless there's a contradiction in the laws—for instance, the literal interpretation of eye for an eye contradicts the literal interpretation of turn the other cheek—I'll follow both Old and New.

My second Big Issue is this: As a Jewish person, how do I treat the issue of the divinity of Christ?

For the bona-fide literal New Testament experience, I should accept Jesus as Lord. But I just can't do it. I've read the New Testament several times, and though I think of Jesus as a great man, I don't come away from the experience accepting him as savior. I've had no Road to Damascus moment yet.

The closest I've come to such a moment was probably during college when I grew strangely envious of my best friend's Catholicism. He went to mass several times a week and did the sign of the cross before every meal. We ate together at least once a day, and I always felt awkward while I waited for him to finish his prayer. And superficial—here he was, funny, smart, but he had something deeper going on than I did. I'd pretend not to look, but I was fixated by the sign of the cross. It's such a simple and beautiful ritual. What if I started doing it with him at dinner? Just to see what it's like? To see if I felt anything? Would my friend be weirded out? Probably. So I never tried it.

Same goes for now. I could adopt the cognitive dissonance strategy: If I act like Jesus is God, eventually maybe I will start to believe Jesus is God. That's been my tactic with the God of the Hebrew Bible, and it's actually started to work. But there's a difference. When I do it with the Hebrew God, I feel like I'm trying on my forefather's clothes and sandals. There's a family connection. Doing it with Jesus would feel uncomfortable. I've come to value my heritage enough that it'd feel disloyal to convert.

Which naturally leads to this quandary: If I don't accept Christ, can I get anything out of the New Testament at all? What if I follow the moral teachings of Jesus but don't worship him as God? Or is that just a fool's errand? Again, depends whom you ask.

The more humanist mainline Christian denominations say yes, it's okay to follow Jesus' ethics without converting to Christianity. Ask a Unitarian or more liberal Lutherans, and they'll tell you there is much to be learned from Christ the moral teacher. This is Christianity with a strong dash of Enlightenment.

The most extreme example of this comes from Enlightenment's archbishop himself, Thomas Jefferson. His version of Christianity is so one-sided it almost seems a parody of this position. In the early 1800s, Jefferson created an edition of the Bible called The Jefferson Bible. He stripped away all the supernatural references. Gone was the resurrection. Gone was the miracle of the loaves and fishes. Gone was the virgin birth. Jefferson's idea was that Christ was a great moral philosopher. So Jefferson only kept Christ's moral teachings—forgiveness, loving thy neighbor and striving for peace. He called them "the most sublime and benevolent code of morals which has ever been offered to man."

The Da Vinci Code tilts the way of Jefferson. Dan Brown doesn't come right out and say Christ was totally human, but a Christ who marries and has kids sure makes him more like us mortal men.

So that's one side. On the other side, most evangelical Christians would say that simply paying attention to Jesus' moral teachings is missing the point. The central message of the Gospels is the Good News; Jesus is the Risen God. You need to accept Him.

The emphasis on faith is a key difference between modern Judaism and current evangelical Christianity. Judaism has a catchphrase: deed over creed. There's an emphasis on behavior—follow the rules of the Torah, and eventually you'll come to believe. But evangelical Christianity says you must first believe in Jesus, then the good works will naturally follow. Charity and kindness alone cannot save you. You must, as the saying goes, be "justified by faith."

Here's an email I got from an evangelical Christian I contacted. He runs a website that tries to reconcile science with Biblical literalism. He wrote:

"It is through being in Christ and following Him that we become transformed. Unless one takes this step, one cannot be truly transformed. So, after your year is over, you will go back to being a man who finds purpose in weird projects and writing assignments. Becoming a follower of Jesus Christ is much more rewarding."

In short, I got schooled.

And yet . . .I still want to explore Christian Biblical literalism. It's not a minor thing. It's hugely relevant to my quest. So here's my revised plan: I'm going to visit some Christian communities that interpret the Bible literally. I will try to learn about them. And, when inspired, and when possible, I've decided I should try to experience some of their teachings firsthand. Overall, it will be much less Do-it-yourself than my trip through the Hebrew scriptures. It'll be more like a guided tour.

Which brings me to my final Big Issue. Where to go on my tour? Christian Biblical literalism comes in dozens of flavors. No way I could cover them all. I'll do my best. But I'll spend much of my time looking at the two poles that shape our moral debate.

1. The Falwell-style conservative fundamentalists, who place a lot of emphasis on the issues of homosexuality, abortion, the Apocalypse and Bush's foreign policy.

2. The Red Letter Christians, a growing evangelical group that focuses on social justice, poverty and the environment.

Both accept the Bible as the word of God, both accept Jesus as their savior, but they come out with radically different agendas.

A disclaimer: I'm going to try to be fair, but I'm probably going to fail. It's the same problem I had when I went to the Creationist Museum. There are limits to how far my mind can leap. I've been a moderate New York liberal all my life. Will I really be able to get inside the mind of a conservative evangelical from Virginia?

Judge not, that you be not judged

MATTHEW 7:1

Day 249. This evening, I spend an hour on the phone talking to pastor Elton Richards. He wants to give me a theological inoculation.

I tell him I'm about to make a road trip to Jerry Falwell's church, and he wants to make sure I know that, in his opinion, Falwell's version of Christianity bears practically no relation to Jesus' message.

'Take what they say, and in most cases, it's the exact opposite of Jesus' message. Jesus' message was one of inclusion. Theirs is of exclusion."

"Okay," I say.

"And they're so focused on the other world and the end times. Jesus cared for the downtrodden and outcasts in this world."

"Got it," I say.

'It's this God-awful certainty that they have."

I promise him and promise him again that I'll spend as much time looking at other, more progressive interpretations of Christianity.

Jerry Falwell is, of course, the perfect person to represent a certain brand of ultra-literal Christianity. Almost too perfect. For decades, he's been the go-to guy when the mainstream media wants a quote from the Christian Right, popping up on TV every couple of months to talk about homosexuals or abortion like a villain in an Aaron Sorkin drama.

Here's my chance to see Falwell unfiltered.

I take a flight to Richmond, Virginia and drive a rental car to Thomas Road Baptist Church in Lynchburg. It's a big week in the Falwell universe. For its 50th year, the church has moved from its 1,000-seat house of worship to a splashy new 6,000-seat one.

At 9:30 a.m., I park my car along with hundreds of others, pull open the glass, mall-like front doors and step inside Falwell's enclave. Like all megachurches, it's not just a church. It's a complex.

There's a massive, brightly lit walkway called "Main Street". There's a playground with a Noah's Ark theme—pairs of wooden zebras and tigers, along with a huge whale's mouth that kids can climb into a la Jonah. There's a Starbucks-ish coffee shop called The Lion and the Lamb Café, where I get a pretty good iced coffee. Nearby, a player piano tinkles Mrs. Falwell's favorite hymns.

Services don't start for awhile, but at 10 a.m., many of the parishioners attend one of the Bible studies in the classrooms off Main Street. There's an astounding range to choose from—34 in all, from a tutorial on the Apocalypse to a meeting targeted at Christian biker dudes.

With the imminent increase in my household, I opt for a class called Growing Families in Room 206. There are about thirty churchgoers already assembled, mostly white, mostly crisply-dressed, engaging in a pre-study mingle.

"Hello, I'm glad you could come." says a fortysomething woman. She eyes my beard. "We welcome people from all, uh, walks of life."

"Thanks."

"Do you have a growing family?" she asks.

"Yes, I have a son—and two more on the way."

"Wow! And you live here in Lynchburg?"

"No," I pause. "New York."

"Great! what are you doing here?"

"Um, just traveling around the South a bit."

Oh man. Biblically, I should have been honest and told her about my book, but I only have a day here at Falwell's headquarters, and I didn't want to waste any time.

"You're here with your wife?"

"Uh, yeah. She's back at the hotel."

Another lie. I didn't want to seem like a lout who abandoned his pregnant spouse, which is what I did.

"She didn't want to come?"

"She was going to, but, uh, she had morning sickness."

And on it grows, the tangled web. She keeps asking questions, I keep spitting out lies.

Mercifully, the meeting starts. The pastor—a man who looks like a thinner, younger, brown-haired Falwell—has some announcements. An upcoming luau, a couple's 20th wedding anniversary—and a welcome to me, soon-to-be-father of twins. The parishioners applaud. I wave a sheepish thank you.

Man, these people are friendly. That's the overwhelming first impression: They're disorientingly friendly. When I walked into the church, an official greeter named "Tip" said "Good morning" with such enthusi-asm, I'd have to append a half-dozen exclamation points to get across his tone. Nobody is aloof. Everybody keeps eye contact. Everyone smiles. In my four hours there, I got more pats on the back, arms on the shoulders, and double-handed clasps than I've gotten in ten years in New York.

Now I know that this friendliness has limits—and disturbing ones. I know that Falwell has offered such bon mots as "AIDS is the wrath of a just God against homosexuals." I know he once commented that "the pagans, and the abortionists, and the feminists, and the gays and the les-bians" helped pave the way for 9/11. I know he recently said that we shouldn't worry about so-called global warming because, in Psalm 119:90, it says God has "established the earth and it abideth." I know his magazine crowbarred poor purse-carrying Teletubby Tinky Winky out of the closet.

Presumably, Tip and others share these views. But that intolerance co-exists with a stunning bonhomie. The place is a study in sweet and sour.

After about fifteen minutes of announcements with no end in sight, I decide I need to get out of there. This was no different than a thousand other churches or temples in America. I need something more spicy.

"Be right back," I lie to the guy next to me, as I slipped out. "I have to go to the bathroom."

I wander down a flight of stairs to the singles seminar. That could be good.

The woman at the singles welcoming table asked how old I was.

"Thirty-seven," I say.

"You're right in there," she points. "It's for singles 35 to 50."

That hurts. I am in the oldsters group. By the way, another fib. I am 38. Vanity.

The leader of the singles group is a burly ex-military guy with a bald head, a gray goatee, wire-rimmed glasses balanced on his forehead, and a huge amount of energy. He seems more into tough love than the folks at the Growing Families class.

He paces back and forth, telling us that we should give up the idea that we're perfect.

"Anyone ever say bad things about other people?"

We nod.

"Anyone ever think bad sexual thoughts?"

Yes.

"Anyone ever have envy?"

Yes.

"Anyone ever lie?"

It's a sermon directed at me.

"Did I ever tell you the story of when I was working as Dr. Falwell's bodyguard?" says our leader. "I handed him the mail one Tuesday, and he says to me 'Did you vote today?'

And I said 'um . . .um . . .um . . .Yeah.' But I hadn't. I lied. I lied to Dr. Falwell. I had forgotten that it was election day. But I know that I have voted in every election since.'"

I can't figure out how this applies to dating, but there's no time for questions. The class ends at 11 a.m., and the featured show begins right after: Falwell's sermon.

The sermon takes place in the an enormous room with comfy, Loews Cineplex-style seats; three swiveling TV cameras; and two huge screens that display the lyrics of the hymns karaoke-style over photos of seagulls and purple orchids.

On the side are two "cry rooms." When I saw the words "cry room" on the church map, I thought it was for parishioners who became too wildly emotional. Actually, it's a soundproof space for screaming babies

Falwell himself walks onto the stage. There he is: He's got that familiar silver hair with the tidy part. He's packing a few more pounds than I remembered. As the 300-person choir sings a hymn, Falwell leans way back on his heels, his hands clasped together in front of him, smiling beatifically.

Falwell starts with some announcements of his own—that the café is open from 8 a.m. to 11 p.m., that Rick Stanley, the brother-in-law of Elvis Presley is visiting today.

And then Falwell puts his hands on the pulpit and begins his sermon proper. And here's the thing about the sermon. It is kind of . . .bland. There was no fire, no brimstone, no homophobic remarks, no warnings of the imminent Apocalypse.

I've read dozens of Falwell's sermons online since that visit. And this wasn't an aberration. About 90 percent of content is run-of-the-mill stuff: the importance of passing the baton to today's youth. The suggestion to keep a prayer journal. A moral lesson about not gossiping, another about having patience—advice that, honestly, is hard to argue with.

I noticed the same thing from watching hours of Pat Robertson's 700 Club. Occasionally, you'll get a crazy "let's assassinate Hugo Chavez"-type comment. But mostly, it's mild stuff—an interview with a gospel singer, or a health segment on the club's weekly "Skinny Wednesday" feature (the wackiest thing I learned there was that Robertson has a side business in "age-defying protein pancakes.")

That's the big secret: The radical wing of the Christian right is a lot more boring than its liberal detractors would have you believe.

Falwell's sermon today ties his church's 50th anniversary to the concept of the Jubilee in the Bible, which occurs once every fifty years. He encouraged us to be 'soul winners' and win over the one million unaffiliated souls in the Lynchburg area.

It's not a particularly offensive sermon, but I will say that it has absolutely nothing to do with the Jubilee the Bible talks about. The Bible's Jubilee year is about forgiving debts and returning all property to the original owner, about social justice, about evening the balance between rich and poor. Falwell's was about expanding the church.

After the service, the curious seeker can get one-on-one counsel with one of Falwell's pastors. I am assigned to Tom, who looks to be in his twenties, and has a spiky boy-band hairdo to offset his suit and tie.

Tom works at Liberty University, Falwell's college nearby the church. It's an amazing place, Liberty, the total opposite of my permissive, grades-optional alma-mater. The Liberty rulebook contains such items as:

"6 reprimands and $25 fine for Attendance at a dance, possession and/or use of tobacco"

and "12 reprimands and $50 fine for Attendance at, possession or viewing of an "R" "X" or "NC17" rated movie, or Entering the residence hallway of the opposite sex."

I decide I have to redeem myself. I have to stop lying, so I tell Tom that I'm Jewish and writing a book about my spiritual quest. He's interested.

I ask if I could gain anything from following the moral teachings of Jesus without being born again.

"It's okay to follow his teachings. It can make you a better person," he says. "But it's not enough. You need to accept Him, to be born again."

"I got saved when I was a freshman in high school," Tom continues. "I was a good Christian already. I went to church. I acted as morally as I could. I had accepted Jesus here." Tom points to his head. "But I not here." He points to his heart. "I was off by twelve inches."

He talks so passionately, so intensely, with such freedom from irony, I feel myself becoming unanchored. Perhaps to counter this, as a defensive measure, I bring up the gay issue.

"I have a lot of trouble with the Bible's stance on homosexuality," I say. Adding somewhat lamely: " I have a lot of gay friends."

"So do I," Tom says.

This takes me aback. A Falwell pastor hanging with Lynchburg's gay community? It turns out, Tom meant formerly gay people trying to overcome their gayness, which made more sense.

"Yes, homosexuality is an abomination," says Tom. "But I'm a sinner too. We're all sinners. You just have to love them."

This is a pretty mild stance—the hate-the-sin, not-the-sinner idea. I'm guessing he toned the rhetoric down for his Northeastern-Jewish audience of one. But still, I find this stance intolerant in its own way. It's like saying we should love Jesse Jackson, except for the fact that he's black.

After about half an hour, my questions slow, and Tom asks if we could pray together.

We close our eyes, bow our heads, put our elbows on our knees and he began addressing the Lord. "Thank you Lord for giving AJ and me the time to talk today. And may you give him more guidance in his spiritual journey, Lord."

More guidance—that I need for sure. We can agree on that.

. . .the men likewise gave up natural relations with women and were con-

sumed with passion for one another, men committing shameless acts with men
and receiving in their own persons the due penalty for their error.

ROMANS 1:27

Day 256. Back in New York, I'm continuing my tutorial in evangelical Christianity. It's Friday night, and I'm sitting in on a Bible study group. The group has been around for 30 years and meets every week on the Upper East Side of New York. Tonight, we'll be delving into Paul's letter to the Hebrews, Verse three. We'll be led by a man named Ralph Blair, who is a hardcore Christian evangelical.

Oh, I should mention one other thing: Ralph Blair is gay. And out-of-the-closet gay. Not, mind you, the I-once-was-gay-but-now-am-cured type of gay. Ralph—and all the other men in his Bible group—embrace their homosexuality with the same zeal that ultra-conservative evangelicals condemn it. They're the anti-Falwells.

"Come in," says Ralph. "You're the first one here."

Ralph has a calming, velvety voice. Which is appropriate—his day job is a psychotherapist. The Bible study meets in his office, which is everything you'd want in a shrink's office: Black leather chairs. Indirect lighting. Dark wood everywhere. The DSM-IV weighing down one shelf, the Sex Atlas on another. And Ralph himself looks pleasingly shrinkish: Bald except for a fringe of gray hair, dressed in a black corduroy jacket, a blue sweater, a tie and chinos.

"I'm glad you found us," he says. "It's not what your average gay man in New York is doing on a Friday night."

I chuckle.

"The New York Times wrote us up in the 1980s, and that's how they started the article," he says.

Ralph has arranged a dozen seats on the edges of the room, each with a thick blue Bible on top. It's more than we'll need. Most of the regulars are out of town, so only three diehards show up: A stout songwriter who grew up in Florida; an architect who looks exactly like Greg Kinnear; and a dance teacher at a New Jersey college who takes copious notes.

They are all members of Evangelicals Concerned, an organization Ralph founded in 1976 for gay and gay-friendly evangelicals. It's not a massive movement: Ralph has 2,000 people on his mailing list. But its existence alone was a surprise.

We begin. Ralph appoints the dance teacher to read some verses from Hebrews Chapter 3 out loud. Ralph stops him to discuss: "Faith is not merely intellectual assent," Ralph says, taking off his wire-rimmed glasses to punctuate the point. "You have to be willing to act on your faith. In other words, talk is cheap. Except in therapy."

Ralph returns his glasses to the end of his nose. He's not overbearing, but he's definitely in charge. He's the analyzer, the parser, the one who knows the original Greek words.

"Go on, says Ralph."

The dance instructor reads: "Yet Jesus has been counted worthy of as much more glory than Moses as the builder of a house has more honor than the house."

This is an important verse. It's at the heart of Ralph's theology—Jesus isn't just a great prophet. He isn't "the fairest flower in the family of humanity." He is God, and the resurrection was literal. Ralph quotes C.S. Lewis here: "A man who was merely a man and said the sort of things Jesus said would not be a great moral teacher. He would either be a lunatic—on the level with a man who says he is a poached egg—or he would be the devil of hell. You must take your choice."

In short, Ralph is theologically conservative. That's what makes him an evangelical. The scriptures' social and humanist message is important, but Blair puts the emphasis on the Good News itself—the divinity of Christ.

The 90-minute session glides by without a single mention of homosexuality. If an evangelist from Thomas Road Baptist Church happened to drop in, he might not even notice anything different. Well, let me revise that. Ralph and his group do, at least, fulfill one gay stereotype: They know a lot about clothes.

At one point, the conversation drifts to buttons, and the dance instructor starts throwing around terms like "placket"—which apparently means the part of a man's shirt that covers the buttons.

Then the architect tosses in a factoid about Eisenhower-style jackets, which were short so as to save fabric in World War II. They had no skirt.

"The skirt," he explains to me, "Is the part of a man's blazer worn below the waist." He looks at Ralph: "You wear a skirt almost every day."

Ralph smiles.

After Bible Study, we go out for chicken kebabs at a Turkish restaurant and I get a crash course in Ralph's life. He grew up in a moderately religious Presbyterian home in Ohio. He knew he was gay early on, certainly by high school. He also knew he loved religion.

In his high school library, he found a catalog to Bob Jones University, the fundamentalist college. He was drawn to it, he says with a laugh, because it was bright yellow. "All the other catalogs were dull colors, black and white."

He liked Bob Jones U's emphasis on Christ, and enrolled in 1964. It didn't go smoothly. For starters, Ralph got chewed out by an apoplectic, finger-wagging Bob Jones Sr. for defending Reverend Billy Graham, who was considered too liberal. "I thought he was going to have a heart attack," he says.

Ralph didn't come out of the closet at Bob Jones U. He went public slowly, steadily, as he criss-crossed the country attending other seminaries and grad schools. He started Evangelicals Concerned in 1975 after the president of an Evangelical college took him out to dinner in New York and confessed that he was a tormented, closeted gay man.

Of course, Ralph's organization is controversial. And at first blush, it makes about as much sense as an Association of Vegan Burger King Owners. It's at once inspiring and depressing. Inspiring that they have found each other, and depressing because they are part of a movement in which the majority thinks of their sexuality as sinful.

But Ralph says you have to distinguish between evangelical Christianity and the religious right. The religious right's obsession with homosexuality comes "out of their culture, not out of Scripture."

"But there do seem to be anti-gay passages in the Bible," I say.

"Yes, the so-called clobber passages," he says. "But I call them the clobbered passages."

Ralph's argument is this: The Bible does not talk about loving same-sex relationships as they exist today. Jesus would have no problem with two men committed to one another. One of Ralph's pamphlets has this headline on the front: "What Jesus said about homosexual relationships." You open the pamphlet up and there's a blank page.

Ralph says if you look at the Bible's allegedly anti-gay passages in historical context, they aren't anti-gay at all. They are actually anti-abuse, or anti-paganism. Consider the famous Leviticus passage: "You shall not lie with a man as with a woman; it is an abomination."

"In Biblical times, there was no parity between men and women. Women and children were just a little bit above slaves. To treat a man like a woman was to disgrace them. It's what soldiers did to their conquered enemies, they raped them."

That famous Leviticus passage is actually merely saying: Do not treat your fellow man disgracefully.

Or take another commonly-cited passage in the New Testament, Romans 1:26–27. Here, the Apostle Paul rails against those who gave into 'dishonorable passions.'

" . . ..Their women exchanged natural relations for unnatural, and the men likewise gave up natural relations with women and were consumed with passion for one another, men committing shameless acts with men and receiving in their own persons the due penalty for their error."

Ralph says that Paul is preaching here against pagan cultic practices—the loveless sex that went on in the idolatrous temples of the day.

I hope Ralph's right. I hope the Bible doesn't endorse gay-bashing. But even if it does, there's another tack religious people can take. This one I learned from Ralph's acquaintance in the Jewish world, a man named Steven Greenberg. Greenberg is the first out-of-the-closet Orthodox rabbi in America. Like Ralph, he's an extreme minority. Most Orthodox Jews still believe Leviticus bans same sex relationships of any kind; Your average far-right Orthodox Jew is just as anti-gay as your average far-right evangelical; in 2006, the ultra-Orthodox Jews held violent demonstrations in protest of a planned gay pride march in Jerusalem, eventually forcing its cancellation.

I call Greenberg. He has plenty to say about the Bible and homosexuality. But the point I find most fascinating is this: God and humans are partners in a quest to reveal new meanings of the Bible. The letters of the Bible are eternal, but not its interpretation.

"The whole Bible is the working out of the relationship between

God and Man," says Greenberg. "God is not a dictator barking out orders and demanding silent obedience. Were it so there would be no relationship at all. No real relationship goes just one way. There are always two active parties. We must have reverence and awe for God, and honor for chain of tradition. But that doesn't mean we can't use new information to help us read us the holy texts in new ways. We don't have to sit back and passively accept that Leviticus bans sex between men at all times and in all ways if other convincing ways of reading can be found."

Or put it this way: Greenberg says God is like an artist who is constantly revising his masterpiece. Sometimes, he nearly erases His whole work—as with the Great Flood. Other times, he listens to what humans say—Moses, for instance, argues with God and convinces him to spare the lives of the complaining Israelites. "It sounds strange to say it," he says, "but in the Bible, God is on a learning curve."

Greenberg tells me "Never blame a text from the Bible for your behavior. It's irresponsible. Anybody who says X,Y and Z is in the Bible—it's as if one says, I have no role in evaluating this."

The idea that we can work with God to evolve the Bible's meaning—it's a thrilling idea. It makes me think back to Mr. Berkowitz and his shoes and the whole issue of religion providing freedom from choice. Greenberg is the other end of the spectrum from Mr. Berkowitz. He says just because you're religious doesn't mean you give up your responsibility to choose. You have to grapple with the Bible.

Give thanks in all circumstances

1 THESSALONIANS 5:18

Day 258. I feel myself becoming an extremist—at least in some areas. Like with my obsession with gratefulness. I can't stop.

Just now, I press the elevator button, and am thankful that it arrives quickly.

I get onto the elevator am thankful that the elevator cable didn't snap and plummet me to the basement.

I go to the fifth floor and am thankful that I didn't have to stop on the second or third or fourth floor.

I get out and am thankful that Julie left the door unlocked so I don't have to rummage for my King Kong key ring.

I walk in, and am thankful Jasper is home and healthy and stuffing his face with pineapple wedges.

And on and on. I'm actually muttering to myself. 'thank you . . .thank you . . .thank you.'

It's an odd way to live. But also kind of great and powerful. I've never before been so aware of the thousands of little good things, the thousands of things that go right every day.

Sometimes my 'thanks' are directed at no one in particular. It's more of an appreciation than a thanks. A reminder to myself: 'pay attention, pal. Savor this moment.' But other times, when I'm in a believing phase, my thanks have an addressee. I'm thanking God, or the universal laws of nature—I'm not sure which—but it gives the act of thanking more weight.

And he lifted up his eyes on his disciples, and said:
"Blessed are you poor, for yours is the kingdom of God".

LUKE 6:20

Day 264. In terms of stereotype-busting, it's hard to beat Ralph Blair and his group of gay evangelicals. What could possibly top that? Evangelicals who don't believe in Jesus? Evangelicals who worship Poseidon? I don't know.

But I do want to spend some time with another group of evangelicals who, in their own way, have camped out far from Reverend Falwell's tent. They're called the Red Letter Christians.

I'd never heard of the Red Letter Christians before my Biblical year. They're still much smaller than the conservative evangelical lobby. They don't have TV shows with millions of viewers and 1–800 operators standing by. They don't have their own universities with facilities like the LaHaye Ice Hockey Arena. And yet, even since the start of my year, I've watched them gain more and more national prominence.

The Red Letter Christians are a loose-knit, like-minded group of preachers, the most prominent of whom are a Philadelphia-based pastor

named Tony Campolo and Jim Wallis, the founder of Sojourner's magazine and author of God's Politics. Bono is an honorary member.

Wallis writes on his website how he came up with the name. He was
doing an interview at a Nashville radio station, and the DJ said:

I'm a secular Jewish country music songwriter and disc jockey," [he]
said. "But I love your stuff and have been following your book tour." He
told me he loved my "riffs" and would like to spend an evening together
just to get some lines for new music. "You're a songwriter's dream."
Then he told me he believed we were starting a new movement, but noticed we hadn't come up with a name for it yet. "I've got an idea for
you," he said. "I think you should call yourselves 'The Red Letter Christians,' for the red parts of the Bible that highlight the words of Jesus. I
love the red letter stuff.

In their own way, the Red Letter Christians are literalists. They probably would avoid that label, since the word has such negative connotations. And true, they accept more figurative language in the Bible than,
say, the Falwell camp. But they are literal in the sense that their goal is to
return to the plain, primary, simple sense of Jesus' words, what Mer-
riam-Webster's literalism entry calls "the ordinary meaning of a term or
expression."

When Jesus said that you should invite the poor, the crippled, the
lame and the blind to your banquets, then you should. When Jesus
talked about non-violence, we should take him at his word. The problem
with a lot of religion, says Campolo, is that people have "interpreted the
Gospel so much, we've started to believe the interpretations instead of
what Jesus said."

Campolo looks a bit like Joe Torre, but balder and with clunky
glasses. He was, along with Reverend Jesse Jackson, one of Bill Clinton's
spiritual advisers during LewinskyGate.

I call Dr. Campolo up, and I immediately like him because he addresses me as "Brother."

"Many of us in the evangelical community believe that evangelical
Christianity has become captured and enslaved by the religious right,"
Campolo says, right off the bat. "Its loyalty seems to be more to the plat-
form of the Republican party than to the radical teachings of Jesus."

Campolo and the Red Letter Christians claim not to be liberal or conservative, Democrat or Republican. Which may be true—but their social policies definitely are more moveon.org than Foxnews. Anti-war, anti-consumerism—and above all, anti-poverty.

They point out there are more passages in the Bible about the poor than any other topic save idolatry—about 7,000, in fact. "The Christian call is to share," says Campolo. "There's nothing wrong with making a million dollars. There is something wrong with keeping it."

Some in the Falwell camp subscribe to a doctrine called Prosperity Gospel. The idea is this: Stay faithful, go to church, pay your tithes, and God will bless you by making you rich. God wants you to be successful. God has nothing against a Gulfstream jet and a private tennis court. The Red Letter Christians call this heresy. "Christianity is not a watered-down version of middle-class morality," says Campolo.

As for homosexuality, Campolo is no Ralph Blair. He doesn't endorse gay marriage. But . . . neither does he publicly condemn it. He believes it's not a major Christian issue. It wasn't what Jesus preached about. It's not something on which we should waste spiritual capital. Jesus was concerned with breaking down barriers and embracing society's outcasts.

At the end of our conversation, Dr. Campolo calls me "brother" again, which I love. If I were in the punditry business, I'd guess that that Campolo and his movement will keeping gaining steam. They may never fill Madison Square Garden and have their own universities, but they'll become a powerful force. They've already gotten enough press to inspire a backlash: Black Letter Christians. These are Christians who say the Red Letter Christians ignore troublesome passages that don't fit their agenda. Jesus may have a message of mercy, but he also has a message of justice. They cite his words in Matthew 10:34: "Do not think that I came to bring peace on the earth. I did not come to bring peace, but a sword."

Regardless, the Red Letter Christians are just one of the cracks in the Republican/evangelical love affair. Some evangelicals don't necessarily go as far as to embrace progressive politics, but say instead that churches should stay out of politics. The New York Times ran an article in 2006 about Reverend Gregory A. Boyd, a pastor of a Michigan megachurch. As the article says, Boyd "first became alarmed while visiting another megachurch's worship service on a Fourth of July years ago. The service finished with the chorus singing "God Bless America" and a video of fighter jets flying over a hill silhouetted with crosses. 'I thought to myself, 'What just happened? Fighter jets mixed up with the cross?'"

He gave a series of sermons saying that Christians should not seek political power, but instead seek to have 'power under' others—winning people's hearts by sacrificing for those in need, as Jesus did."

A thousand members of Boyd's flock were offended enough to leave the congregation. But another four thousand stayed on.

Jesus said to him, "If you would be perfect, go, sell what you possess and give to the poor, and you will have treasure in heaven; and come, follow me."

MATT. 19:21

Day 268. I bought The Purpose-Driven Life today. This is the guide to a Christian life by Hawaiian shirt-wearing megachurch minister Rick Warren that has been on the New York Times bestseller list for about half a decade now.

When I get it home and started to read it, the first thing I notice is that Warren had trademarked the phrase "Purpose-driven." It has a little ® after it. This made me angry. Did Jesus trademark "Turn the Other Cheek® Did Moses trademark "Let my People Go?™

But then I see that, in fine print, it says that Warren gives away 90 percent of the Purpose-driven profits. Ninety percent. He reverse tithes. Now I just feel small.

It reminds me that I have to finish my own tithing for the year. I go online and donate the final chunk of my 10 percent to a place called Warm Blankets Orphan Care, which builds orphanages in Asia. The Bible commands us to take care of the fatherless, plus this charity got the maximum four star rating on charitynavigator.org.

As with that first tithing back in September, I felt a mixture of God's pleasure and my own pain. But I think, or hope, I felt less pain than before. It comes back to the idea of surrendering. I still haven't been able to fully surrender my spirit or emotions, but I have at least surrendered some of my bank account. I have to embrace the surrender.

But I won't say another word about it. I've already violated Jesus' teaching: :

"So when you give to the needy, do not announce it with trumpets, as the hypocrites do in the synagogues and on the streets, to be honored by men."

Love . . . keeps no record of wrongs.

1 Corinthians 13:5 (NIV)

Day 270. There's a passage in the New Testament that I keep coming back to. I think about it every day. It's not nearly as famous as the Sermon on the Mount or the Good Samaritan parable. It's mostly known for being read at weddings.

In the passage, the Apostle Paul is writing to the Corinthians, and tells them that "Love is patient, love is kind. It does not envy, it does not boast, it is not proud. It is not rude, it is not selfseeking, it is not easily angered, it keeps no record of wrongs."

I think this passage speaks to me because I violate this one so literally, especially that last part.

I keep a record of wrongs.

It's in my Palm Treo in a file I've labeled "stuff." I figured the name "stuff" was vague and dull enough that if someone found it on the subway, he or she wouldn't bother to look at the file. Because I knew it's not something I should be proud of.

The problem is, Julie is always insisting that I have a terrible memory. She says I'm constantly getting things wrong. I respond that my memory is about as good as her memory—decent, but not great. And that she gets things wrong a lot too. Then she demands an example, and I can never think of one. So I've started to keep a list.

I'm aware of the irony that I have to consult a list to prove that I have a decent memory.

Here's a sample from my list.

—Vichyssoise is a potato soup like I said, not a fish soup like Julie said.

—That the animated android Max Headroom did commercials for

Coke like I said, not Pepsi like Julie said.

—That we saw an Irish movie called Waking Ned Devine on our second date like I said, not another charmingly quirky movie called Saving Grace.

You get the idea. I've only actually put my list into action one time. This is because it's kind of difficult to look at the list in public without exposing the secret of the list. During an unpleasant argument about who left the microwave door open, I sneaked into the bathroom, clicked on my Treo, then re-emerged with an example of the time she left the keys in a rental car and we had to call Avis.

In short, the exact kind of thing Paul was preaching against. I decide not only should I erase my "Stuff" file, but I should confess to Julie about its existence. So that's what I'm doing.

When I show Julie my list, she looks at it for a good 10 seconds without talking.

Then she laughs.

"You're not angry?"

"How could I be angry?" she says. "It's just so heartbreaking that you need this."

"Well, I have trouble remembering things in the moment."

I take the Treo back from her, highlight the 'Stuff' list, then press delete. I feel good. I've cleaned the slate on my Treo, and I've cleaned the slate with Julie. I know it may seem like a small thing, but the 'Stuff' incident made me realize my worldview is too much about quantification. It consists of thousands of little ledgers. Everything—people included—comes with a list of assets and liabilities. When I forgive, I file the other person's wrongs away for possible future use. It's forgiveness with an asterisk.

The Hebrew Scriptures encourage forgiveness—Leviticus says "do not hold a grudge"—but it's fair to say that it's a bigger theme in the New Testament. Start over. Be born again. Become a new creature in Christ.

Consider Jesus' Parable of the Prodigal Son. Here's how the New Catholic encyclopedia describes it:

"The story of the son who took his portion of his father's goods and squandered it by riotous living. When reduced to the depth of misery and obliged to eat the husks thrown to the swine, he bethought himself of his father and resolved to return to him penitent. The father was watching for him, greeted him affectionately and killed the fatted calf to make merry over his return. The elder son resented the father's rejoicing. The father silenced him by the reminder that: "thou art always with me, and all I have is thine, but. ..thy brother was dead and is come to life, was lost and is found."

When I first read the Parable of the Prodigal Son, I was perplexed. I felt terrible for the older brother. The poor man put in all these years of loyal service, and his brother skips town, has a wild good time, then returns and gets a huge feast? It seems outrageously unfair.

But that's if you're thinking quantitatively. If you're looking at life as a balance sheet. There's a beauty to forgiveness, especially forgiveness that goes beyond rationality. Unconditional love is an illogical notion, but such a great and powerful one.

The eyes of the LORD are in every place, keeping watch
on the evil and the good.

PROVERBS 15:3

Day 271. A spiritual update: Back when I was in seventh grade, I had this delusion. I thought that the girls on whom I had crushes might be watching me. Not at school, mind you. They ignored me there. But in my room, when I was alone, they were watching. I wasn't sure how the logistics of this worked (psychic powers? Hidden cameras like the Truman Show?) but it put a lot of pressure on me. I had to make sure to act cool in case Kim Glickman was observing. I'd put on an LP of David Bowie not because I wanted to hear Bowie, but because I wanted Kim to think I wanted to hear Bowie. I'd brush my teeth in a rakishly nonchalant manner, just so she knew I was cool even when doing dental hygiene. Maybe she likes the tortured artists, I thought. So sometimes, I'd channel Sid Vicious and do something crazy, like throw my three-ring school binder across my room and watch the pages splatter on the floor. (I'd then spend fifteen minutes cleaning up and putting the pages back into the rings).

Sad, I know. Luckily, I got over that in ninth grade. But now, I'm starting to have a similar feeling. Kim can't see me. But maybe something can. Something is keeping track of my life, of all of our lives. My existence is not a meaningless collection of actions, so I should take seriously every decision. I don't know what the payoff will be, if anything. But someone is writing this all down in the Book of Life.

> *When they had rowed about three or four miles,*
> *they saw Jesus walking on the sea and drawing near to the boat.*
>
> JOHN 6:19

Day 272. My brother-in-law Eric does not embody the Biblical virtue of humility. He's a prideful man.

When I went on Who Wants to Be a Millionaire? and Eric was my Phone-a-Friend. It seemed a good choice. He went to Harvard and will lecture you on anything from the SALT II treaties to symbolism of Zola's novels. Well, when I called him on the air, he choked and lost me $32,000. Did that dent his ego? Not a bit.

He still believes he's the smartest man alive. I'm sure if Eric were around in Biblical times, he'd be chief architect of the tower of Babel. These days, he's getting his PhD in behavioral psychology at Columbia, which means he says things like this: "Humans are a fascinating species." As if our struggles are all for his intellectual amusement.

Eric came over to lunch at our apartment today. And within five minutes, he's already tried to puncture my project.

"So, did you hear about that study about Jesus walking on water?"

"No."

"This scientist says it's because the conditions in the Mediterranean at the time caused ice floes on the Sea of Galilee."

"I see."

I haven't seen that study, but I'd seen many like it.

There's a whole miniature industry devoted to the business of explaining miracles with science. You can buy several books on the subject.

The rivers of Egypt turning blood-red? It was likely the red algae volcanic ash. The darkness sweeping over the land? It was the khamaseen, a hot wind of the Saraha, churning up the sand. When Moses sweetened the bitter desert water at Marah with a tree? He might have been using an ion exchange resin. Not that I know what that means. But it sounds convincing.

In any case, I wish Eric would shut his Harvard-educated trap. I don't need to hear scientific explanations of miracles. It plays too perfectly into my skeptical side, which still runs deep.

I know plenty of religious people who see miracles as myths, not literal truth. They say that we don't need to believe that Joshua actually stopped the sun in the sky so he could finish a battle; the story can still have beauty and meaning even if Joshua didn't not get a divine extension. And I imagine that, if I go religious at the end of this year, that's the camp I'll belong to.

But if I'm going to be literal, I must at least try to believe they happened. That God overturned the natural order. It's a heck of a mental hurdle and, as with creationism, one I'm not sure I can clear.

I take some measure of consolation from a book I just read. It's called the Battle for God by former-nun-turned-religion-scholar Karen Armstrong.

Armstrong makes the contrarian argument that people in Biblical times did not believe the miracles happened. Or not in the same way that fundamentalists today do, anyway. Armstrong says that the ancients viewed the world simultaneously in two different ways. One was logos, the other mythos. Logos was the ancient's rational and practical side, the factual knowledge they used in farming or building houses. Mythos were the stories that gave their lives meaning. For instance, the story of the Exodus was not to be taken as factual, but as a tale filled with significance. The ancients didn't necessarily believe that it happened exactly as told—with 600,000 men trudging through the desert for 40 years. But it was true in the larger sense, in the sense that it gave meaning to their lives.

Fundamentalism, Armstrong says, is a modern phenomenon. It's the attempt to apply logos to mythos, to turn legend into scientific truth. I don't wholly buy Armstrong's thesis. It smacks of wishful thinking to me. I don't think the distinctions in the Biblical minds were that black and white. But given the choice between her theory and fundamentalism, I'll take hers.

> *"Whoever strikes his father or his mother shall be put to death."*
>
> EXODUS 21:15

Day 273. When Jasper wakes up from his nap, I go to retrieve him. He is standing at the edge of his crib, his hair sticking up in back, Alfalfa-style. In his hand, he is clutching a plastic bowling pin, which is his version of a security blanket.

I lift him out.

Jasper grins—it is a grin meant to convey that he was about to do something spectacularly witty—and then he hits me in the face with a bowling pin.

"Don't do that," I say. I have on my stern James Earl Jones voice.

He takes that to mean do it again, but harder. So he winds up and delivers another blow to my face. And another. These ones were powerful, leave-a-red-mark-on-my-forehead hits.

"Jasper!" I said. "Say you're sorry."

Jasper just grins.

"You do not hit people in the face with bowling pins. It's very dangerous. That's a no-no."

He looks at me bewildered, then angry. How could I not see the humor in a flawlessly-executed-bowling-pin-to-the-face maneuver?

"Apologize to me please."

"No."

"Apologize."

"No."

This is going to be ugly.

The Hebrew Bible says that hitting your parents can be punishable by death. Instead, I turn the other cheek. I ignore my son.

Ignoring a rebellious son is, coincidentally, a strategy recommended by a secular parenting book I read months ago. So I put him on the ground, turn my back to him, and cross my arms. I look like a model posing for the label on the Mr. Clean bottle.

He starts to whimper.

"Say you're sorry and we can go play," I say.

"No."

"No hitting people," I say. I say it with decisivenss, confident that I have thousands of years of tradition behind me.

I keep my back to him. He grabs my leg.

"AJ!" he says. "AJ! AJ!"

There's something ineffably heartbreaking about a two-year-old call-ing to his father, and the father not answering. And I am that father. It's killing me. But Jasper is still too stubborn to say "sorry."

The Bible talks about the importance of punishing your kids if you love them. And I think there's something to that paradoxical advice. The best punishment should be a sacrifice—you sacrifice a pleasant after-noon, you sacrifice some in-the-moment affection, to give them a better future.

Jasper stomps, he sulks, he mutters to himself. It's the longest fight we've had. Finally, four hours later, he tracks me down in the living room and gave me a sad little downcast-eyes "Sorry."

"Great!" I say. "I'm so proud of you for apologizing. What should we play?"

But Jasper would not be playing with me tonight. He would play alone. He goes to bed all mopy and martyr-like

It probably sounds like a minor skirmish, but for me, the War of the Bowling Pin was an epic one. The next morning at about 7:15, I heard Jasper screaming into the monitor: "AJ! AJ!" I opened his door, stuck my head in. I picked him up, he gave me a grudge-free hug around the neck. Yes, our relationship survived my dispensation of justice. It's a good les-son for me. I still spare the rod, but I'm trying not to spoil the child.

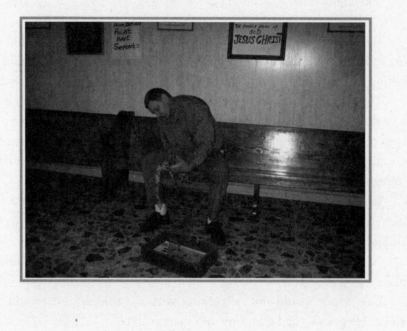

Month Ten: June

"Nor should there be any obscenity, foolish talk or coarse joking,
which are out of place"

EPHESIANS 5:4 (NIV)

Day 277. "How was the birthday party," I ask Julie.

She and Jasper had just returned from a party at a preschool on the East Side.

"Okay. But they had this rabbit for the kids to pet, and there was rabbit shit everywhere."

"Huh."

I am shocked at her language. And then I am shocked that I am shocked.

When I first met Julie, she rarely cursed, whereas I had no filter whatsoever. I chose a particularly adolescent curseword as my default computer password. I enjoyed watching TV with the closed captioning, because the captioners sometimes type in the dirty words that are bleeped out for the apparently more-delicate non-hearing-impaired community.

But for the last two months, inspired by Orthodox Jews and evangelical Christians, I haven't used a single naughty word. And it startles me when others do.

What is a Biblically naughty word? Well, there's two genres: blasphemy and profanity.

Blasphemy is the subject of the third commandment, which orders us not to take the Lord's name in vain. The question is, what makes for a "vain" utterance? Is it when you say the word "God" in any secular context? Or when you invoke God's name when you are lying under oath?

Or when you speak God's holy name, the word Yahweh? All three theories have their supporters.

If you want to be supremely safe, as I do, you should only use the word "God" when praying or talking about the Bible.

As for profanity—the S-word and the F-word and regular old bodily-function-themed cussing—things are even less clear.

In fact, as science writer Natalie Angier points out, the Bible itself uses some adult language. In 2 Kings 18:27, the men "eat their own dung and drink their own piss." The word Beelzebub—a synonym the devil— is actually thought by many to be a dirty pun meaning "Lord of the Dung."

Still, there are parts, especially in the New Testament, that such language should be avoided. Consider the passage from Ephesians I put at the top of this chapter.

"Nor should there be any obscenity, foolish talk or coarse joking, which are out of place" Ephesians 5:4 (NIV)

Or else, this one from Ephesians 4:29:

"Do not let any unwholesome talk come out of your mouth."

So to be totally protected, I've scrubbed up my vocabulary. My current cursewords are: Fudge, sugar and shoot. When I say one of my new cursewords, Julie usually responds with something like, "Hey, Opie. You going fishing this morning?" Or just whistling the Andy Griffith theme song.

She can mock me, but the weird thing is, I think my G-rated language is making me a less angry person. Because here's the way it works:

I'll get to the subway platform just as the downtown train is pulling away, and I'll start to say the F-word.

I'll remember to censor myself. So I'll turn it into "Fudge" at the last second.

When I hear myself say "Fudge' out loud, it sounds so folksy, so Jimmy Stewartish and amusingly dorky, that I can't help but smile. My anger recedes. Once again, behavior shapes emotions.

Fudge seems clearly within bounds, but what about words like "heck?" Those are more morally ambiguous, but probably should be avoided as well.

In the 1600s, "criminy" was considered a curse word for being too close to "Christ." Same with "gosh" and "golly" in the 1700s, which were meant to evoke God and God's body respectively. Later, "Jiminy Crickets" and "Gee Wilkins" were wicked codewords for Jesus. "Tarnation" began as an offensive combination of "eternity" and "damnation." And heck was an only slightly better alternative to "hell."

A minister's daughter recently told me that, when she was growing up, they used "Cheese and rice" instead of the name of her savior, which I imagine would also have been banned in the 18th century. Land mines lurk everywhere in the English language.

> *Jesus said to them, "Render to Caesar the things that are Caesars,*
> *and to God the things that are Gods."*
>
> MARK 12:17

Day 278. I've been dropping in on another evangelical Bible Study class—a straight one. They meet on Tuesday nights in the back room of the American Bible Society in Columbus Circle.

The dozen or so other members have been very welcoming of me, though a little perplexed at the same time, since I look more Jewish than your average diamond dealer on 47th street. I'm glad they let me listen as we drill deep on a different passage from the Gospel of Mark each week. It's always humbling. I can keep up with them on the Old Testament—I can quote Deuteronomy and the Proverbs—but I'm still a third-string minor leaguer when it comes to the New Testament.

Anyway, I bring this up because last week at Bible study, the co-leader—a tall, precise, white-haired man named Kevin—was talking about how he tries to be a good and law-abiding person.

He told us that a he was recently driving from New York to Ohio for business, and he had a battle with himself. He'd keep gunning his car up to 65, then he'd feel guilty for breaking the law, and slow back down to 55.

'I said to myself, 'do I really need to speed?' he said. 'What's it going to save me? An hour? Is it worth it in the long run to break the law?'

There is scriptural justification for strict observance of civil law, speed limits and otherwise. You can see it in one of Peter's letter to his followers in the New Testament, where he tells them to obey the emperor:

> *"Be subject for the Lord's sake to every human institution, whether it be to the emperor as supreme, or to governors as sent by him."*
>
> 1 PETER 2:13–14

When I ask the pastor out to pasture Elton Richards about whether to obey every human institution, he cautions me: You can find the opposing idea in the New Testament as well. There's a story about Peter and John preaching God's word, and they are told by the authorities to shut up. They do not. They say, in effect, 'we answer to a higher authority."

Author Marcus Borg says the two themes run throughout the Bible. Call them statusquo theology and liberation theology. Statusquo theology tells us to support our earthly leaders. God appointed our leaders, so we shouldn't question them—or even speak ill of them ("You shall not . . .curse a ruler of your people," Exodus 22:28). Liberation theology encourages God's people to throw off the yoke of oppression, and flee the Pharaoh, or his modern-day equivalents. Liberation theology says that God is with the people.

So which to choose? Well, in the case of traffic laws, Bible-study-leader Kevin has got a point. I'm not doing any noble Gandhi-like civil disobedience by going 70 in a school zone. I'm just trying to get home faster to take a nap.

This month, I have pledged to try to really follow New York's street laws. To the letter. This has changed my life in a more dramatic way than I could have imagined. Just try not to jaywalk in Manhattan. It's almost impossible. I wait on the corner, usually alone, or, if I'm lucky, with a German tourist couple and a class of first graders on a field trip. The rest of New York pedestrians see the traffic lights as helpful suggestions, but lacking authority.

I won't pretend it's fun. It's a pain in the butt. It takes me about 30 percent longer to walk anywhere. And it's another source of stupid—but increasingly intense—arguments with my wife. Yesterday, we got out of a cab in the middle of the block, and I refused to cross the street there. I walked to the end of the block, waited for the light to change, marched over the zebra crossing, then walked back up the other side. Conveniently, it was raining. Julie was waiting for me under an awning.

"Hope you had a nice walk," she says, her voice more tired than angry.

Driving is just as bad. Until I started to pay attention, I didn't even know speed limits existed in New York. I figured the rule was: Gun your car to get to the next light as fast as possible, then jerk to a stop, then repeat. Or, more likely, sit in traffic and go 5 mph. But if you look hard enough, you can find them. Actual speed limit signs—30 mph on most avenues. So whenever we rent a car to visit Julie's brother in New Jersey, I've made sure to cruise at a nice, smooth 25 mph down Columbus Avenue.

When we get to the highway, things get more complicated. Often, I'm the only one putt-putting along at 55, certainly the only one without a World's Best Grandpa bumper sticker. I should probably have my hazards on. Cars whiz by me. They honk. They swerve. The drivers look at me like I'm the lone Red Sox fan at a Yankees game. The first time I drove on the highway, I couldn't stop laughing—I'm not sure out of nervousness or out of the absurdity of it or both.

So in general, the whole experience has been a pain. But there are two upsides.

1. I've come to see obeying traffic laws as an urban version of the Sabbath. It's an enforced pause. When I stand alone on the corner, I try to spend the time appreciating the little things New York has to offer. Look at that—the street signs have changed from yellow and black to a much more pleasant green and white. When did that happen? Or else I watch the FedEx truck drive by and notice the secret white arrow embedded in its logo (it's between the F and the E).

2. I have freedom from worry. No one I know has ever been arrested for jaywalking. But whenever I violated the "Don't Walk" sign, there was always a tiny, faint pang from knowing that I was doing something wrong. I no longer have that. I feel in control. It's that same feeling of

cleanliness, of relief, that I get when I actually fold all the sweaters in my closet or clean out all the emails in my in-box.

. . .Not in the passion of lust like heathen who do not know God

1 Thessalonians 4:5

Day 286. Julie is seven months pregnant with the twins, and wildly uncomfortable. She can hardly move. She gets out of breath opening the refrigerator door. When I asked her a couple of weeks ago if she wanted to be intimate, she said the following:

"I can't think of anything I'd rather do less."

No sugarcoating there.

Speaking of sex, I think I dismissed the whole lust issue too glibly. I found a way to rationalize it—I told myself, well, the Hebrew Bible has pro-sex parts, so I don't have to bother with all that modesty business.

I took the easy way out. The truth is, there are plenty of sections of the Bible that do encourage restraint of the sex drive, sometimes even abstinence. Jesus says not to even think about other women aside from your wife:

"You have heard that it was said, 'You shall not commit adultery.' But I say to you that every one who looks at a woman lustfully has already committed adultery with her in his heart."

Matthew 5:27–8

And the Apostle Paul implies that celibacy is the ideal; marriage is a second-best solution, a concession to our urges. As he says in Galatians 5:24:

"And those who belong to Christ Jesus have crucified the flesh with its passions and desires." So I decide I should try to be ascetic for my final few weeks, and, as Paul says, put to death those parts that are human.

My previous strategy of censorship didn't work. We saw that with the CleanFlicks fiasco. It was too passive. I have to attack lust head on. I have to change my way of thinking about sex. So after much reading, I've developed four strategies.

Last night, I had the chance to road-test all four. I went to a fashion show that Uri had invited me to. He said the designer is an Orthodox Jew who grew up in Brooklyn, and I figured, Orthodox fashion? Sounds pretty tame. Lots of bulky, shapeless, earth-toned dresses. Perhaps a scandalous glimpse of exposed ankle. I could handle that.

I know I am going to be tempted from the moment I arrive. The event is held in Chelsea at the "Frying Pan," a rusty boat docked off 23rd street. The crowd is thick, packing both sides of the catwalk. Yes, there were a sprinkling of Orthodox Jews, but mostly it is gorgeous twentysomething fashion types with back tattoos, and bare shoulders/midriffs/thighs. (There is also a man in a pink suit, pink shoes and pink bowler hat, and on said bowler hat, a tiny billboard—about the size of a license plate—with a functioning electronic text scrawl. This did not make me lustful, but thought you should know).

I start out with Strategy Number One. Here you to think of the woman in question as out of your league. You remember this advice from the medieval rabbi from way back in the first month? You have to think of yourself as a peasant, and her as a princess. She's so beyond your grasp, you can admire aesthetically, but not lustfully.

I try this out within the first five minutes. When Uri and I took our place, we noticed a woman with a small leopardskin skirt, small bustier and very large cleavage.

"You don't see that too much in Crown Heights," says Uri.

Interestingly, this strategy has gotten much easier for me with my current appearance. A year ago, I might have deluded myself that I had a shot at Leopardskin Bustier Woman. Nowadays, not so much.

Strategy 2: Think of the woman as if she were your mother.

This is another tip from the medieval rabbi. So I do it. I think of Leopardskin Bustier Woman as my mom, and I feel revulsed. I feel like Malcolm McDowell in A Clockwork Orange when they made him look at pictures of women in stockings, then zapped him with 5000 volts. This is more effective than strategy number one, and also more disturbing.

Strategy 3: Recite Bible passages to yourself.

After a few minutes, the fashion show itself starts, and the temptations get worse. The models aren't hidden behind modest muumuus. They stomp down the runway with their exaggerated hip swivel, wearing about in alarmingly skimpy outfits that look like kimonos during a fabric shortage. One dark-haired model has no shirt or blouse whatsoever. The only thing around her chest is what appears to be an extra-large rubber band.

Here, I try strategy number three. This one I picked up from a book called When Good Men Are Tempted—a guide to controlling your lust by an evangelical Christian named Bill Perkins. He suggests you recite Bible passages:

"I've found that memorizing large sections of the Bible gives me a safe mental focus when I'm tempted. By the time I recite a paragraph or two to myself, my spirit is strengthened and my mind is cleared."

So I do that. I mouth to myself one of the verses he suggested. It worked in a way. My brain was so busy with its recital project, it didn't have time to focus on the rubber band. The meaning of the passage is almost beside the point. I could have probably recited the lyrics to the Mikado and gotten a similar benefit. It's all about keeping your mind distracted.

The show ends and I tell Uri I should probably go. He says, "You sure you don't want to just hang around for a few minutes?"

"Well, just a few minutes."

We bump into a friend of Uri's. She is blonde, Israeli, cute, and very drunk.

"She has a weird fetish," Uri whispers to me. "She likes to fondle payot."

As in the side locks? Uri nods.

Oh man. Uri introduces me to her.

"I'm very drunk," she says.

I smile noncommittally.

Was she checking out my side locks? I think so.

Here, I try out Strategy Number Four: Do not objectify. This one I got from downloading an excellent sermon about lust by a Unitarian minister. The minister suggested that you can battle your urge to objectify women by focusing on them as a complete person. So I looked at Fetish Girl and thought about everything but her body: Her Israeli childhood, what might be her favorite novel, how many cousins she has, whether she owns a PC or Mac.

But she won't stop looking at my payot. This isn't working. In a panic, I switch to the less evolved but more efficient method: Think of her as your mom. I felt nauseated. Victory.

I've also noticed a strange phenomenon. I figured it'd get more and more difficult to suppress my sexuality. I figured it'd be like water building up behind a dam. But quite the opposite—it's more like my sex drive has evaporated. I'm sure it'll come roaring back like a dragon—to use the metaphor in my book When Good Men are Tempted. But for now, it's pleasantly tranquilized.

I love feeling dead below the belt. I feel spiritually spotless. It makes me realize I have a hidden Puritan streak. On some level, I do consider sex dirty, or else why would I feel so buoyant when I've stamped it out? There's something lovely about putting your libido in deep freeze.

And there's another advantage: The thousands of watts of energy devoted to sex are suddenly free for other pursuits. Sublimation is real. I've never been so productive as I have in these past weeks. I can crank out 2000 Esquire words a day on this no-sex-diet.

Lord, how often shall my brother sin against me, and I forgive him?

MATTHEW 18:21

Day 287. Tonight, at 9:15 p.m., Julie leaves our bedroom door open. I have repeatedly asked her not to do this. I can't sleep unless the room is Reykjavik-level cold, so I always shut the door at 7 p.m. and flip the air conditioner on high. Julie, who could sleep anywhere and anytime, always forgets, leaves the door open, and lets my precious cool air slip out.

I snap at her.

"Please shut the door!"

Huh. That came out a little too sharply. To soften things, I throw in a Biblical literalism joke.

"I forgive you this time. But if you do it another 489 times, I won't forgive you."

Julie shuts the door without asking me to explain my wryly cryptic statement. So let me do it here.

I was referring to a passage in Matthew 18:

"Then Peter came up and said to him, 'Lord, how often shall my brother sin against me, and I forgive him? As many as seven times?'

Jesus said to him, 'I do not say to you seven times, but seventy times seven.'"

In other words 490 times.

When I first made my list of Biblical rules, this was actually part of my plan. I'd take everything literally, even those sentences that were clearly metaphorical. I would forgive someone 490 times, despite the fact that Jesus almost surely meant you should forgive an infinite number of times.

I revised that plan for a couple of reasons. First, it would involve chopping off various parts of my body (see below), which I was reluctant to do. Second, it soon became clear that I could make my point—that Biblical literalism is necessarily a selective—without intentionally warping the meaning of the Bible.

But here is a sample of the even more bizarre life I could have led.

—I could have plucked out my eye, since Jesus says "And if your eye causes you to sin, pluck it out; it is better for you to enter the kingdom of God with one eye than with two eyes to be thrown into hell." (Mark 9:47) This is generally interpreted by Christian leaders to mean you should get rid of those things in your life that cause you to sin. "If you are addicted to Internet pornography, you should consider getting rid of your computer," says Dr. Campolo. Though as with most passages, there have been people who have taken it at its word. A psychologist of religion named Wayne Oates writes of mental patients who plucked out their eyes in literal compliance of Jesus' words.

—I could hate my parents, since Jesus says "If any one comes to me and does not hate his own father and mother and wife and children and brothers and sisters, yes, and even his own life, he cannot be my disciple." Luke 14:26. Here, the idea is that: given the difficult choice between God and your family, you should choose God—not that Jesus condoned parent-hating.

—I could avoid uttering the word 'good' for the rest of my year, in literal adherence to this passage:

And a ruler asked him, "Good Teacher, what must I do to inherit eternal life?"

And Jesus said to him, "Why do you call me good? No one is good but God alone.

This approach reminds me of one of my dad's wacky practical jokes: He'll start pouring a glass of water for one of my friends, and tell the unsuspecting chump "just say when." The chump will say 'stop' and my dad will keep pouring. The chump will say 'that's enough' and my dad will keep pouring. My dad will keep pouring till the water spills over the edge of the glass and splashes onto table. Then my dad will look at him in faux bewilderment and say: "You never said 'when.'" A classic.

And here's the amazing thing—those who overliteralize the words of God get mocked . . .in the Bible itself. I learned this while reading a book called Rescuing the Bible from Fundamentalism by the Episcopal bishop John Shelby Spong. He writes this about this passage in the Gospel of John:

> *In reply Jesus declared, "I tell you the truth, no-one can see the kingdom of God unless he is born again."*
> *Nicodemus—a Pharisee responds:*
> *"How can a man be born when he is old . . .Surely he cannot enter a second time into his mother's womb to be born!"*
>
> JOHN 3:3–4 (NIV)

Nicodemus is like a sitcom dunderhead here. Born again? How is that possible? How can an adult squeeze back into his mother's uterus? He can't see that Jesus' words were figurative and poetic and he becomes the butt of a joke.

the truth will make you free.

JOHN 8:32

Day 290. Ever since my lying spree on the Falwell trip, I've recommitted myself extreme honesty. In response, Julie has come up with a way to make my honesty more palatable. She's started to ask me a singularly terrifying question: What are you thinking about?

We'll be walking to the playground, and she'll spring it on me:

"Hey. What are you thinking about?"

I can't just respond "nothing much." I have to tell the truth, the unvarnished truth.

"I'm thinking about that rude guy at the Judaica store on Broadway, and how I should have told him, 'You just became a villain in my book.'"

"Sounds like vengeance. Isn't that Biblically forbidden?"

Julie loves her new trick. It's as if she's found a peephole into my soul and can discover who she's really married to, no deceptions. Or, as she puts it, "I feel like I've picked up the Opportunity card in Monopoly."

We'll be unpacking groceries, and suddenly I'll hear:

"What are you thinking about?"

"Oh business stuff."

She's not falling for that. "What business stuff?"

"That I wish I could time travel back to 1991 and buy up hundreds of Internet names like flowers.com and beer.com and cabbage.com, then I could sell them for millions of dollars to the flower and beer and cabbage industries, and then I'd never have to work again." (This is an alarmingly common fantasy of mine).

"That's the saddest daydream I've ever heard. Plus, that's greed."

She's right. I'm wasting my time with greedy and angry thoughts. Not always, mind you. Sometimes, when Julie pops the question, I'll be thinking about something noble, like the environment or our son's future. In fact, compared to my pre-Biblical life, the percentage of brain-space allotted to gratitude and compassion has inched up. But I still have way too many thoughts like this:

"What are you thinking about?"
"The Bible, actually."
"What about the Bible?"
"The story of Esther."
"What about the story of Esther?"

"Well . . .what it would be like to be the king in the Esther story, and get to spend the night with each of the most beautiful women in the kingdom, like a test drive or something, and then get to choose your favorite."

"You've really evolved."

In the last couple of days, I've been focusing on cleaning up my brain. It's possible God is monitoring my thoughts, but it's certain that Julie is. So I've commanded myself to think positive thoughts. And today, it paid off.

"What are you thinking about?"

"How lucky I am to have a healthy wife and a healthy son and two so-far-healthy babies."

Julie pretends to gag. But it was true, that's what I was thinking.

Of making many books there is no end

ECCLESIASTES 12:12 (NIV)

Day 292. I've got a decent Biblical library going now. Perhaps 50 books or so. And I've divided them into sections: Moderate Jewish. Fundamentalist Jewish. Moderate Christian. Fundamentalist Christian. Atheist. Agnostic. Religious Cookbooks.

I've tried to keep the conservative books on the right side and the liberal ones on the left. When I started my year, I thought nothing would go to the right of my Falwell collection. But of course, I was wrong. I just got in a book called A Handbook of Bible Law by a man named Charles Weisman.

I'd try to summarize it, but the subtitle does a pretty good job, so I'll just type that in: "An Indexed Guide to Over 1500 Biblical Laws, Commandments, Statutes, Principles, Admonishments, Exhortations & Guidelines Under 22 Different Subject Headings."

When I found "The Handbook of Bible Law: An Indexed Guide to Over 1500 (etc. etc.)" it seemed the perfect Fodor's guide to my spiritual trek. All the laws in one place! It was so well-organized, I figured it might be worth talking to the author. His name is Charles Weisman. So today I Googled him. And I found out that he probably does not want to hear from me. And vice versa.

Weisman runs a small publishing company in Burnsville, Minnesota that distributes such gems as The International Jew, a collection of Henry Ford's anti-Semitic rants. You can also buy a tome called America: Free, White & Christian, and books about how the "white Adamic race have (sic) been the innovators and builders of all advanced civilizations throughout history." You get the idea.

And when Weisman publishes the handbook of Bible law, it's not out of academic interest. He wants a theocracy in America now.

Weisman's got company. There are thousands of beyond-the-pale-fundamentalists who want to set up a Biblical government based on both Testaments. As in a society that executes homosexuals, adulterers and blasphemers. As in one that shuts down every synagogue, mosque and moderate church. They are the American Taliban. Not all are racist like Wiesman—in fact, most claim not to be—but all scare me. Unlike mainstream Christians, they don't believe that Christ's death voided much of the law. And unlike mainstream Jews, they don't mute the harsher Hebrew Bible passages, the executions for adultery and blasphemy and the like.

So they are on the fringe, yes. But perhaps not as much as I'd hoped. The movement is called Reconstructionism or Dominionism (the differences are subtle, but as far as I can tell, Dominionism is for the slightly less extremist extremist). And writers such as Gary Wills and Slate's Michelle Goldberg argue that the Dominionism has undue influence on some more respectable members of the Christian right. It's an influence they say far outweighs their numbers: They were a driving force behind the homeschooling movement and have helped shape Pat Robertson's worldview.

They're doing what I'm doing, but they aren't doing it as part of a spiritual quest/book project. They make me appreciate the comparative graciousness of the Falwell folks even more.

"They will pick up serpents."

MARK 16:18

Day 299. If you want to slam Christian Biblical literalism, I've noticed, the go-to epithet is "snake handler." As in "Jerry Falwell is a knuckle-dragging snake handler."

Actually, Falwell has condemned snake handling. But it's easy to see why this small sect has become shorthand for religious extremism in America. You watch the Appalachian snake handlers on the Discovery channel, and they look as weird as the guy on Coney Island who hammers six-inch nails into his nostrils, or Nick Nolte after a couple of vodka tonics.

I knew the basic idea behind serpent handling. I'd once assigned an *Esquire* article on the topic to Dennis Covington, a writer who penned a wonderful serpent-handling memoir called *Salvation on Sand Mountain*. As Dennis explains, the serpent handlers take their inspiration from a passage spoken by Jesus in Mark 16:17–18, which reads:

"And these signs will accompany those who believe: in my name they will cast out demons; they will speak in new tongues; they will pick up serpents, and if they drink any deadly thing, it will not hurt them."

Most Christians read the phrase "they will pick up serpents" to be a metaphor—faith will help you overcome life's 'serpents,' its challenges and bad people and temptations. The serpent handlers don't see it as figurative. They show their devotion to Jesus by picking up snakes—venomous snakes—during their services.

You may criticize them for a loopy interpretation, but one thing is

for sure: These are not the type of Biblical literalists who had a precon-
ceived political agenda and then dig up a few Scriptural passages to back
that agenda up. They simply read a passage in the Bible and did what it
said. They are the ultimate literalists. I needed to visit them.

I called up a man named Jimmy Morrow, whose phone number I got
from a professor of religion at the University of Tennessee. Jimmy was
happy to hear from me, and told me to come on down anytime.

"Will I have to handle snakes?" I asked.

"Absolutely not," said Jimmy. "You can come to the church for 1,000
years and not handle a single snake."

After church, "if all goes okay," Jimmy says he's having a picnic, and
I'm invited. If all goes okay. That's a scary concept. These snakes are
real. Though it's uncommon, people do get bit and die—more than 60 of
them in the last century.

So on a Sunday morning, I fly to Knoxville, Tennessee, drive 90 minutes to Clayville, one exit past the Wal-Mart, and pull up into the driveway of the Church of God with Signs Following. It's a small, wooden
one-room structure. Outside, a white painted sign quotes Mark
16:17–18.

Jimmy arrives minutes later. He hugs me and invites me inside. He's
a tall, gray-haired fifty-one-year old with a big jutting Clintonian chin.
And he has the thickest accent I'd ever heard. It took me awhile to adjust
my ears—for the first half an hour, I have to strain the same way I do
when Shakespearian actors first start spouting their Elizabethan English.

Jimmy is the humblest fundamentalist you'll ever meet. Even his
slightly stooped posture radiates humility. "I'm just a mountain man,"
he tells me. He peppers his speech with a lot of "Well, I think" and "it's
my interpretation"

"I just tell the word of God, and people can take it or reject it," says
Jimmy. "I've had Mormons here—I treat 'em good. I've had people from
Finland here—I treat em good. I don't say anything against 'em. Just tell
'em the word of God."

Jimmy was saved when he was 13. He saw a snake in the road, and
the snake tried to bite him, but "God locked the snake's jaws. So that's
when I knew it was true."

Since then, he's amassed what he believes is the largest archive of serpent handling material in the world. He unlocks a church storeroom to
show me. It's crammed with yellowed newspaper clippings, black-and-
white photos, and videotapes of National Geographic documentaries.
Here, you can read about how serpent handling started—in 1908, when
a Tennessee preacher and ex-bootlegger named George Hensley heard
the word of God. You can read about how, since then, it's spread to nine
states and a handful of countries with about 2,000 followers.

Jimmy gets out his Bible. It's the King James Version, and nearly
every passage has been highlighted in one color or another: pink, yellow,
blue. He shows me Mark 16:17 and reads it so fast it sounds like it's one
long word.

I ask Jimmy what else serpent handlers believe. Some practitioners
also drink strychnine because the passage says "you shall drink a deadly
thing." They also avoid jewelry in accordance with 1 Timothy 2:9—
"Women adorn themselves in modest apparel, with shamefacedness and
sobriety; not with braided hair, or gold, or pearls, or costly array." Some
greet each other with a Holy Kiss—a kiss on the cheek or mouth—as instructed by Romans 16:16.

Jimmy's handled thousands of poisonous serpents. Most of them he
picks up in the mountains right outside his house. He's taken up copper-
heads, cottonmouths, rattlers, an eight-foot King Cobra and a two-step
Vietnamese viper. "If you get bit, you fall in two steps. But God gave me
victory over him."

He has been nailed, though. Twice. First, in 1988. "It was just like a
blow torch. I couldn't sleep for five nights. It throbbed like a tooth ache."
The second time, in 2003, a Northern copperhead got him in the chest.
But he didn't feel a thing.

Jimmy built this church himself. It's a simple church: There's a
linoleum floor, an electric organ, some wooden benches, and a dozen or
so tambourines, some with crosses on them, one with a Fisher Price tur-
tle. Since I told him I'm Jewish, he points out a Bible passage on his wall
written in Hebrew. "We believe the Jews are the chosen people," he says.

The Church of God with Signs Following doesn't quite fit into my
oversimplified liberal vs. conservative evangelical schema. Politically,

Jimmy's a fan of LBJ-style Democrats. Theologically, they're more in line with Falwell, with an emphasis on End Times.

The parishioners are trickling in. And I do mean trickle. Only about a half-dozen show up, which makes me kind of sad. Jimmy doesn't seem to mind. "One time nobody showed up. I still got up on the pulpit and preached. And this guy walking by, he stuck his head in and said 'What are you doing? No one's here. No one can hear you.' And I said, 'Well, you heard me, didn't you?'"

A couple of minutes past 11, Jimmy asks his friend Matthew to do a warm-up sermon. Matthew steps up. He's young—28—and looks a bit like Steve Buscemi. He walks back and forth, his key chain jangling from his belt. He starts to preach.

"People say to me, 'I keep the Ten Commandments.' That's good. But there are many other commandments besides those ten. We should keep everything the Lord says."

Matthew's voice fills the church. He preaches hard, hunched over, his back almost parallel with the ground, as if he were doing a Groucho Marx impersonation.

"I've heard people say the Bible means this or the Bible means that. But my friends, the Bible means exactly what it says. If God wanted it changed he would have had the prophets change it."

"C'mon!" says Jimmy, who is sitting on a chair behind the altar. He lifts his hands in the air. "Amen!"

Matthew's carrying a blue handkerchief. Every minute or so, he wipes his brow or the saliva from the corner of his mouth. He's working on three hours of sleep—he preached late last night at another church.

Matthew was supposed to talk for only a few minutes, but it's been twenty minutes and he's going strong. He jumps from topic to topic, wherever God takes him: healing, the chastening hand of God, his son's injured leg, Jesus' mercy, the war in Iraq ("We shouldn't be in Iraq, and God will punish President Bush.")

The Catholic and Lutheran services I've been to have been like well-orchestrated Bach concertos. This is like Ornette Coleman free jazz. All spontaneous.

"I was trying not to get started again," says Matthew, "but I believe in obeying the holy spirit . . .huh."

Matthew punctuates every sentence with a pronounced exhale. HUH. In the beginning, it was distracting, but now it seems sort of natural.

"Today is the day for salvation HUH. Right here in this church HUH."

It's been an hour now. Jimmy is stamping his feet. Jimmy's wife, who is sitting behind me, is weeping and saying "Praise Jesus." Another woman a few pews back is speaking in tongues "shamamamamama," she says. Then her body jerks. "shamamamam."

I feel myself getting hypnotized by those repetitive HUHs. I feel like the top of my head is being swept upwards. For a minute, everything fades to white except for Matthew, and his shirt sleeves and his blue handkerchief and his Godly riffs.

I snap myself out of it. It was too much. How could I come back to New York and tell Julie I was saved at a serpent handling church in Tennessee? I force myself back down. I'm not ready to surrender yet.

Matthew preaches for an hour and a half before the spirit moves him to stop. The warm-up act had gone on so long there was no need for Jimmy's main event. Jimmy wraps up the service by anointing his parishioners with olive oil. Jimmy feels badly that I had come all the way down and missed the big show. Not a single snake had been handled, no Strychnine drunk.

"Let me see if the Holy Spirit moves me," he says.

From under the altar, Jimmy slips out a wooden box with a clear plastic top. Inside, a copperhead, about three feet long, slithers over itself, flicking its tongue.

Jimmy tells me he takes good care of the snakes—"I clean 'em, care for 'em, water 'em and feed 'em mice." And afterwards, he lets them go back to the mountains. (Regardless, my animal activist Aunt Marti was furious at me for coming down here at all).

Jimmy sits on a bench and closes his eyes. "Ack-ack-ack-ack-ack." He says. He's speaking in tongues, a descending scale. "Ack ack ack ack."

Jimmy opens his eyes and reaches down for the copperhead. He picks it up with one hand near the head, one near the tail, moving his hands in slow little circles.

'ack ack ack ack.' The snake just flickers its tongue.

He does this for a minute, holding the serpent at eyes' height. Then slowly, carefully returns the snake to its box.

Jimmy is out of his trance. The weird thing is that his appearance has completely changed. He looks happier, fuller, transformed from two minutes ago. Maybe that's how Moses glowed when he came down from the mountain.

"How did the snake feel?" I ask.

"Not cold and slimy. More like velvet."

"And what did you feel?"

"It's joyful," says Jimmy. "Like a bucket of warm water pouring over your head."

I don't handle the copperhead myself. I had promised Julie I wouldn't. If I really needed to fulfill that literal part of the Bible, she pointed out I could always handle a garter snake, since the Scriptures never specify "venomous snakes."

Afterward, Jimmy takes me to a picnic at his friend's house. We eat cake and chicken and look at his friend's brightly-colored Chinese bird. We talk about family and grizzly bears and the Apocalyptic times we live in. And then Jimmy hugs me and tells me I have to come down and stay with him for longer.

As I drive back to the airport listening to a country song about Moses' showdown with the pharaoh on AM radio, two things strike me: First, when you're there, when you're in that one-room church, serpent handling doesn't seem as bizarre as I had expected. It's like that great quote I once read: religion makes the "strange familiar and the familiar strange." Here, the strange had been made familiar.

My second thought is: I wish Jimmy would stop handling snakes. I know. My college anthropology professors would be appalled. So would Ralph Hood, the religion teacher who hooked me up with Jimmy in the first place. He wrote a culturally relativist essay about how serpent handling is a valid mode of worship, how it lets the handler embrace life by conquering death. Judge not, lest ye be judged.

But I still have my risk/reward mindset, and here the risk to Jimmy's life cannot outweigh the reward of transcendence. He's one of the favorite people I've met this year, and almost every Sunday, he's tempting death. And why? Because of a literalist interpretation of Mark 16—a passage that some New Testament scholars argue was not in the original scriptures. I want Jimmy to find transcendence through dancing or hymn-singing or Sufi spinning. Anything.

Well, there's an old mountain saying that Ralph Hood quotes: "If you don't believe in serpent handlers, pray for them." That I can do.

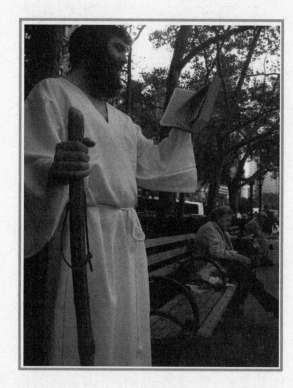

Month Eleven: July

If any one thirst, let him come to me and drink
JOHN 7:37

Day 306. I spend the morning at the Holy Apostles soup kitchen again. I've been studying who gets which job and why. I've noticed something: The beverage station—which is the very first stop in the main room, right next to the front door—is almost always given to . . .a hot female volunteer. Is this a coincidence? Or are they trying to give the place a little sex appeal?

My hunch is the latter. Which could be un-Biblical. Aren't we supposed to be concerned with the spirit, not the flesh?

Today, I am stationed right next to today's official pretty lady. I pour the pink lemonade, she hands it out. She's a short, blonde woman in a yellow T-shirt. She's the leader of a Church Youth Group from Abilene, Texas.

She hands out lemonades with a "have a great day" and a smile out of cruise line commercial.

She seems to be doing well, but the soup kitchen elders can be tough.

"Don't step forward when dispensing the lemonade," snaps a veteran volunteer. "It slows up the line. Just hand it to them."

The blonde nods, chastened.

There's almost always a church youth group at the soup kitchen. I have yet to see a Atheist's Youth Group. Yeah, I know. Religious people don't have a monopoly on doing good. I'm sure that there are many agnostics and atheists out there slinging mashed potatoes at other soup kitchens. I know the world is full of selfless secular groups like Doctors without Borders.

But I got to say: It's a lot easier to do good if you put your faith in a book that requires you to do good. Back in high school, my principal—a strict guy who wore disconcertingly festive pink glasses—started something called 'mandatory volunteering.' Every week, students had to spend two hours doing good if they wanted to graduate.

We students were outraged. Mandatory volunteering is oxymoronic! You can't legislate morality! It must be cultivated naturally. Plus, the policy came from the administration, so it had to be wrong.

But I wanted to graduate, so I went to a soup kitchen and cleaned trays. And it wasn't so bad. Looking back, I realize mandated morality isn't such a terrible idea. Without structure, I would have been at home playing Star Raiders on Atari 800 or looking at my dad's censored Playboys. Maybe Congress should take a page from my high school—or Mormon missionaries or the Israeli army—and require good citizenship from Americans. You graduate high school, and you get shipped off to Americorps for a year—it's the law.

make an incense blended as by the perfumer

EXODUS 30:35

Day 309. Only two months left to go, which freaks me out. I have way too much to do. There are dozens of commandments I have yet to follow. And despite my shepherding and locust-eating, I still haven't submerged myself enough in a primitive lifestyle. This month I vow to do just that. With the help of a thin, brown hardcover called Daily Life in Bible Times, I do just that:

—Incense. I've started burning myrrh every morning. As you probably know, myrrh is one of the three gifts the wise men brought to Jesus. It's also mentioned several times in the Old Testament—God told Moses to make a sacred anointing oil using myrrh, along with cinnamon, aromatic cane, cassia and olive oil (the recipe is so sacred, you were executed for mixing it wrong).

I bought my myrrh at a shop on Broadway, a cramped place filled with oriental rugs and brass jewelry and a surly guy behind the counter who is angry that I was wasting his time by having the gall to purchase items from his store when he had important sudoku to attend to. The myrrh comes in several congealed cones the size of a chocolate truffle, and I light one on the kitchen table when I wake up.

Julie scrunches her face and says: ""It smells like a Cathedral in here."

Yes. That's exactly what it smells like—the apse of Notre Dame or St. Paul's. It's not a frivolous smell. It smells old and serious and holy.

—Hospitality. They knew how to treat a visitor back in Biblical times. If you're looking for the best host in history, Abraham has to make the short list. When three strangers appeared at Abraham's tent door, he ran and got them bread, veal, cakes and milk. He sat them under the shade of a tree. He stood nearby while they ate, just in case the veal was undercooked or they ran out of cake.

This turned out to be a clever move. The strangers revealed themselves to be two angels and the Lord, so Abraham's hosting was not for nothing.

The zeal for hospitality continues in present-day Middle East. When I was in Israel, it got to be oppressive, quite honestly. I peeked into a shop in the Old City section of Jerusalem, and the shop owner insisted that I come in, sit down and have tea with him.

"I'd love to, but I actually have to run."

He looked at me like I had just neutered his dog without permission.

"Sit down and have tea."

It was not a request. I sat down and had tea.

Food and drink aside, the proper Biblical host offered something else: water for the guest's feet. Everyone wore sandals, it was desert conditions—it's a nice thing to do. For the last two weeks, I've been trying this out.

"Come in!" I said to Julie's friend Margie. "Can I offer you food? Drink? Care to wash your feet in a bowl of water?"

In modern times, this always comes off creepy, no matter which gender I'm offering it to. I've realized footwashing is a surprisingly intimate and private thing, like gargling. In other words, no one's taken me up on footwashing. Margie went the furthest—she agreed to have a bowl of water brought out, but it just sat there forlornly on the table.

—Olive oil lamp. An olive oil lamp isn't just Biblical, you'll be happy to know. It's also environmentally friendly. As it says on the appropriately-named treehugger.com

"Olive oil lamps are a pleasing way to light your home. Olive oil is a renewable, non-petroleum fuel which burns without fumes or odor. You can also burn any vegetable oil, or liquid fat or grease in these lamps."

I ordered a replica of an ancient "Samaria" lamp from Israel—it's terra cotta, about the size of a grapefruit, comes with a thick white wick, and looks like a genie might puff out of it at any minute.

I use it at night. I'm typing right now by olive oil lamp. The flame is solid and steady and casts a healthy glow over the table, but it's also alarmingly high. I can't figure out how to properly adjust the wick, so I've got this thing that could be used in the opening ceremonies of the Olympic Games. I burn through a lamp-full of olive oil in half an hour. Perhaps it's not so economical after all.

—The Robe. I've been wearing white for a few months now—or off-white, by now—but I started to feel that wasn't enough. Before the end of the year, I wanted to sample some real Biblical attire.

I ordered a white robe off eBay, but when I tried it on, I looked like I was about to sing in a gospel choir. It wasn't working at all.

The only genuine-ish Biblical robe that didn't cost several hundred dollars was at a Halloween costume store. There it was, next to the Roman emperor togas: A shepherd's robe. It was white, with a V-neck, a belt rope, and is suprisingly comfortable. A man rarely gets to walk around in public with his legs unencumbered by pants. It's a nice change.

When I took it for a spin this week, I learned a robe is a polarizing garment. At times, I was treated as if I was a D-list celebrity—two Austrian teenagers asked to have their photo taken with me. At other times, I engendered not just the usual suspicion, but flat-out hostility. As I was passing this man on the street, he looked at me, snarled and gave me the finger. What was going through his mind? Does he hate shepherds? Or religion? Did he just read Richard Dawkins's book?

I've felt absurd many times throughout in the last 10 months, but wearing a white man-skirt was a particularly embarrassing part of the experiment. My beard has drawn attention, but it is also, paradoxically protective since it shields my face. A robe is not. A robe makes me vulnerable.

My friend Nathaniel told me about a rabbi in the 19th century who made his students do ridiculous things. He'd make them go into a bakery and ask for a box of nails. Or go into a tailor and ask for a loaf of bread. The idea was that he was trying to break down their ego, which he saw as a hurdle to true spirituality. That's what I try to think of when I walk around with my shepherd's robe, which sometimes billows up like Marilyn Monroe's white dress: I am breaking down the ego.

—The Slave/Intern. My slave-slash-intern started a couple of weeks ago. And it could be among the top 10 best things that ever happened to me.

I've had assistants before, but this is a whole other league. Kevin is a nice Quaker boy from Ohio. He's well-scrubbed, has blondish hair, and looks like he stepped out of a commercial for herpes medication (I mean that as a compliment, by the way; they always cast the most vigorous, American types, you know?). He's also part of an a capella group that sings Jay-Z tunes. I heard them on his iPod and they're really good.

And man, has he thrown himself into this role of Biblical slave. Yes, he does a lot of regular intern stuff—researching, making phone calls, data entry (he set up an eBay account for me so I could sell some of my possessions—mostly DVD's and clothes—and donate the proceeds to charity).

But he also sends emails like this:

"Need any shopping done? Any baby clothes or things like that?"

Or

"I'm willing to work 8 hours a week or 80."

I felt a bit guilty at first, but that faded soon enough. It's hard to complain when a guy zips off to the hardware store whenever a light bulb blows out.

He also sent me this email yesterday:

"If I can use your kitchen—mine's too small for these purposes—I'd love to bake you a loaf or two of Ezekiel bread tomorrow morning or afternoon, so that you can enjoy them over the weekend and on the Sabbath. Is this okay?"

Today, I come home from a meeting, and Kevin was in my kitchen, his hands covered in flour, a mortar and pestle and various plastic bags of grain on the counter. Ezekiel bread is one of the few recipes in the Bible. God told the prophet Ezekiel to bake a bread made with wheat, barley, beans, lentil, millet and spelt. Kevin's Ezekiel bread was quite good. It reminded me of a less-crunchy Graham cracker. Kevin later confessed he tweaked the biblical recipe and added honey, but I felt it would be petty to rebuke him.

"Maybe we should give some to your neighbors," Kevin says. "That would be the Biblical thing to do."

We knock on some doors but no one's home. Well, actually, my neighbor Nancy is home, but she calls out from inside: "I'd love some, but I have a cracked rib, so I'm not getting up." I remind myself: I've got to get to work on that Hendrix proposal when she's better.

Kevin says he'd like to take a portion of bread to give away on his walk home. He's like the good servant in Jesus' parable. A master left for a trip, and gave five bags of money to his good servant and five to his bad servant. The good servant invested the money and doubled it to ten bags. By contrast, the bad servant buried his bag of money, which meant no increase at all. A good servant is proactive. Kevin would have doubled the money, maybe tripled it.

If a man begets a hundred children . . .

ECCLESIASTES 6:3

Day 314. We go out to Chinese restaurant with Julie's dad and stepmom. Julie is big enough now that the top of her stomach juts out at a 90 degree angle. She slides into the booth with impressive grace.

The waiter takes our orders. I get the steamed vegetables—bland but Biblically safe. A few weeks ago, I decided I'd make my Berkeley-based aunt Marti proud and go vegetarian. It wasn't so much an ethical decision as a pragmatic one. It's just so much easier to keep the Bible's food laws if you steer clear of the animals. Plus, according to the Bible, the human race started out as vegetarian—Adam, Eve, Cain, Abel, all the way up to Noah never ate of the flesh. So avoiding meat is not un-Biblical.

I've also tried to cut out eggs. This is because of something I learned while interviewing a Karaite—that sect of Judaism that follows the Bible as strictly as possible.

"Let me drop an atom bomb on you," said this Karaite—his name is Nehemiah Gordon, and he runs the Karaite website, karaitekorner.org. "You can't follow the Bible literally because we'll never know what some of the words mean."

In Leviticus 11, there's a list of birds that are an abomination: the eagle, the vulture, the osprey, the pelican, etc. Problem is, those birds are just our best guess. The true identity of the birds have been lost in the haze of time. So to be safe, some Karaites don't eat eggs or poultry at all. It's a profound insight—and it has made my diet even more extreme.

Anyway, that was my dinner: vegetables that had been steamed into tastelessness. The conversation consisted mostly of Julie's stepmom trying to console Julie about the overload of Y chromosomes in our household.

"If you have another baby, I bet it's going to be a girl."

When we got home, I ask Julie about the helpful insight.

"You think we should?"

"No. Absolutely not," she says. "These ovaries of mine are done."

"My thoughts exactly."

"Though we do have a frozen embryo at the clinic, right?"

I don't know. Do we have another frozen embryo? I can't believe I don't know. I should have been on top of that. The next day, I call the clinic and get a nurse on the phone. No, we have no embryos left. Nothing survived besides the two in Julie's alarmingly swollen belly. Which is a relief. I don't have to figure out what to do with an extra embryo. One fewer moral decision to make.

The ethics of embryos—stem cells and abortion—are, of course, incredibly complex. Reasonable people disagree. And frankly, the debate is beyond the scope of this book. So I won't try to argue for one side or the other. You can probably guess my position—it's typically liberal.

But I will say this: When I read the Bible, it didn't seem to support either side. Religious tradition, church doctrine, rabbinical interpretation—those all weigh in on stem cells and abortion, and weigh in mightily. But the literal words of the Bible are, I believe, neither pro-life or pro-choice.

Some Pro-life advocates disagree. They point to several passages to prove that life begins at conception. Among them:

> *"For Thou didst form my inward parts; thou didst knit me together in my mother's womb."*
>
> PSALMS 139:13

> *(This passage is cited to prove that God is working on the fetus even as it is in the womb, thus making the unborn child sacred)*

> *"The LORD called me from the womb, from the body of my mother he named my name."*
>
> ISAIAH 49:1

> *(Here the prophet Isaiah says that God made him sacred him before he was even born. Again, God is at work in the womb)*

> *"And when Elizabeth heard the greeting of Mary, the babe leaped in her womb, and Elizabeth was filled with the Holy Spirit."*
>
> (LUKE 1:39–41)

> *(Here, John the Baptist's pregnant mother meets the Virgin Mary, also pregnant. John The Baptist jumps for joy—which is cited to show that unborn children have emotions).*

To base a major ethical decision on passages like these seems overreaching. They're too vague. They can be interpreted any number of ways—and naturally, pro-choice Christians and pro-choice Jews do just that.

But pro-choicers go father, which I wasn't expecting. They cite passages of their own. I read an article called "The Bible is Pro-Choice" from a magazine called Humanist Perspectives. The article talks about this quote from Ecclesiastes 6:3–5.

"If a man begets a hundred children, and lives many years, so that the days of his years are many, but he does not enjoy life's good things, and also has no burial, I say that an untimely birth is better off than he

Here, an untimely birth is interpreted as a phrase for miscarriage. This is meant to show that sometimes it is better that a life not be lived at all.

And there's also a controversial line in Exodus 21:22. This one says that if a man hurts a woman while she's pregnant and she "loses her offspring", the man is liable. His punishment: He shall be fined some money. This, it's argued, shows that the unborn child is not considered human. If it were human, the punishment would be more severe. He'd be put to death.

Naturally, the pro-lifers have rebuttals to this. And their opponents have rebuttals to the rebuttals. (If you want to see a more in-depth look at the back-and-forth arguments, I recommend a website called religioustolerance.org). The abortion and stem cell debates always remind me of a William Blake quote. I wish I could say I read the quote while perusing Blake. Heck, I wish I could say I read the quote while reading a book by a Yale Divinity School professor. The sad truth is, I read it in a book called Don't Know Much About the Bible. But it's still a great quote:

Both read the Bible day and night,
But thou read'st black where I read white
　　He who is glad at calamity will not go unpunished.

                                                    PROVERBS 17:5

Day 325. I don't know what's happening to me. My friend Paul emailed me a YouTube video. I clicked it open. It showed of a female newscaster reading some stock market news, when suddenly a huge stage light falls, smacking her on the head. She crumples off her chair and out of sight.

All the viewer comments said "LOL" or "laughing my ass off." But I didn't get it. It just seemed upsetting. I spent twenty minutes on Google trying to find the name of the poor newscaster so I could email her a get-well-soon or hope-you-win-your-lawsuit note. I couldn't track her down.

What's going on? What kind of a overly virtuous sap am I turning into? Next I'll be renting Pay It Forward.

> *By day the heat consumed me,*
>
> GENESIS 31:40

Day 331. It's a hot, hot summer New York weekend. I'm sweating heavily in my beard and tzitzit. Jasper's face is lobster-red. So when our friends—who have a plastic blow-up kiddie pool in their courtyard—invite us over, it sounds like a good idea.

Jasper's right now splashing around in the pool with their daughter Lily, and he's having the time of his 2-year-old life. He's laughing like Ray Liotta in Goodfellas. He's showing us how he can jump from one side of the pool to the other.

I, on the other hand, am not having the time of my life. It's not good, this jumping. He's going to break his kneecap, crack his skull—something. I want to dial 9–1 and keep my finger poised over the other 1 in preparation for the inevitable disaster.

After three minutes of watching, I can take it no longer. I slip off my shoes, roll my white pants up to my calves, get up from the table and step into kiddie pool.

"What are you doing?" Julie calls out.

"I'm spotting our son," I say, as I wade toward Jasper.

"Helmet," says Julie.

"Really?"

"Yes, helmet."

Fudge. Maybe she's right. Remember the example set by God, I tell myself. Remember that he gave humans free will. Which was a crazy generous thing to do. But God knew that humans are part-divine, so He wanted to give us the divine ability to make decisions. And just as importantly, to mistakes.

So I should do the same with Jasper. Slowly, reluctantly, I step out of the kiddie pool. I sit down on a sticky white plastic chair and watch Jasper. Who eventually smacks his knee on the pool bottom, appears dazed for about 10 seconds before returning to jumping like a maniacal monkey.

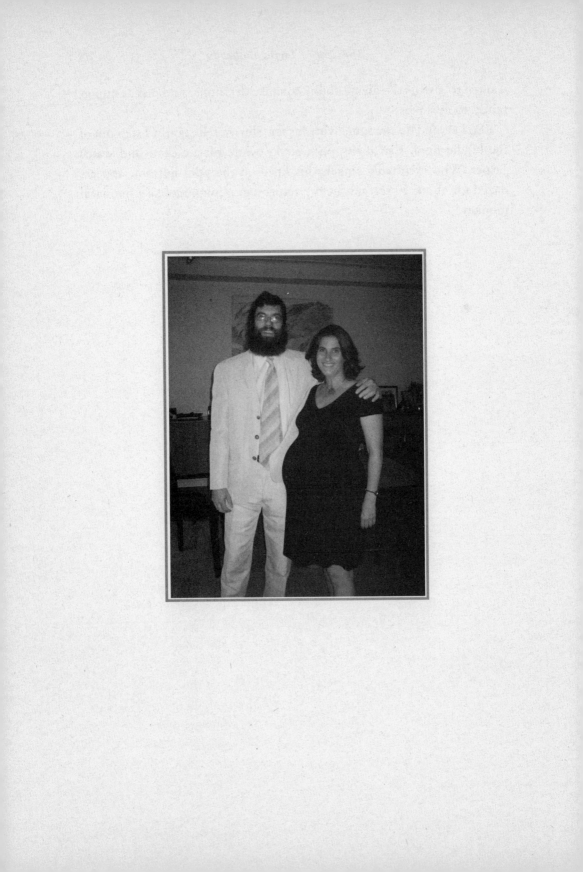

Month Twelve: August
(and some of September)

Honor widows who are real widows

1 TIMOTHY 5:3

Day 336. Today, I met my great aunt Joelle for lunch. Joelle's the only other religious member of our family besides my Orthodox aunt Kate. She's a practicing Catholic who happily thanks God, even when surrounded by agnostics like my family. She's a former actress and singer (when our family sings happy birthday, her vibrato gives it a professional sheen), and the single most talkative person I've ever met. Her husband—a sweet Navy veteran—died a few of months ago at their house in Miami.

The Bible says to comfort widows, which was one of the reasons I invited her to lunch. But as is often the case, I think was more helpful to me than I was to her.

She talked about God's love, his unconditional love. "Sometimes I can't believe how much God loves me. I think, How can he love me that much? I don't love myself nearly as much as he loves me." Even if life turns sour, or Joelle botches something up, she can count on the unconditional love of God.

When I left the lunch, I felt at peace for the first time in a week. Last week, you see, I had a bit of a mental breakdown about my Bible project. In the final stretch, I've been frantically trying to read every single book on religion, trying to interview every religious leader, trying to figure out how to obey every rule. What if I miss an insight? What if I overlook a potential translation? I haven't paid God five shekels to redeem my firstborn son. I haven't talked to a Seventh Day Adventist yet. What if they have the secret? I've barely made a dent in the Bible.

But maybe God will forgive me for my lack of omniscience. If Joelle is right, He'll still love me. I'll never know everything. I can't compete with Him. And if you want to see what happens when you try, just look at the overachievers behind the Tower of Babel.

Again she conceived and bore a son

Genesis 29:34

Day 359. Today is the birth of our twins. The date is our choice. We scheduled to have them emerge onto God's Green Earth today, August 24, at 9 a.m. It's right there in Julie's computer calendar, like a root canal with the dentist.

It seems highly un-Biblical. I can't imagine Rachel scheduled the birth of Joseph for the third day after the barley harvest. But our kids are positioned butt-first in the womb, so the doctor says there's no choice but a Caesarian section.

It's all very civilized, this birth. Nothing like Jasper's. This time, Julie has no contractions and lets out not a single lupine howl. She is wheeled on a gurney into the Operating Room with a little shower cap on her head. The anesthesiologist numbs her from the neck down, and that is it, she is ready to give birth.

I strap a surgical mask over my nose and mouth and join Julie in the OR.

"Uh-uh," says the nurse. "You need one for your beard."

She escorts me out and gets me a second mask for the bottom of my face. I return.

"We're going to take off your wife's gown now," the nurse says. "So if you want to leave, now is the time . . ."

"No thanks," I say.

An odd offer, I think. Oh wait. She believes I'm an Orthodox Jew and might not want to see my wife's nakedness.

The atmosphere in the O.R. is an odd mix. It is, on the one hand, frighteningly gory. I'm stationed by Julie's head, and the doctor has hung a little curtain in across the stomach so as to block the really messy stuff, though I still see enough to nearly make me pass out. On the other hand, the atmosphere is almost relaxed. The doctors are chatting about weekend plans like they are having a chicken salad at the cafeteria.

Hold my hand," says Julie.

"Well, you're impure for 30 days after the birth, so I can only hold it before the birth."

"Please don't-"

At 9:50 a.m., our doctor reached in and scooped out one little man. At 9:52 she reached in and scooped out another. I officially have a whole bunch of sons.

I look at my boys as they squirm around under a huge heat lamp. The boys themselves are another strange mixture. On the one hand, they're such little animals—tiny, naked, slimy little animals. They even sound like animals. Their crying isn't human—it sounds like ducks quacking. On the other hand, I can already see something transcendent in them. When they pry their eyes open—blue eyes on both of them? where did that come from?—I spot what a nun I know calls God's DNA. Those eyes are alive.

When the doctor plucks out our sons out one after the other, I flash back to perhaps the most unforgettable delivery in the Bible. Yes, even in the O.R., the Bible still colors my thinking. This was the birth of the twins Peretz and Zarah. It goes like this: There was a struggle between the sons to see which one could be born first. One son—Peretz—stuck his hand out of his mother's womb, and the midwife tied a red ribbon around his wrist. Then he pulled his hand back inside. The second son then maneuvered around him and got out first. But since the first son had breached the womb, he was considered the oldest, sort of like how an NFL player gets the touchdown if he can just get the ball over the line.

I'm glad I flashed to this story. Not because of the red ribbon twist. But because, if you remember, their conception is a good metaphor for my boys. Those ancient twins were conceived in complicated circumstances—the offspring of Judah and his daughter-in-law Tamar, who disguised herself as a prostitute. Mine too have a complicated origin. But that doesn't, I hope, doom them.

And now that I type this up, I'm wondering if the Peretz-Zarah story could be a Big Metaphor for my year. Maybe it applies to the Bible itself. The Bible may have not been dictated by God, it may have had a messy and complicated birth, one filled with political agendas and outdated ideas—that doesn't mean the Bible can't be beautiful and sacred.

Little children, you are of God . . .

1 JOHN 4:4

Day 362. They released Julie and the twins from the hospital at 11 a.m on the third day. It would have been sooner, but we lost about 45 minutes to the hospital guards who double-checked and triple-checked our wrist bracelet IDs and social security numbers to make sure we haven't swiped the wrong babies.

We've been home for two days now, and I've been spending the majority of that time snapping these little body suits on them. Man, these things have a lot of snaps. What the fudge happened to good old zippers?

Jasper has been dealing with his brothers with an interesting strategy: complete denial.

He refuses to acknowledge them. won't even look at them. they can be screaming right in front of his face, but he'll use his X-ray vision to stare right through their skull.

As for me, I know this will surprise you: I'm deliriously tired. Yesterday, Julie was making a sandwich in the kitchen and I playfully patted her on the butt when I walked by. The only thing was, it wasn't Julie. It was my mom. My mom was visiting the twins. And in my bleary-eyed state, I had confused Julie for my mom. This is definitely forbidden by Leviticus.

I've barely been able to do anything Biblical since the birth. I'm losing valuable time. I decided to extend my project another month, but Julie bargains me down to two weeks.

It doesn't help matters that the boys—Zane and Lucas—are on completely different schedules and refuse to cooperate. Their rivalry is, yes, Biblical.

The younger one is tiny—barely five pounds—and the older is a big lug, almost seven, and they're constantly battling each other to get access to Julie's milk supply.

The younger one is sneaky. I think he can sense when the older one is stirring, and he'll start howling to make sure he gets first crack. He's the Jacob to his brother's Esau—the mischievious underdog. Is it bad that I root for him? I've rooted for underdogs all my life, so I almost can't help it. I'm sure it's temporary. It better be. I've seen what favoritism can do— Jacob favored Joseph and it got Joseph tossed in a ditch by his jealous brothers.

Forgive, and you will be forgiven

Luke 6:37

Day 363. I finally told my parents that I had met Gil and was including him in the book. I emailed them the sections with Gil.

They weren't happy. They told me I didn't expose Gil's dark side enough. They asked if I had to make him such a prominent part of the book. They wanted me to be clear he was an ex-uncle. They disputed the part where I said Gil was the most exotic creature in the family (my mom said that our cousin who was a shepherd in Switzerland is weirder).

But in the end, they were forgiving. They didn't make me change a thing. "We'll live with it," Mom wrote. "We love you." Their son did the equivalent of eating the husks thrown to the swine, and they welcomed me home with a hug.

"He that is eight days old among you shall be circumcised

Genesis 17:12

Day 367. My twin sons have been in this world for eight days, which means today is the day to perform one of the first Biblical commands: Circumcision.

I actually knew quite a bit about circumcision even before my Biblical adventure. Perhaps too much. For a year or so in my early career as a journalist, I wrote a surprising number of magazine articles about circumcision. It was my first real beat.

I was living in San Francisco at the time, and my eccentric aunt Marti introduced me to some anti-circumcision activists who saw the snipping of the foreskin as cruel and unnecessary. As Marti put it: "It's the only men's issue I care about."

The hardest of the hard-core didn't just want to outlaw circumcision; they wanted to reverse their own circumcisions. I remember attending a support group meeting that was bizarre even by the standards of San Francisco support groups. They called themselves RECAP, short for Recover A Penis (a rival group was called BUFF—Brothers United for Future Foreskins).

The meeting was held in the basement of a church—either an extremely liberal church or a church that didn't know to whom they were renting space. A dozen men sat in folding chairs arranged in a circle. Some were pony-tailed hippies, some looked like the Leather Dude in the Village People, a few were just normal guys who could have worked in the loan department at Citibank.

"I don't feel whole," said one. "I want to feel whole again."

Another asked: "Can you imagine what it's like to have sex with a foreskin? It must be like watching color TV." (I never was able to confirm this, but the claim is that circumcision blunts the sensation).

Most of the time was spent discussing homespun methods that would allow the men to regrow their foreskins. I'll spare you the details. I'm sure the Internet has plenty more information for those who are interested.

The Recap movement hasn't caught on, but, in general, circumcision seems to be on the decline in America. The American Academy of Pediatrics makes no recommendation either way. There are some studies that point to medical benefits of circumcision—it reportedly lowers the rate of penile cancer and HIV—but they're apparently not convincing enough for the AAP to take a stand yet.

So when our first son Jasper was born, I had mixed feelings about circumcising him. I didn't think he'd end up in a San Francisco basement venting his anger, but why put him through the pain? There's no rational reason for it.

My aunts fueled my confusion. I was subjected to dueling campaigns. On the one hand, my Orthodox aunt Kate left voicemails encouraging us go ahead with it. On the other, Marti sent pamphlets with stomach-churning stories of circumcisions-gone-bad.

In the end, Julie put her foot down. Jasper would have a circumcision, and it would be at our apartment, and it would be done by a family friend Lou Sank, a New Jersey pediatrician who also has mohel credentials.

When the day came, and the family gathered, I did my best to ignore what was actually happening. I deluded myself into thinking of it as bagel-and-cream cheese brunch, with a short detour into some minor medical procedure.

I distanced myself with jokes. Of which Lou—like all mohels—had plenty.

"Did you hear the one about the guy who converted to Judaism as an adult?" he asked. "He has to get a circumcision, but he's nervous about it. So he asks his Jewish friend Abe, does it hurt? And Abe says, "Oy. When I had mine done, I couldn't walk or talk for a year.""

The only terrifying moment was when I spotted a knife on the table the size of a small machete. It turned out to be for the cutting of the ceremonial bread. So that too turned into something of a joke.

With Jasper, Julie and I refused to watch the actual cutting. We both went into our bedroom and shut the door, and held hands, and talked very loudly about whether the dolphin-themed mobile took AA batteries or C batteries so as to drown out the crying.

Two and a half years later, circumcisions two and three are upon me. And despite the existence of bagels and the mohel Lou, these feel different: This time, I plan to watch. If I'm choosing to do this to my sons— this, the fifth and final law on my list of Most Perplexing Rules in the Bible—I can at least face up to my choice.

Circumcision is a huge part of the Bible—it merits 87 mentions. It was seen as the way to seal the covenant between God and humans. A signature in blood. Abraham was the pioneer. God appeared to him and instructed him to circumcise all males in his house, and all newborns after eight days. Abraham had no newborns at the time, so the first inductees were his elder son Ishmael (who was 13 years old) and Abraham himself, who was all of 99 years old.

In the New Testament, circumcision becomes optional, at best. The Apostle Paul—whose mission was to expand the Christian faith beyond the Jewish people—said that circumcision wasn't necessary. You didn't need the physical proof as long as you changed your heart. The phrase he used is "Circumcise the heart." Some passages do indicate that Paul is fine with circumcision for those who are direct descendants of the Israelites.

"So are you going to do the circumcision yourself?" asks Julie's brother Eric.

"I hear there are some nice flint rocks in Central Park," adds her other brother Doug.

"Very good," I say.

I'm not in the mood for jokes, I'm too anxious. My forehead is damp.

I mutter something about how the Bible doesn't mandate that the father perform the ceremony.

Actually, we're about as far from a flint rock as possible. Lou has come with a case full of gleaming metal equipment, which he's laid out on our dining room table. He snaps on his white surgical gloves, ties on a yellow apron, and pulls out a box of alcohol wipes.

"Who's first?" asks Lou.

"Zane?" I say.

"Okay, bring him over."

He looks so tiny on the table, as small as a soup bowl at a dinner setting.

I glance around the room. My sister-in-law is staring out the window. My mom is flipping through a Thomas the Tank engine brochure. Julie has her back to the table. No one is looking at Zane.

I gaze back at my son, who has started to cry. A bus rumbles by in the background. My teeth are clenched. I'm squinting, some sort of compromise between open and closed eyes.

Lou attaches some clamps. More crying. He takes out a brown leather strap. And scalpels. Drops of blood stain the towel. Zane is now wailing, open-mouthed.

In a sense, it's all very hygienic, medical, sanitized. And yet . . .nothing can disguise the fact that what is happening on that table is deeply primitive. It's the most primitive thing I've seen my entire Biblical year.

There, on a patch of white gauze, is a piece of my son. He has sacrificed a part of his body to join an ancient community. Julie and I stand side by side and read a prayer from a Xeroxed sheet of paper. "Blessed are you, He who blessed our fathers, Abraham, Isaac and Jacob, Moses and Aaron, David and Solomon, bless this tender infant . . .

These are no longer just meaningless names. These are the men I'd spent my year with. Abraham, Isaac, Jacob. This was a chain that—if Julie and I continued spouting names for several hours—would presumably reach Charles Jacobowitz and Arnold Jacobs and A.J. Jacobs. Who am I to break thousands of years of tradition? Circumcision is a crazy irrational ritual. But here's the thing: It's my heritage's crazy irrational ritual. So maybe I shouldn't dismiss it.

So whatever you wish that men would do to you, do so to them.

MATTHEW 7:12

Day 372. A few days ago, right before Labor Day weekend, the hallway outside our apartment began to smell.

"It's like rotten turnips" Julie said. "You smell it, don't you?"

I did, but told Julie it was probably nothing. Our mysterious neighbor in 5R—a woman I've never met—loves to cook exotic dishes made from animals unknown. This was probably just a recipe gone awry.

But the smell didn't fade by morning. Julie called the building staff; they "checked it out" and found nothing.

Over Labor Day, our neighbors all left Manhattan. The building was empty except for me, Julie, our kids and that smell. Which got worse. And worse. You couldn't tell where it was coming from—it seemed to soak the hall.

When Julie and I would go out for a walk, we'd dart from our apartment to the elevator, our mouths and noses covered with our shirt collars.

Julie called the maintenance staff again. They promised to look into it.

On Tuesday morning, I woke up to banging in the hallway. I cracked our door and peeked out. The building handyman Victor was outside apartment 5I—the one owned by our sweet hippy neighbor Nancy—trying to pry open her front door with a hammer. I could hear Nancy's dog barking. Four medics lingered nearby, occasionally clicking their walkie talkies and speaking in low voices.

I knew before one of the medics asked me that question: 'Have you seen your neighbor in the last few days?"

It took Victor half an hour of pounding before he broke down the door. He went in, reemerging a few minutes later.

"Alive?" I asked.

He shook his head.

They wheeled Nancy's body out on a stretcher covered with a sheet. They snapped a padlock on the door, along with yellow police tape ribbon and a Day-Glo sticker warning people not to even consider trying to come inside. They brought an industrial strength fan at the end of the hall to clear the smell.

I told Julie when she woke up. She sat down on the couch and put her face in her hands and didn't talk for what seemed like two full minutes. Finally, she looked up, her eyes red.

"I saw her a week ago and she was all worried about me and how I was holding up."

I just shake my head.

"What'd she die of?"

"They don't know yet."

"I told them there was a smell," saidd Julie. "I told them. This is what I was afraid of."

Whenever something happens, I always try to think of a biblical precedent, a story that will help me put it into perspective. But with Nancy's death, there is none, really. The Bible doesn't talk much about living and dying in solitude.

Adam starts out alone, but God doesn't let that last long: "It is not good for a man to be alone." In Biblical times, the smallest unit of society wasn't the individual. It was the family.

Nancy had no family, no husband, no children, just a handful of friends, few of whom she saw very often.

That night, Julie and I lie in bed, too spent to do much reading.

"Maybe we could . . .say a prayer."

Julie looks at me like I had just proposed a threeway with the waitress at Columbus Bakery.

"You serious?"

"A prayer of thanksgiving. I find them helpful. We don't have to call it a prayer. We just give thanks."

Julie paused. "Okay."

"Maybe we'll start out simply."

"I'm thankful for our health and our kids," Julie says.

"I'm thankful we got to know Nancy," I say.

"I'm thankful you're ending your project soon."

The memorial service is held a couple of days later. It's in the apartment of a woman who knew Nancy just a little bit—they were both members of the building's informal dog-owner's clique. Since Nancy had no family, Julie did most of the organizing—tracking down her few friends, posting a notice in the lobby.

About ten people show up. Her high school friend Dan reads letters she'd written over the years, painfully honest notes about her loneliness and how she still has "the bends" after emerging from the sixties. We pass around the album cover she designed for Jimi Hendrix. Several people say something along the lines of:

"She had a troubled life, but at least she found some peace at the end with her dog Memphis."

And we talk about the crushing irony, a twist that sounded like it was out a Chekhov play but was true: She died of heart failure and asthma. The asthma was brought on by her dog.

If you try to literally follow Leviticus 19:18—you shall love your neighbor as yourself—well, you can't. That would mean putting your neighbor's dreams, career, children, pets and finances on par with your own. This is why it's usually reinterpreted in the less extreme—but infinitely wise—version known as the Golden Rule: "Do unto others as others would do unto you."

While she was alive, I didn't do so well with the Golden Rule and Nancy. Here she was, my literal neighbor. Two doors down. And I had made a half-assed effort. I never invited her to dinner. I never rolled up my sleeves and helped her get her Jimi Hendrix book published. I never got her a gift to repay her for the ones she bought Jasper. I never fulfilled my mission to do a mitzvah for her.

I got my chance to partially redeem myself. Nancy's beagle Memphis still wasn't adopted. He had a temporary home at another neighbor's apartment, but that family couldn't keep him long. So the next day I began a frantic quest: Find Memphis a home, and in so doing, make me feel less powerless.

I clicked onto Craigslist to put up a dog-adoption notice. But while there, I read a notice from the ASPCA. It warned of psychos who adopt dogs and then, for amusement, shoot them or toss them in the river. This doesn't help my mood. Instead, I send an email blast to everyone I can think of. I include a photo of Memphis. I had snapped the photo earlier in the day—the dog was born with a droopy face, but now it was positively dragging on the ground. Will anyone adopt such a forlorn-looking mutt?

A friend of a friend responded. He wanted to meet the forlorn dog. He came over, dressed in a suit and tie, his wife and children in tow.

"Let's think about it," said his wife, as the kids scratched Memphis head.

She may have had a prudent idea. But the kids weren't about to wait, so just like that, Memphis was off to a suburban house with a yard and a porch.

The next day, I felt like I'd at least done something Nancy would have liked. But I also flashed back to a question Nancy asked me months ago:

Did I help because the Bible told me to, or because I really wanted to?

Was finding the dog a home a pat and tidy way to quantify some moral progress for my book? Quite possibly.

I consulted one of my spiritual advisers about this—Greg Fryer, a Lutheran minister who lives in my parents' building. He told me the following:

"C.S. Lewis said the distinction between pretending you are better than you are and beginning to be better in reality is finer than moral sleuthhounds can conceive."

In short, pretending to be better than you are is better than nothing. Not only was this a great quote, but it also included dog imagery, so I thought it must be fated. I thanked Reverend Fryer and C.S. Lewis for letting my conscience off the hook.

A few days later, three men in white hazmat suits came to clear out Nancy's apartment. They had stuffed everything—her clothes, her frying pans, her papers—into black plastic garbage bags, about a dozen of which lined the hall. And they were just getting started.

I tied a red bandana to my face, put on some yellow dishwashing gloves, and stepped past them into the apartment.

"Just looking for something real quick," I said, before they could ask for identification or permits.

I wove my way through the mess on the floor, and there, on a table in the corner, I found a stack of papers. I flipped through it. It's a very rough draft of her memoir. I took it.

"Thanks!" I said, as I walked out.

When I got back to my apartment, I sat on my couch and read the handwritten pages. It's a tough but lovely book. It's also highly unfinished, sometimes with but a sentence fragment scribbled on top of a page. I don't know if it'll ever get published. I hope so. But in case it doesn't, here's a sentence on page 41 that stopped me short. It is about her painting of Jimi Hendrix, the one that became the cover to one of his albums.

Eventually, I sold the original to the Hard Rock Café, not only because I needed a little money, but because I was afraid that, if I would die, it would be put on the street, like all stuff is put on the street when people die, in a black plastic bag. Now it was safe.

It was in my mouth as sweet as honey.

EZEKIEL 3:3

Day 377. My niece Natalia is having her bat mitzvah in New Jersey today. As you probably know, the most important part of a modern bar or bat mitzvah isn't the Torah portion or lighting the candles. It's the theme. You've got to have a theme—sports, Camelot, whatever. I recently went to a bar mitzvah called Zach Wars: Revenge of the Torah, which seemed at odds with Leviticus' ban on vengeance. Natalia's theme is Willy Wonka's Chocolate Factory.

She and her mom have gone all out. The invitations were wrapped around a chocolate bar. Her mom spent weeks making 22 papier mache oompa loompas. Bowls of Skittles and M&Ms cover the tables.

Jasper is getting fidgety, so I carry him onto the dance floor, where we joined all the 13-year-old classmates and 68-year-old cousins twice removed. We are dancing to some Beyonce song, and I feel something happen. I feel something envelope me and then envelop Jasper. And then I feel it keep going. I feel it spread out like a drop of cranberry juice in a glass of water, sweeping through the room, swallowing my nieces and nephew and Julie and my parents. Here I am, at this gloriously silly ritual, surrounded by giant Twizzlers and Milk Duds, my defenses down, and this feeling has seeped out of my brain through my skull and filled the room. And kept going. For all I know, it has swept out the doors and windows and into the parking lot and through the driveway.

I'd had some close calls this year. There was that hypnotic trance while watching the serpent handling preacher. But I've never fully let myself go, always hovering a few feet above-ground like a hot air balloon still stuck to its a tether.

So at this suburban Jersey country club, my son's hands locked around my neck, his head pressed against my shoulder, I chose to accept this feeling and ride it to the end. To surrender.

I had to label it, I'd say the feeling is part love, part gratefulness, part connectedness, part joy. And that joy was like joy concentrate, far more intense and warmer than what I felt that night of dancing with the Hasidim. Maybe now I've finally felt what King David felt when he danced before the Lord. During those moments, nothing could have bothered me. If my garments flew up around my waist like King David's did, it wouldn't have mattered. At least to me. The joy would steamroll right on through.

My altered state only lasted all of 10 seconds. Maybe less. And then it faded away. But not totally. There's still some background radiation—which I hope to God stays for weeks, months.

Driving back to New York, I ask myself, why did that just happen? Did it have something to do with my frazzled state after Nancy's death? Maybe. Was it because my project is about to end and I forced myself into the state? Yeah, probably. But even if it was manufactured, it was still real. Farm-bred salmon is better than no salmon at all. Or to put it another way: My year was a controlled experiment, but sometimes experiments produce results precisely because they create extreme circumstances. If Gregor Mendel (a monk, incidentally) had let his pea pods grow willy-nilly, he would never have understood genetics.

Without my year, I wouldn't have been open to that feeling I got on the dance floor. And for that alone, all the craziness and Handy Seats and locusts and snakes might have been worth it.

The end of all things is at hand

1 PETER 4:7

Day 380. One day to go. I've given up trying to go on a Bible binge this last day. I don't want to waste it running around like a kaparot chicken. I try make it a slow day, a day of meditation. I want try to get a little perspective. Such as:

Did the Bible make me a better person? It's hard to know for sure, but I hope it did. A little at least. The other day, I handed out flyers to a

Save Darfur rally, but then got angry at the people who walked by without acknowledging me. I came up with elaborate revenge fantasies in which they read about the rally in The New York Times and felt guilty for not taking my flyer, even tracking me down to apologize. In other words, I'm pretending to be a better person, which is a good first step, if C.S. Lewis is to be believed.

I'm more tolerant, especially of religion, if that helps my case. Here's how I know this: When Jasper was born, my Orthodox aunt Kate gave him a bunch of building blocks with Hebrew letters and paintings of Biblical scenes. I didn't want Jasper using them because I was worried the blocks would somehow imprint on his brain and eventually convert him to Hasidism. Nowadays, I'm not just okay with him playing with his Bible blocks. I like it. I want him to know his religion.

And the Bible itself? What do I think of it after my year-long immersion?

When I started my project, Elton Richards made that majestic food analogy: He said my quest was like a banquet table, and not everyone would sit with me at my banquet table, but I have a hunger and thirst, so I deserve to nourish it. I loved the way he talked. I decided that by year's end, I would employ an extended food metaphor of my own. I think I have one now. It may not be majestic, but here goes:

There's a phrase called "Cafeteria Christianity." It's a derisive term used by fundamentalist Christians to describe moderate Christians. The idea is that the moderates pick and choose the parts of the Bible they want to follow. They take a nice helping of mercy and compassion. But the ban on homosexuality? They leave that on the countertop.

Fundamentalist Jews don't use the phrase "Cafeteria Judaism," but they have the same critique. You must follow all of the Torah, not just the parts that are palatable.

Their point is, the religious moderates are inconsistent. They're just making the Bible conform to their own values.

The year showed me beyond a doubt that everyone practices cafeteria religion. It's not just moderates. Fundamentalists do it too. They can't heap everything on their plate. Otherwise they'd kick women out of church for saying 'hello' ("women should keep silence in the churches, for they are not permitted to speak," 1 Corinthians 14:34) and boot out men for saying "Tennessee Titans" ("make no mention of the names of other gods," Exodus 23:13)

But the more important lesson was this: there's nothing wrong with choosing. Cafeterias aren't bad, per se. I've had some great meals at cafeterias. I've also had some turkey tetrazzini that gave me the dry heaves for 16 hours.

The key is in choosing the right dishes. You need to pick the nurturing ones (compassion), the healthy ones (love thy neighbor), not the bitter ones. Religious leaders don't know everything about every food, but maybe the good ones can guide you to what is fresh. They can be like a helpful lunch lady who . . .okay, I've taken the metaphor too far.

Now this does bring up the problem of authority. Once you acknowledge that we pick and choose from the Bible, doesn't that destroy its credibility? Doesn't that knock the legs out from under it? Why should we put stock in any of the Bible?

"That's the big question," says one of my rabbis, Robbie Harris. I asked Robbie as well as every other member of my advisory board. There's no simple or totally satisfying answer. But let me offer two interesting ideas from them:

The first is from the pastor out to pasture Elton Richards. Here's his metaphor: Try thinking of the Bible as a snapshot of something divine. It may not be a perfect picture. It may have flaws—a thumb in the lens, faded colors in the corners. But it still helps to visualize.

"I need something specific," says Elton. "Beauty is a general thing. It's abstract. I need to see a rose. When I see that Jesus embraced lepers, that's a reason for me to embrace those with AIDS. If He embraced Samaritans, that's a reason for me to fight racism."

The second is from Robbie himself. He says we can't insist that the Bible marks the end of our relationship with God. Who are we to say that the Bible contained all the wisdom? "If you insist that God only revealed himself at one time, at one particular place, using these discrete words, and never any time other than that—that in itself is a kind of idolatry." His point is: You can commit idolatry on the Bible itself. You can start to worship the words instead of the spirit. You need to "meet

God halfway in the woods."

Which brings up another question: Do I believe in a traditional Bibli-
cal God? Well, not in the sense that the ancient Israelites believed in
Him. I could never make the full leap to accepting a God who rolls up
His sleeves and fiddles with our lives like a novelist does his characters.
I'm still agnostic. But in the words Elton Richards—I'm now a reverent
agnostic. Which isn't an oxymoron, I swear. I now believe that whether
or not there's a God, there is such a thing as sacredness. Life is sacred.
The Sabbath can be a sacred day. Prayer can be a sacred ritual. There is
something transcendent, beyond the everyday. It's possible that humans
created this sacredness ourselves—but that doesn't take away from its
power or importance.

I come away from this year with my own cafeteria religion. I'll be
doing things differently than I did 13 months ago, things both big (resting on the Sabbath) and small (wearing more white clothes). And I'll
keep on saying prayers of thanksgiving. I'm not sure whom I'm thanking, but I've become addicted to the act of thanking (see the overlong ac-
knowledgments section).

> *There is . . .a time for every matter under heaven*
>
> ECCLESIASTES 3:1

Day 381. My favorite book, Ecclesiastes has these famous lines:

> *There is a time for everything . . .*
> *A time to give birth and a time to die;*
> *A time to plant and a time to uproot what is planted.*

This is the Time for me to uproot my topiary.

I've been anxious about this for weeks. First of all, I'd heard night-
mare stories about kids who didn't recognize their fathers post-shave.
Some of these kids went on extended crying jags. They'd scream about
this strange man in their house. The relationship took weeks to recover.

I'm so paranoid about this, I came up with an idea of how to prep

Jasper for the day of defoliation. It involved breaking the second commandment—thou shall not make any images—but I did it anyway. a couple of weeks ago, I went to Kinko's and printed out a large color photo of my face circa 2005—from the era of smooth cheeks. I attached the photo to a popsicle stick. Then, every morning, for an hour while I fed him breakfast, I'd hold the photo in front of my face like a mask. I made holes for the eyes and mouth. He seemed a little weirded out.

Now the day is here. I spend the morning inspecting my beard. I went into the living room to get in some last-minute prayers. Julie's in there. I'm depressed.

"You okay?" says Julie.

"Not really."

"Well, you're making me really happy. Try to focus on that.'

The shave itself is scheduled for 2 p.m. on September 18. The publisher sent a photographer over to get a before and after shot, so I spent the a few minutes staring at the camera and trying not to look too much like a terrorist so I don't scare off potential book buyers.

Luckily, the photographer doesn't ask me to smile. This would have been hard. My mood is black for several reasons. First, there's always an immediate post-partum depression after finishing a big project. I felt it when I read the entry on Zywiec in the encyclopedia. I feel unmoored and a little scared. What do I do? I don't have structure. Second, beard has been with me for so long, it's taken on its own identity, almost become a living organism. I feel like I'm losing a pet rabbit.

And third, I'm not just shaving my beard, I'm amputating a large part of my identity. In a couple of hours, I won't be Jacob anymore. I'll be back to being a regular old unremarkable New Yorker, one of millions.

It's 2 p.m. when I take the first snip out of my beard. It's not easy, the logistics of shaving this thing. You can't just put on some cream and whip out the razor. First, I hack away at the beard for 45 minutes with a big silver pair of scissors. The clumps of hair float down, turning the sink black and making the floor look like a Supercuts franchise. The beard eventually shrinks down to the length of putting green grass. I sweep it up all the tufts and stuff them into a gallon-sized Ziploc bag.

Not sure what I'm going to do with this bag of hair. Maybe give away patches with the first 100 copies of the book.

And now, for the razor. Actually, I bought a new razor for the occasion at the pharmacy. In this year, a lot has happened in the razor industry. Back when I was shaving regularly, they had a mere three blades. Now these newfangled five-bladed ones have popped up.

I lather up, jut out my chin, and put the razor to my neck. I hear that familiar scrape. A stripe of skin appears. And another. After ten minutes, I wash off the rest of the shaving cream, and there it is. My face.

Man, I look weird. I feel naked, vulnerable. My cheeks are tingling, like my face just got out of a year-long steam bath.

Julie has been watching the last five minutes.

"You look like you're 14!"

And it's true. Maybe it's an optical illusion—like how a little circle looks even smaller when it's next to a huge circle—but I could pass for an eighth grader.

Julie grabs my cheeks and pulls me towards her. I kiss her for the first time in two months. Which was lovely. I had forgotten how her lips felt.

The photographer was kind enough to bring champagne. He pops it in our sink and pours some glasses for me, him and Julie.

I'm about to take a sip, when I pause. I say a silent prayer of thanks for the champagne.

The prayer feels good, different, unforced. I'm off the clock.

He shall restore what he took by robbery

LEVITICUS 6:4

Day 388. It's been a week since the shave. The first day was the worst. I felt unanchored. Too many choices. It reminded me of the overwhelming freedom I experienced on that first day of freshman year at college, but without any of the exhileration and double the dread.

Oh, and lots of guilt. I felt like I was getting away with all sorts of transgressions. I went to the barber and I had my hair washed by a woman. All the while I was thinking, can I really do this? Can I really flip through the People magazine while she's trimming my sideburns? Can I really buy a banana on the way home without worrying if it's from a tree that's more than four years old? It still seemed wrong.

Every day, the guilt recedes a little. Every day, I get a bit more accustomed to choice. Choice isn't necessarily a bad thing, I tell myself. And at least my year gave helped narrow my choices.

I'll never be Jacob again. I'll never live with so many restrictions. But a part of my Biblical alter-ego has carried over. If my Bible self had a foot-long beard, what remains is barely a five o'clock shadow, but it's there. I think it'll always be there.

Right now, I'm at the Post Office, Jasper in tow. I told him I was running an errand, and he insisted on coming, since he's somehow gotten the idea that 'errands' are as exciting as the Central Park merry-go-round. We wait fifteen minutes before getting to the front of the line. I slide a brown bubble wrap package onto the scale. Six dollars to go to Monte Sereno, California. I pay my money. In three days, my ex-girlfriend will open her mailbox to find her black leather Bible with its tissue-thin pages and faded gold embossing, the 1,536 pages that have shaped my year.

Jasper and I leave the post office, turn left and head towards home for a quiet Friday night.

All the events in this book are true. Some of the sequences have been re-arranged, and a few of the names and identifying details have been changed. Unless otherwise specified, the Bible quotations are from the Revised Standard Version.